HEARTH
AND
HOME

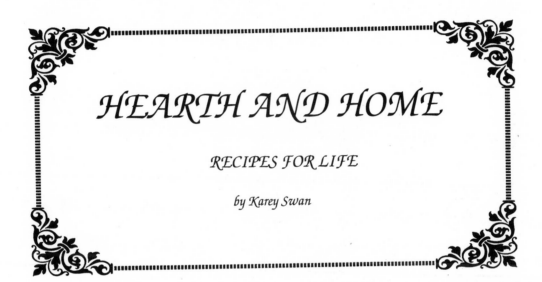

HEARTH AND HOME

RECIPES FOR LIFE

by Karey Swan

LOYAL PUBLISHING
WWW.LOYALPUBLISHING.COM

HEARTH AND HOME

Recipes for Life

ISBN 1-929125-06-2
Printed in the United States of America

This book is dedicated
to those kindred spirits out there who passionately and whimsically write on pages of their lives words analogous to these:

HYMN TO A GOOD WIFE

Who can find a wonderful wife?
She is not an impossible dream,
But is far greater in value then earthly treasures.
Her husband's heart confidently trusts her,
As she blesses him with her homemaking skills.
All the days she lives bring good to him.
She searches for wool and cotton,
Creating with her hands as she knits and sews.
She seeks treasures from afar,
Bringing wonderful surprises to her family.
She rises before the sunrise,
And prepares breakfast for her family,
And anyone else dwelling under her roof.
She is skilled and shrewd in business,
And invests her earnings in the future.
She exercises, rests and eats wholesome foods
To strengthen her body.
She knows the creations of her hands are good,
Made through discipline and hard work.
She is knowledgeable and skilled
In the crafts of hearth and home.
She freely reaches out ot the needy
And personally gives them the fruit of her labors.
She is not afraid of the cold and snow,
Because she clothes her family with warm coats.
She decorates her home in fine fabrics,
And wears beautiful clothing she has made.
Her diligence and skill in home affairs
Free her husband to pursue his place in public life.
She sells her handmade textiles,
And brings the sweaters she has knit to the local shops.
Home economic prowess and character
Give her confidence as she faces the future.
The words she speaks are worthwhile,
And filled with wisdom and kindness.
She inspires her family to be creative and productive,
And is diligent in her responsibilities.
Her husband, who is filled with joy and gratitude says,
"Many daughters have done well, but you excel them all."
Although the works of her hands are great,
And provide charm and beauty to her household,
True wisdom and God-centered reality is seen,
Only as she lives her life in wholehearted obedience,
To God's revelation in His Word.
Encourage her and festoon her life with praises!

Paraphrase of Proverbs 31: 10-31
by Monte Swan, 1999

5

ACKNOWLEDGMENTS

A "Great Big Thank You" needs definitely to go to my family. I've read acknowledgments in other books' beginnings before, but you can't fathom, can't empathize, until you have walked in similar shoes. I've heard tell it's hard on a marriage and on relationship, when building a house. What about building a book? Well, we've built two houses together, a book in song, and now this book. We're still best friends.

I authored this book, but . . where do I end and Monte begins, or Monte ends and I begin! Picture each of us as individual circles. When analyzing the shared likes, the synergism, our circles would overlap. A Venn diagram would show our intersecting sets so together, you'd have to look closely to see the separate circles. In other words, Monte is in reality co-author.

Our sixteen-year-old son, Travis, is almost unreal. His knowledge of the computer boggles my mind. He does know the inside workings of it, having helped clean them at one of his jobs. But he knows nothing of Page Maker and yet was able to help me so much. With all the new-fangled devices these days, Monte and I call upon Travis all the time. I even called Travis quite a bit at work. In fact, his employers and co-workers are so curious by now, that they all want my book!

Heather has taken up the slack around the house. I've not required her to cook yet. I still feel responsible for putting food on the table, though the fare has been simple. Heather has helped in picking up the clutter and keeping the kitchen clean. Though almost an adult, she has not lost the ability to play. This trait has been good for Dawson's sake.

Dawson is the spark in our life. Many adjectives could be used to describe him. He has such an infectious zeal for life. Independence is a trait so different from the older two at his age. He is able to do so much on his own, even cooking, that I forget how old he is. Awesome Dawson is actually six going on sixteen.

Does one acknowledge God on a page such as this? Is He a separate entity to be thanked? "I am not" without Him. Going back to the venn diagram circle sets, I am a subset, an inner little circle within His bigger circle. His story is ongoing. This book shares my story, our story, which is a part of His story.

There are many people outside of our immediate family who have been inspiring this work and helping in the process. Kathy von Duyke, Gayle Graham, Pam and Phil Lancaster, Jessica and Wade Hulcy, Pat and Lura Roberts, and Ruth Beechick are the ones who come to mind. And then Gayle Bibee and Bill and Karen Cormier who helped edit.

To list all who have impacted our lives would be impossible. I will list those who are more directly related in one way or another to this work:

Betty Swan
Donna Henley
Kelly Nolen
"Lives of the Wives" Swan group
"The Pink Ladies"
KONOS sisters
Stan and Sue Keith

Bruce Cripe
Gary and Giselle Smith
John Newkirk
Doug Fox
Vicki Brady
Peter Heitt
Yvonne Osterwald - "Page Maker Lady"

TABLE OF CONTENTS

FOREWORD

Our family's first visit to the Swans' home nestled in the mountains outside Denver remains forever etched in our memories. Imagine walking into a friend's house for the first time only to be confronted with a 200-pound side of elk stretched out on the kitchen table!* What do a bunch of city slickers from back East do when first facing a side of elk? Sit down and join the carving party, of course! The next few days were to be life changing!

For one thing, we soon learned Karey cooks everything from scratch. There's not one single store-bought can of anything in her pantry. I checked! Now, like many of you, I've never considered grinding my own wheat kernels to bake melt-in-your-mouth breakfast sweet rolls, or pulverizing my own coriander with a mortar and pestle since it tastes better that way!

But life at the Swans' is more than delicious, healthy home-cooked meals. It's singing after dinner beside the wood cook stove. It's listening to Monte and Karey philosophize about marriage and family relationships. It's hiking through mountain passes, collecting quartz and marveling at the handiwork of our Creator God. It's learning to can pears from the farmer's market, and making homemade soap with lye and olive oil. It's absorbing old-fashioned wisdom from a loving, tranquil woman of God.

Who hasn't longed for a simpler lifestyle in our complex world? Not all of us can move to the country and build a log cabin. But we can start where we are! Karey says she first raised vegetables in a small garden-style townhouse in Arizona. Maybe I could begin by sprouting seeds under my kitchen sink! Our daughter Heather remarked, "Mrs. Swan's such a good mother. She's right there for her children, quilting and baking, taking care of the home." Karey says she learned the secret for creative homemaking by staying out of the car! Perhaps I could start combining errands so I wouldn't have to leave home more than one day a week.

I couldn't copy Karey's recipes fast enough when I visited her. Life at the Swans' is an experience you wish you could share with all your friends. "Please write your thoughts and recipes on paper for the rest of us," I begged. The next thing I knew, Monte had talked Karey into hostessing a regular radio segment on creative homemaking, and she was compiling those reflections into a book! So much the better for all of us!

Enjoy this peek into the Swans' home. Listen to Karey's musings as she kneads her bread. Step into her root cellar or read her yearly calendar posted on the wall for all to see. And expect the experience to be life changing!

Gayle Graham
Richmond, Virginia

*PS: Where do you think one stores a whole elk until you can put it all up?

INTRODUCTION

Speak the things which are proper for sound doctrine . . .
the older women likewise, be reverent in behavior. . .
teachers of good things—
that they bring the young women to their senses
to love their husbands, to love their children,
to be discreet, chaste, homemakers, good,
obedient to their own husbands,
that the word of God may not be blasphemed.

Titus 2:1-6

This book is something I've toyed with writing for a long time. Why? Why do most people write books? Many are probably written because people have encouraged them, saying "You have something to share." "We like this. Can you give us some more?" Some people have probably been doing workshops, classes or talks and eventually accumulate enough loose notes and paperwork to compile. If people attending those sessions really benefited, then there are others who may like the information too.

My first workshops have been around the kitchen table, initially while practicing hospitality with friends and guests. People were always taking home recipes or craft ideas. They would say, "My family likes all your recipes, would you share some more?" "You should do classes." So I started doing classes, mainly cooking classes, but those often overflowed with crafts as well. I've done some quilt-piecing classes too. Kathy von Duyke, a friend and writer, said I should write a book - and the best way to begin is to write articles. So I wrote some articles for a national newsletter she was currently publishing. Then, my best friend and husband, Monte, who is always encouraging me and helping me to grow and stretch, started telling various persons about my abilities, and surprise . . . I'm doing radio segments!

The first little ditties could be considered my abstracts. They are actually some of my radio segments. I thought to leave them intact and at the beginning of this book because they sum up so well what my articles have been based on. And they must have tantalized listeners because it has been necessary to respond to many people. This last response has been the incentive to finally produce a compiled work. Many of the recipes were initially printed for my baking classes. Then as I prepared them for written articles I had to remember what we talked about during the class process and subsequently added those details - the hows and whys and tips. Through the process of trying to put this all together, other memories of interesting topics were added.

Solomon said, "There is nothing new under the sun." Are my ideas new? No. "What has been done will be done again." My ideas surely are not new, but maybe the way in which I present them is new. I have stood on the shoulders of many and see from a slightly different perspective than they. This really is not complete by any means. It is a beginning. Hopefully a good beginning for you. Our life, our family, our story is still in progress. More additions may follow as I put more thoughts and recipes on paper (computer!). Enjoy my chattiness and ramblings throughout.

Homemaking Life Skills

Our children's education should not be limited to the three Rs, but should include life skills necessary for functioning in the adult world. One life skill that many of my friends were not taught as they grew up in the 60s and 70s is cooking. Since most of our daughters will, no doubt, become wives and mothers some day, training in the art of cooking should be a part of every home, and sons should at least be taught cooking survival skills.

Some of you may say, "What does she mean by the art of cooking?" Well, serious cooking requires knowledge of basic physics and chemistry, as well as nutrition. Knowing your ingredients and the importance of freshness and quality combined with culinary skills and proper training in the use of kitchen tools, brings cooking to the level of craft or art. Edith Schaeffer refers to it as one of the *Hidden Arts of Homemaking*! For many of us, if the goal of our home cooking class lies beyond "Mundane Microwave 101," my guess is that we may well be learning the art of cooking right along with our children.

Cooking from Scratch

Cooking from scratch is how grandmother used to do it. It is a life skill that should be taught in every home. Cooking from scratch is simply putting a recipe together using whole, fresh food rather than purchasing processed food. It is grinding your own flour, mixing it with baking powder, eggs, and milk instead of using a packaged pancake mix. It is making your own soup stock and cutting up fresh vegetables instead of reaching for canned soup.

The higher nutritional value and lower cost of cooking from scratch is substantial, not to mention the superior taste. The average family would cut 30% to 50% off their grocery bill and at the same time improve their health by cooking from scratch. With the availability of bulk whole food we enjoy today, kitchen machines that do most of the work, and the mountain of *how to* books, cooking from scratch is within the reach of virtually every family.

ART OF HOMEMAKING

Bread Making

Bread making is one of the most important life skills to include in our home training. Our family not only has saved nearly $4000 dollars over the last 18 years in bread costs, but has greatly enjoyed the health benefits, and loves the taste of bread made from freshly ground flour.

In bread today, the germ, along with other parts of the whole grain, are removed so the bread will have a long shelf life — nutrition comparable to that of saw dust. Once whole grains are cracked and the insides exposed to the air, nutrients are lost, and worse yet, the germ of the grain becomes rancid. It is similar to what happens to the fresh sweet taste of sweet corn a couple of days after it has been picked. There are some 26 known nutrients in wheat. Would you feel cheated if someone took $26 from you and only returned $6? That's exactly how the flour you buy is made, stripped of its nutrients, synthetically enriched and, if lacking preservatives, probably rancid.

Many families view breadmaking as a novelty or luxury they can't afford. Our family is blessed with servants who help with our bread making. When we were first married, not having these servants, I used to make bread by hand. Kneading whole wheat dough by hand takes time as it is critical to knead it thoroughly. About 18 years ago I discovered the Bosch bread kneading machine and view it as my bread-making servant. I have tried several types, wanting to make the most of my efforts. The Bosch kneads six loaves at once! Additionally, I grind my own grains with a Grain Master Whisper Mill to maximize the nutritional value.

Grinding your own grains and baking your own bread saves the average family $400 per year in bread costs. Ten minutes of machine kneading is equal to one hour of hand kneading and is the key to a soft, well-textured whole grain bread.

Avoiding the Center Aisles

Avoiding the center aisles of your grocery store can save you as much as 50% in your grocery bill and ironically improve your family's diet. The grocery store's center aisles contain expensive, processed and pre-prepared foods like potato chips, cold breakfast cereals, and soft drinks. These foods are largely responsible for the chronic health problems afflicting our modern society. Did you know that you are paying nearly 3 dollars per pound for the potatoes in a bag of potato chips compared to 10 cents per pound for fresh potatoes?

On the other hand, whole fresh foods such as carrots, grains and apples are found in the perimeter of the grocery store. Or they can be purchased at even less cost from farmers' markets or food co-ops. If optimum health and the family budget are priorities, these should make up the bulk of our diets. Knowing these basic, fresh, whole foods and how to use them is a life skill I would recommend for every home's curriculum.

Fat Calorie Calculation

I'm sure you have all heard that lowering your fat intake is the most important step you can take toward improving your diet and controlling your weight. But how do you do it? Since many people love the hands-on, discovery approach to learning, let me suggest that each family member keep a diary or record of his/her fat calorie percent intake per meal per day for a week. Here's a three-step recipe for this family project:

1. Add up the total calories you consume during the day.

2. Add up the total grams of fat consumed and multiply the total grams by nine. This is your total calorie intake from fat.

3. Divide your total fat calorie intake by your total food calories. This is your fat calorie percentage.

If it is under 30% or better yet 20%, congratulate yourself, because your diet is probably filled with grains, legumes, vegetables, and fruits - essential keys to good health and weight control. If it is above 30% you now know how to lower it. Actually, all this wouldn't be necessary if we avoided processed and fried foods.

Carbohydrates

When I was growing up, "carbohydrates" had a negative connotation, particularly in the minds of people who were overweight. But empty carbohydrates in foods such as bleached white flour and sugar are the villains. Their carbohydrates have been refined to a simpler chemical state and, as a result, their calories are empty calories, because important vitamins, minerals, and fiber have been processed out for the sake of texture and shelf-life.

Natural whole carbohydrates, on the other hand, are good carbohydrates and should not be a threat to overweight people. They are contained in foods such as whole, fresh grains, fruits, and vegetables. Recent research has shown that these carbohydrates and the nutrients that accompany them in whole foods, pave the road to optimum nutrition. As we teach our children nutrition, we go beyond the facts with a concrete, hands-on approach by touching their palates. When it comes to nutrition, an educated palate, in our opinion, is as important as an educated mind.

14

Homemaking Beyond Maintenance

     I saw a stitchery years ago that said, "If a mother's place is in the home, then why am I forever in the car?" Some mothers have responsibilities that take them away from home everyday, but for most of us, daily trips are really unnecessary and can be a serious distraction. I've learned to keep lists and consolidate our trips, I find that *I* need to remain home for long stretches of time in order to get beyond the maintenance part of homemaking (stuff like cleaning, laundry, and ironing). If I don't stay home, I miss the creative part of homemaking, which for me is needlework, crafting a dried flower wreath, training a young heart, or giving hospitality to a tired friend. Without these I'd go crazy and burnout would become a serious threat.

Behold, I have given you every plant bearing seed,
which is upon the surface of all the earth,
and every tree which has fruit yielding seed;
to you it shall be for meat.

Genesis 1:29

Part of the secret of success in life is to eat what you like
and let the food fight it out inside.

Mark Twain

Adam and Eve ate the first vitamins, including the package.

ER Squibb

He who laughs, lasts.

Mary Poole

On the seventh day God ended his work which he had done;
and He rested on the seventh day.

Genesis 2:2

Chapter One
HOMEMADE HEALTH

I have always had an interest in nutrition, particularly practical insights into health. I probably inherited this tendency from my grandmother, who was a nurse. She left the medical world - when it began focusing on synthesizing medicine and "putting bandaids on symptoms" - and became a homeopathic nurse. She would be quite in demand today considering the current homeopathic revival. I gleaned a lot of tidbits from her, since she was always throwing them about. My mother got interested in health foods when I was in high school, so I had exposure there too. In college, I started out majoring in nutrition, but switched to landscape architecture.

When I got married in 1975, I developed a love for reading cookbooks. My husband, Monte, has nurtured this love by stocking my kitchen with 199 cookbooks. I taught myself to make foods from scratch, how to garden, and preserve and store food. I am the type of person who likes to understand the hows and whys of everything — to know the basics and the bottom line. When you know your ingredients and how each affects the finished product (the "tools of learning" cooking), you understand what things go together to make something really good. It becomes a craft, an instinctive art. With a thorough understanding of the basics you will be able to make anything. (I even read about how to make marshmallows . . . as a result I don't care to eat them now!) In 1978 I began investigating machines that grind grains and help in making bread because I felt grinding one's own grains would be most nutritious, besides being cost and time effective. These machines help me do the best job possible as a homemaker and are important tools for a "domestic engineer." At the time, bread was the one food my youngsters would always eat, and I wanted it to be the best bread possible! Of course bread isn't the only thing these machines can be used for, but that was my initial purpose.

Several years ago while doing baking classes for some friends, I gave them a homework assignment that turned out to be life-changing for one family. The assignment had everyone's family analyze its fat calorie percent intake per meal, per day. Our own family had done it and it proved to be an eye opener. In the process I lost pounds and now am at the weight I was when I got married. Heather, now eighteen, still (after three years) omits butter on her toast. Travis, sixteen, raids the pantry of pretzels or other non-fat fillers to raise his non-fat calorie percent which brings down his butter and cheese-induced fat calorie percent. We learned that unspecified calories are not the main consideration in dieting - the key is your fat calorie percent. Monte made up a fat calorie calculation/record-keeping chart that I now give to everyone who attends my baking classes. Everyone learns a lot because it is personal, hands-on, discovery, real-life, learning - besides having major implications for improving the quality of your life and preventing diseases! Our family originally planned to do this chart for a week but after only a few days we saw the light, or the big picture.

1. Keep track of all you put in your mouth (and swallow, of course) for the day and add up all the calories (from fat, carbohydrates, protein, etc).

2. Next, add up the total grams of fat for everything you ate that day and multiply the total by 9. This number is your total fat calorie intake for the day.

3. Then divide this number (total fat calories) by the total calories for the day. This is your fat calorie percentage.

For example, if the total calories of food is 100 and the grams of fat 3.3, then the fat calorie percentage is 30%, because:

(9 calories/grams of fat) x (3.3 grams of fat) = 30 fat calories.

(30 fat calories) ÷ (100 total calories) = 30 % of total calories from fat.

FOOD	Total Calories	Fat x 9 = Fat Calorie	Fat Calories ÷ Total Calories = % Fat
Breakfast			
Lunch			
Supper			
Snacks			
Day Totals			

Around 30% fat calories is what the FDA recommends. We really should consume closer to 20% or less, especially if we have a weight or health problem. The bottom line and what our children learn, is to consume an abundance of grains, beans, vegetables, and fruits to bring down (dilute) the fat calories percentage. Eating 15 to 30 grams of fat per day will keep your average under 20% fat calories if you eat between 1200 and 2600 calories. Count calories of fat, not total calories!

Don't be fooled by labels either. When ham or ice cream, etc. say 95% fat free, you are only told the percent of fat by weight. The total fat as a percentage of calories is usually over 60%!! — twice as high as your maximum should be. But you can earn the "privilege" of eating this fat by eating a lot of rice or some other low-fat food. Popular 2% milk contains 38% fat calories. One percent milk contains 18% fat calories and skim milk contains 3% fat calories.

> Don't just count Calories! Count Fat!

18

I refer to children learning, but we adults are learning right along with the kids (and modeling, remember)! One mom in my class, a very good friend of mine, decided to take it all seriously and put it into practice. She is very overweight, or I should say *was*. She was tired of cooking and wanted a change. She bought "kitchen servant machines" I mention, (see bibliography) took my recipes from my classes, and jumped in. Her first comments to me were, "Everything I've made has turned out great! Everyone loves everything!" Then she decided to continue keeping track of her fat consumption and clamped down. After almost a year, she is still thanking me, and has lost 70 pounds(!) and plans to continue. She recently told me that people can do it by learning how and what to eat and by not making excuses like ". .but my husband . . but my kids . . but we had this wedding, and this company, etc." She's accountable for herself. You have to learn to eat right. Diets, starvation, and drinks do not teach you *how to eat* and you will just put it all back on and more. You can have a "feast meal" once a week if you feel deprived of certain foods, otherwise you may lose the motivation as you keep heading toward a long-term health-promoting change. Another note here is that there are a lot of skinny, unhealthy "fat" people walking around too. The goal is to design a strategy that will work for you.

We made a Nutrition Target poster. The children put foods closest to the bulls-eye that are least adulterated and processed, generally WHOLE foods, and the worst foods, highly processed, around the rim. This target comes from studying healthy world cultures. Without exception, 50% of healthy world cultures' foods are grains, nuts, seeds, and beans; 30% vegetables; 10% fruits; 6% dairy products; and 4% meat. Many of us grew up with the four food groups circle and seem to put most of our focus on meats and dairy products. We need to change our approach to meal preparation and focus on the grains, beans, and vegetables with meat as an accompaniment.

Nutrition Target

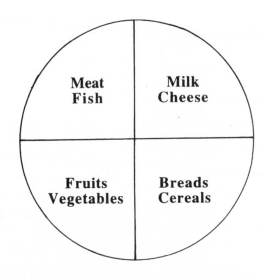

Four Food Groups Circle

19

The Battle of the Pyramids

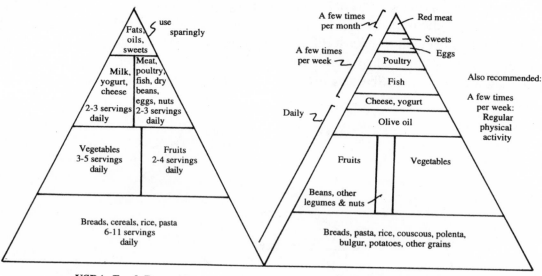

USDA Food Pyramid

The Mediterranean diet

We now have the food pyramid, as of 1992, but I heard the head of the USDA say he still doesn't feel it's the best visual approach — our eyes are drawn to the point rather than the bottom, where the grains are. We've also grown up with negative connotations of carbohydrates. A negative emphasis should be placed on empty carbohydrates, while natural whole carbohydrates need to be top priority! [The July 4, 1994 edition of *US News & World Report* had an article on the new Mediterranean diet which breaks down the food pyramid further by illustrating what to consume daily versus weekly versus monthly along with other details — like bringing beans down closer to the grains, dividing the dairy and meats, and adding olive oil (which is your best source of fat since it is mono-unsaturated — all animal products contain saturated fat).]

Along with this Target poster's nutrition, we analyzed the costs of these foods. My kids have learned that a bag of grain prepared as cooked cereal goes a lot further financially than packaged, cold cereals. Our pressure cooker brings preparation time down to minutes. Oat groats, millet and flax seed is one of our favorites. Homemade breads, and other homemade items, are generally going to be much more nutritious and trivial in cost compared to packaged mixes and pre-made items.

About the time I thought I had nutrition pretty much understood - at least the major aspects of it - the Paleolithic diet was published in *The Zone*. This book challenges the high-carbohydrate diet as unnaturally out of balance and a threat to maintaining proper hormone and insulin levels. The diet recommends low-fat protein and low-density carbohydrate fruits and fiber-rich vegetables. The MIT researcher, Dr. Barry Sears, developer of this diet, says we should be eating like cavemen not cows. By eating so much grain, he claims, we are fattening ourselves the same way we fatten our grain cattle for slaughter. But how does this relate to Genesis 1:29? In recent years our family has slowly moved toward the high-density carbohydrate diet. But at the same time, continuing to use primarily the low-fat wild game (elk and fish) as our meat source. So to a large degree we have followed the Paleolithic diet - possibly combining the best of both diets. Diets are highly personal. The common sense guidelines in my book use whole, fresh, and balance as the key. Special health problems demand special diets.

What we do need to realize is that all too often, we look at what different cultures eat, and then pick and choose. Imagine putting together jigsaw puzzles. There's a puzzle of Mexico, a puzzle of the Mediterranian area, a puzzle of Alaska, or China, or Africa. Can we take pieces from each of these and make a new puzzle that fits together into a new clear picture? There are other variables involved in these regions' health. To pull out a variable here and there may not work for us. A possible key to this puzzle is presented in another book, *Eat Right for Your Type*. The research on which the book is based sorts diets according to your blood type.

Speaking of nutrition, again, our nation's food system developed as more people moved from the country to the cities. Food needed to be shipped and stored for the masses. The loss of nutrients comes primarily from needing to lengthen the shelf-life of foods. Once whole grains are cracked and the insides exposed to the air, the germ of the grain (that life-giving element that allows the grain to reproduce itself) becomes rancid (oxidizes) within days. As a result, the germ, along with other parts of the whole grain, is removed to lengthen its shelf-life (a shelf-life comparable to saw dust). This means all flours, mixes, and pre-made foods are nearly devoid of nutrients. We have become so accustomed to highly processed flours we forget that earlier cooks knew only whole-grain flours. Dr. A. J. Carlson, a leading investigator on foods and nutrition, graphically stated, "When rats and gray squirrels are given corn in abundance, they eat the germ and leave the rest. People leave the germ and eat the rest." The flour you buy is stripped of its nutrients by bleaching (chemical residues remain), and enriched (probably synthetically), and then the whole grain flours, unless you know they've been ground and immediately frozen, have lost most of their nutrients and gone rancid. This is why I grind my flour. When vegetable oil (part of the grains' germ) goes rancid, it may be

Genesis 1: 29
Behold, I have given you every plant bearing seed,
which is upon the surface of all the earth,
and every tree which has fruit yielding seed;
to you it shall be for meat.

difficult to taste the spoilage, but do not be fooled, it produces free radicals which, if ingested, do dangerous cell damage to your body. Rancidity is the chemical change in fat or oil produced by the combination of oxygen from the air, with unsaturated fatty acids in the oil, producing substances called aldehydes (or free radicals) which are harmful to your health. They are present in many popular health foods such as wheat germ, vegetable oils, and sesame seeds, for example. Without preservatives it is important to make sure these foods are fresh.

When it comes to shopping for your food, try to think WHOLE. That is how God made food. Recent nutrition research unanimously concludes that whole food is the best way to go. Buy your herbs and spices whole and grind with a mortar and pestle when needed - superior flavor! Would you sit and eat 10 apples, plums or oranges, or 300 grapes in one sitting? (Result: the "runs" or canker sores!) But you ingest that when drinking juice, without the benefit of the pulp and fiber. Our family dilutes juice or drinks it in small quantities. God made the whole and we often take only a part of it, usually leaving out necessary elements. If you keep a list of items running low on your shelf and learn to stock the basics (remember: think WHOLE) and how to make things from scratch (you may need a better cookbook), you will not be running to the store every day. Also, when you keep and use the basics you do not need to be utilizing the center aisles of the grocery store; just keep to the perimeter and you'll find your grocery budget brought way down and the general health of your family brought way up.

I am not a physician nor a certified dietician. I have my opinions on lots of things; I am a mom, who simply loves to read books. The majority of my knowledge is self-taught from a wide range of books and years of jumping in and trying things. Monte has always encouraged me to do this. He is a scientist. Our family doctor refers to Monte as "Dr. Swan," since he usually has every ailment diagnosed before the doctor does. Anyway, Monte is always trying to unravel the ultimate cause of everything and the philosophical implications of these causes. While most of the medical profession prefers to treat the condition with medication, I prefer lifestyle modification, which includes positive changes in diet, exercise, attitude, etc. When it comes to cooking, food preservation, gardening, sewing and crafting, etc. (all parts of our lifestyle), I can speak from my trial and error experiences. Over the years many people often respond "How do you know and do all you do?" My frequent reply is that I **jump in and do** — literally!

A lot of people give excuses like, "Oh, when I can move to the country and have lots of room and a big kitchen and lots of storage . . ." Believe me, if you don't jump in and "do" where you are, you'll never "do!" You've heard the sayings: "Bloom where you are planted." "He that is faithful with his little, will be given more;" and, "Moses, what do you hold in your hand?"

Another point I bring up is that you need to remain home for long stretches of time in order to get beyond the urgent or simple maintainence, in order to be creative. I saw a stitchery years ago that had in the middle, "If a mother's place is in the home, then why am I forever in the car?!" The border showed many activities: soccer, ballet, gymnastics . . .

From the beginning we have tried to protect our family lifestyle. For example, I believe children need long stretches of time to complete their "play" thoughts. In our culture, we daily uproot our children, often many times a day, to run here and there and everywhere. And then we wonder why they have short attention spans (of course TV ["Sesame Street" included] contributes to this). I also thought about us women. We come out of twelve years of school and maybe college. After all those years of daily stimuli, we get married and *try* to stay home (TV images don't help here either)! We're addicted. We are conditioned to an unnatural way of life and are driven by self-imposed external forces.

22

and what do we choose? We often look for an image in someone else's mirror, and so have avoided seeing our real selves. The Bible does give us guidelines to use as a grid to filter, measure and evaluate all that comes our way. As women our primary job descriptions are relational and nurturing. I do want to be a help-mate, not a half-mate; a husband-lover and child-lover. We need to focus more on *being*, than on doing. "Being" does mean becoming, but we run so fast . . . it is only when we slow down, when we seem to stop, that we move away from the selfish self towards the real. The most real people are able to forget their selfish selves and have true compassion; a giving of oneself away unselfconsciously. The bottom line is "a woman who fears the Lord, she shall be praised" - a wife rightly related to her Lord, will be rightly related to her husband and others. She fears the Lord, not society, not friends.

Who do we try to please? What ideals have we set before us? Where did they come from? Am I looking in the wrong mirrors? Are we getting substitute images for reality? At times we don't take the Bible seriously, thinking it doesn't really relate to where we're living. In reading, I've found the New Testament days were very similar to our days. Corinth, Ephesus, and Athens were major metropolises for tourism - highly sophisticated and wealthy. Many of their deities were female. Paul was writing to families dealing with many of the same issues, stresses and problems as today. The stoics and epicurians of Paul's day had embraced the same philosophy as naturalists and pantheists of today and had merged them together into a post-modern New Age-like philosophy. Women as well as men were embracing independence. They were autonomous. The institution of marriage was in retreat and family life was in shambles. Their response was as today - when good institutions are abused, throw the baby out with the bathwater! Home was an option for the woman. Paul was stepping out against what was popular when laying out relationship principles. If we are told "We can do it all" (do-it-yourself-ism) - something has to give. With all our options, how

Do I ever ramble! When you evaluate and prioritize, just remember, the hand that rocks the cradle still holds the greatest influence in this world. And in order "to train up a child in the way he should go" we ourselves need to be chewing on something to pass on and model.

Everything has been thought of before, but the problem is to think of it again . . .
It is the great triumph of genius to make the common appear novel.
JW Goethe

All the really good ideas I ever had came to me while I was milking a cow.
Grant Wood

The best time for planning a book is while you're doing the dishes.
Agatha Christie

To lengthen thy life, lessen thy meals.
Benjamin Franklin

Chapter Two
BREAKFAST ANYONE?!!

Breakfast may not be your favorite meal, but it may be your most important meal. Today people lead dangerously busy lives and often overlook and even skip!! breakfast. Also, their concept of breakfast is the all-American "traditional" breakfast of eggs and bacon, which is unfortunately, time-consuming and unhealthy, especially for sedentary people. One hundred years ago when people physically worked long hours they could get away with a fat-rich breakfast, not only because of the exercise element but because they diluted the fat in their diet with vast amounts of carbohydrates from non-processed foods. Starting the day nutritionally right is very important! Let me give you two good reasons:

1) Food is fuel, and you cannot run on empty for long. Have you ever wondered what the word "breakfast" means? It means that you are *breaking your fast* of the night. Eating a simple something breaks the inactive sleep cycle - starting the body's metabolism, and preventing the mid-morning slump that sends most people looking for a quick fix — usually of fats, sugars, or even caffeine. Your body actually craves more food as the day progresses, to catch up on the needed nutrients missed earlier in the day. When you skip meals, your body activates a starvation defense and stores fat for survival and lowers your metabolic rate (calorie burning) which leaves you with a *fat metabolism*. By eating regular meals and nutritious snacks, you can actually raise your

metabolic rate and begin to burn more calories creating a *lean metabolism.*

2) Food is fuel, and when I say "eat a simple something," I mean a whole-grain and whole-fruit breakfast, which sounds simple but is surprisingly full of complex nutrients. Recent research (nothing new to my mother) suggests that the incredible complexity of whole foods may be a key to cancer and heart disease prevention, whereas enriched processed foods supplemented with highly-concentrated vitamins may not be a quick fix answer. This thinking is consistent with the idea that God knew what He was doing when He created grains, vegetables, fruits, and legumes. Something as simple as whole wheat toast or a dish of oatmeal and an apple will make a big difference in your energy level for the day and will even affect your other food choices throughout the day. Fat-loaded foods put major stress on your digestive system and possibly even your immune system. Some would say that your blood, in a sense, becomes "sticky," resulting in sluggish circulation through the brain. What we need are complex carbohydrates. Whole grains provide a steady release of glucose into our bloodstream, thus stabilizing blood sugar, emotions, and nerves. A simple nourishing breakfast gives high, long-lasting energy for the whole day and reduces the urge to snack or overeat later. Keep in mind that refined carbohydrates (sweets and white flour products) will make you feel hungry within a short time because of their effect on your blood sugar levels. Whole grains comprise much of the base of the food pyramid and form the cornerstone of

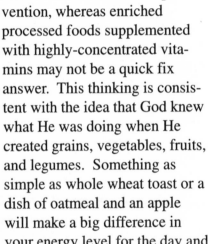

MENU

**oatmeal
apple
wheat toast**

good health and weight control. The more food we eat in its natural state the healthier we will be.

The nutrient value of whole food varies according to the quality of the soil, how it was grown, when it was harvested, and how fresh it is. Although it is difficult to control the first few variables, the last variable is really only a matter of education. For example, a grain of wheat is sealed and stable until it is ground. Grinding mixes oxygen with the wheat which causes its complex nutrients to react with the air (oxidation). Additionally, the wheat germ oil in the wheat will go rancid (free radical formation) within a few days. This scenario occurs in all vegetables, fruits, and legumes. Thus eating whole fruits, grinding your own grains, and generally avoiding processed foods, such as store-bought breakfast cereals, is a stepping stone to optimum health. Remember the cost factor of whole grain cereals versus store-bought processed cereals. All of your whole grains are a bargain and have not lost their nutrients as processed cereals have!

We may be attached to certain foods. I for one love store-bought cold cereals! This may be because some foods represent the comfort and security of our childhood home. So some of our eating habits are due to emotional factors or even sugar and fat addiction. We may be eating for reasons other than physical hunger: i.e. comfort, pleasure, anger, boredom, stress and the like. I associate drinking mugs of hot beverages with warm conversations and fellowship. My son Travis associates curling up and reading a book with snacking, especially eating ice cream!

Another commonly overlooked ingredient in breaking your fast is water. Drinking several glasses of pure water (lukewarm not icy cold) immediately after waking can do wonders for your health. Most Americans are chronically dehydrated. Our voice teacher says drinking several quarts of water per day is the best way to keep your vocal cords healthy. Did you know that water is crucial for your brain to function at its full potential? It is also the key to solving many of our digestive problems. Keeping your body hydrated and starting up your digestive system gently with water makes sense. Sitting down a little later to a relaxed wholesome breakfast is the ideal way to nutritionally start your day.

Breakfast has always been my favorite meal of the day. There is no way I would skip it! And it has never been just a doughnut-coffee meal either. I do love the taste of coffee and I do drink it. Have you ever tried fasting, and found you have gotten a headache?! Sometimes it is due to not eating, especially if you have hypoglycemic tendencies. But most likely, it is because you missed your regular morning coffee. In fact, earlier in our marriage I used to think I was allergic to church, but decided my head ached because we slept later on Sunday, therefore had coffee later.

Begin now to incorporate more wholesome foods into your breakfast. Make a conscientious effort to eat a WHOLEsome breakfast every day. Your tastes will change, as will your health and weight! So here's to a satisfying and energetic morning with some of our favorites!

Waffles need the extra oil to prevent sticking. I often make waffles for a supper and use the frozen extras for a breakfast.

Blending whole grain kernels in the blender works only in Bosch or Vitamix type blenders; no other typical American brands will work! Believe me I've tried it.

When making pancakes, I like to sprinkle poppy seeds on top of the still moist batter before turning; a nice crunch.

I multiply this recipe 3 or 4 times when making waffles to have frozen extra for toaster waffles!

When no fresh pears are available, I use my home canned pears or dehydrated pears, but you need to remember to re-hydrate these by soaking.

Vanilla Yogurt
> *1 1/2 cups plain yogurt*
> *2 tsp vanilla extract*
> *1 1/2 Tb maple syrup*

Whole Kernel Pancakes / Waffles

2 cups flour
or 1 1/2 cups whole grain kernels (oats, barley, buckwheat, corn . . .) Grind in blender (see side note) with the following water on high for 4 minutes.
2 cups water
1/3 cup powdered milk
1-2 eggs
1 Tb baking powder
1/2 tsp salt
1/3 c oil (can use less for pancakes)

(I often add a handful of sesame and flax seeds to the batter)

Mix it all together thoroughly. (This gets very thick in the blender so after the initial grain grinding pour it into a bowl. Most of the time I grind all the grains in the grain mill and then mix up the batter.) For pancakes, I dilute with more water so they are thinner. We don't like thick, cakey, gooey pancakes.

We usually serve our pancakes and waffles with maple syrup, or with home frozen or canned rhubarb and yogurt. This pear sauce is great on waffles:

Maple Pear Sauce

3 pears
2 Tb maple syrup
1/2 tsp vanilla extract
1/4 cup sliced almonds
1/8 cup wheat germ
1 Tb butter

Slice pears in thin wedges and cut into bite size pieces. Mix all of this together and either bake in the oven at 350° for 10-15 minutes or zap in the microwave, stirring to heat through. This served with maple syrup flavored yogurt and vanilla extract is heavenly!

Yogurt

We make our own yogurt and it is very easy to make:

I use all milk that I make from non-instant nonfat dry powdered milk (non-instant powdered milk needs to be blended in the blender). Most recipes have you add 1/3 cup powdered milk to a quart of milk. In a stainless steel, glass, or enameled pot, heat the milk to 180°. Remove the milk from the heat, let it cool to 110°, and add 3 Tb of fresh, room temperature yogurt with an active culture. Mix well to distribute the starter evenly, but do not beat or whip. Set the mixture to incubate at 110-115°. The easiest way to maintain a constant temp is in an electric yogurt maker. However I've heard of using a warming plate covered with a towel, your oven, a thermos, etc. Check your yogurt after 3 hours. It could take up to ten hours to set. Look for it to be just barely setting because it will firm more in the refrigerator. The longer the yogurt remains in the machine the more tart it becomes. The less the time the sweeter. Flavor your yogurt after refrigeration. You can use homemade jams, teaspoons of frozen juice concentrate, juice nectar, maple syrup, etc.

Use all non-fat, or 1% milk. The less fat, the better the usable calcium.

In the past, I always purchased yogurt for a starter, but lately it seems most yogurts are adding other ingredients that must be inhibiting it from thickening. A starter can be bought, usually powdered, from a health food store and then your own homemade yogurt can be used as starter. Just remember to save some!

Yogurt is your best dairy source for calcium. It is basically milk with "friendly bacteria." It's an outstanding source of protein and vitamins including your Bs. Yogurt boosts the immune system and has a natural antibiotic effect. I had penicillin a lot as a kid and my homeopathic grandma kept telling my mom to give me yogurt! Synthesized antibiotics kill not only your body's bad bacteria, but also the good bacteria. Yogurt also helps aid food digestion because it is "pre-digested" by the bacteria culture it contains and tends to "crowd out" bacteria associated with indigestion.

Whenever a recipe calls for sour cream or mayonnaise I use yogurt. It can also be substituted for buttermilk.

Fresh Granola

I have to give the credit for this recipe to Kathy von Duyke. Her 15-year-old son Brian, made it once for breakfast when we had a lot of homeschool families from across the North American continent at our house for a "camp" week.

Toast 2 cups thick rolled grains (oats, barley, rye, wheat, etc.) in a dry skillet. Remove from the skillet into a bowl. Melt 2 Tb of butter in the skillet and add 1/4 - 1/3 cup molasses and let bubble together awhile. Add the toasted rolled grain. Brian added slivered almonds and chopped fresh apple.

28

I rarely do wheat for homemade cereals, or pancakes and waffles. We use so much wheat for other baked goods that I think it best to use a variety, get a balance. We like oat, barley, millet, and corn.

For a nuttier taste variation toast the grains in a dry skillet before cooking. You could also add raisins, dates, dried fruit pieces, etc. to the water before adding cereal, which sweetens the liquid.

In any of these kinds of baked recipes such as the Flake cereal, cookies, crackers, muffins, etc, if your flour is freshly ground it has a lot of air space and you may need to measure in more flour than the recipe calls for, otherwise it will be too sticky. For all cooking other than bread baking, I have fresh ground flour sit a day to settle and all the recipes work, especially with the white wheat.

These kinds of recipes usually call for rolling between two pieces of plastic wrap but I prefer to roll directly onto the pan.

We like to eat cereals with molasses or maple syrup, though I've always been a nut for brown sugar. The boys use milk. The rest of us use Rice Dream. Sometimes, Monte uses yogurt. I like my yogurt separate on the side.

Hot Cereal - Cream of . .

(If done in blender see note on blender under whole kernel pancakes. Blend on high 2-3 minutes [depends on coarseness you want])

> 1 cup whole grain flour
> or   3/4 c whole grain kernels—any grain or mixture of grains. If doing whole grains in blender—see note on blenders under Whole Kernel Pancakes, pg. 27. Blend with following water—2-4 minutes depending on the coarseness you want.
> 1 1/2 cups water

Start heating in a saucepan:
> 1 1/2-2 cups more water
> 1/2 tsp salt

Pour in water/flour (or blender) mixture and cook for about 20 minutes, stirring occasionally. You can oil the sides of the pan to help prevent sticking. Or cook in a covered double boiler. (Raw taste is the result of <u>under cooking</u>.) Or see note on microwave cooking in cornmeal mush recipe on next page.

Lately we've been cooking the cracked grains in a pressure cooker for about 5-10 minutes and then blending the cooked grains in the blender.

Flake Cereal
> 2 cups flour
> (oat, barley, corn, buckwheat, wheat . .)
> 1/4 cup dry milk
> 1/2 tsp salt
> 2 Tb honey or molasses
> 1/2 cup water

Combine in mixer using wire whips and mix well. Divide into 3 or 4 parts. Roll out onto cookie sheets as thin as possible. You have to use cookie sheets without sides or the rolling pin handles won't allow you to roll it thin. Bake at 350° about 10-20 minutes until lightly brown.

I usually break off outside pieces and put the rest back in the oven for the center to brown since we like well-browned flavor. Break into small pieces and eat as regular cold cereal.

Quinoa & Buckwheat

Toast 1 cup quinoa & 1 cup buckwheat in a dry skillet, stirring occasionally. (You'll hear little popping noises once it gets going.) At the same time, in a large saucepan, bring 4 cups salted water to a boil. When boiling, slowly pour in the grain. (It always foams up, so I slide the pan halfway off the burner until it's all in and stirred.) Lower the heat and simmer with the lid on for about 20 minutes until all the liquid is absorbed, stir occasionally.

We eat this cereal with plain yogurt and maple syrup.

Home-Made Grapenuts

> 2 cups water
> 1/2 cup milk powder
> 1/2 cup honey
> 2 tsp baking powder
> 1 tsp salt
> about 3 1/2 cups flour

Mix all well. I use my mixer with wire whips. Add the last cup of flour slowly so as not to get too stiff. I usually switch to the kneading arm if any batter gets too stiff. Pour and spread batter onto lightly greased cookie sheet. Bake at 350° about 35-45 minutes. Cool, then break into pieces and put through the meat grinder. Put crumbs on cookie sheet and toast at 300° until dry and crisp; or you can dehydrate the crumbs to finish them off instead of baking in the oven. This cereal can become quite hard. The real store-bought Grapenuts taste too malty and salty for me now.

Cornmeal Mush

Mix 2 cups cornmeal with 1 tsp salt. Stir in 2 cups cold water. Bring 3 1/4 cups water to a boil and gradually stir in cornmeal mixture. Cook, stirring constantly, over low heat, until thickened.

My new way to make this is in the microwave. Combine all the ingredients in a glass casserole dish. Cover and cook on high for 5 minutes, stir, cook 5 minutes again, stir. Let sit to thicken. Since all microwaves are different, you may need to cook a minute or so longer. Microwaving works for all hot cereals.

30

I crave Quinoa & Buckwheat. The kids really like it now too, but it took awhile. It's different! You'll think it has a slightly burnt flavor, but this is normal.

Raw buckwheat tastes better when toasted. If you buy kasha buckwheat, it is already toasted. Some bitter residues may be left on quinoa. It is usually washed prior to sale, but it is still suggested to rinse before using. I don't rinse the quinoa for using in this cereal. Toasting helps to eliminate any bitterness and provides another dimension in flavor. I toast the quinoa and buckwheat in the pressure cooker base, add the salted water, bring to a boil and pressure cook a few minutes.

Bosch has now come out with cookie whips for stiff batter.

I've heard of grating it while it is still warm, but I don't know how this works.

Store this in a big glass jar on the pantry counter. Guests always ask what it is (as they do other stuff in my pantry!).

I've always loved this cereal, but always made it with store-bought cornmeal. This is a different consistency than with fresh-ground corn flour. We prefer the fresh-ground corn flour. Corn is good sweetened with honey.

This is also good to chill in a loaf pan, slice, coat in cornmeal or flour and fry on griddle. I used to do this for lunches with the leftovers, but now we don't have leftovers.

French Toast with Tofu

1 pkg tofu - 10.25 oz
2/3 - 1 cup water
dash of salt
dash of nutmeg
1 - 3 tsp cinnamon
2 tsp -1 Tb vanilla
3 eggs
1 Tb oil

This is a favorite of our guests as well as our own family.

The best tofu I've found is the MoriNu brand. It is so creamy, not grainy like others. We even use it in shakes, blended with frozen fruit, honey and water.

Tofu is so good for you and is said to reduce cancer. It has no cholesterol, and is rich in protein, calcium and potassium. Tofu has no flavor and takes on whatever seasoning you add. It is very versatile and can be used as sandwich spread, dip, or baby food. Thawed tofu has a meaty texture.

Blend in blender until smooth and creamy. Place mixture in a shallow dish and dip slices of whole wheat bread into it. Fry on griddle until brown on both sides. (My griddle needs no oil so I don't *fry* mine, just brown.) Serve as you like. This recipe really cuts down on eggs, in fact, you can use less if you like.

Oven French Toast

Fill a greased 9 x13 baking dish with 1 inch slices of bread.

Blend together in blender till creamy:

    1 pkg of tofu
    3 eggs
    1 cup milk powder
    3 cups water
    2 tsp-1Tb vanilla
    1/2 tsp nutmeg
    1/2 - 1 tsp cinnamon

Pour mixture over bread slices. Cover and refrigerate overnight.

Make topping (set aside till time to bake):
Melt together:

    1/3 - 1/2 cup butter,
    1 1/3 cup brown sugar
    3 Tb molasses

Sprinkle 1 cup nuts over toast and spread topping.

Bake at 350° for 50 minutes until puffed and golden.

Oven Oat Pancake

Put 1 Tb butter or oil in #10 cast-iron skillet on low heat with 2 Tb brown sugar or honey while you mix up the pancake batter.

2 eggs, separated

Whip the egg whites first and transfer them to another bowl to add later.

Beat egg yolks well and add:
1 cup rolled oats
1 cup yogurt
1 Tb sugar

Mix. Add:
1/4 tsp baking powder
1/4 tsp baking soda
1/4 tsp salt

When all mixed, gently add beaten egg whites. Pour in the skillet and put in a 350° oven for 20 minutes.

I keep saying this is a favorite for so many, but this is!

I now double this recipe and bake in a larger dish, like a 9 x 13, melting the butter with brown sugar in the heating oven.

Pankaka

2 cups milk
4 eggs
1 Tb sugar
1 cup flour

Mix all together with a wire whip and pour into a well-greased 9 x 13 dish. Bake at 400° for 20-30 minutes.

Another Oven Pancake. Pankaka was always made at Monte's grandma's house on washday, because the cookstove was fired up to heat washwater and she utilized the hot oven. It was and still is a family favorite and company loves it.

I know that "Pankaka" sounds gross, but it truly is a Swedish word and means "cake in pan." This is so easy!

If you make with unbleached flour, it really puffs up and the center settles at the table like those at Village Inn or a Scandinavian pancake house. It doesn't rise as much with whole wheat, but we still like it. Sometimes I'll melt a cube of butter in the pan while cutting up 4-6 apples in thin wedges and put them in the butter sprinkled with some brown sugar, then pour the batter over and cook as usual.

Rye Cornmeal Pancakes

3 eggs
1/3 cup molasses
1 1/2 cups milk
1 cup rye flour
1 cup cornmeal or flour
1/2 tsp salt

Stir all together. If you like a stiffer batter reduce the eggs to 2 and milk to 1 cup and add more rye flour. Spoon or pour onto heated griddle. Brown on both sides.

Breakfast Bread

Put 3 cups hot water in the blender with
(1 whole orange, quartered & seeds removed
(do not peel) and blend well)
2 cups raisins / dates

Let sit a bit and then pulse to chop the fruit. Pour into the bowl.
Then add:

2 cups more hot water
(or orange juice if orange omitted)
2 Tb instant yeast
1/3 cup oil
1/3 cup honey
1/4 cup molasses
2-3 Tb cinnamon
1/4 cup buttermilk powder
6 cups whole wheat flour
(1/4 cup pure gluten)

Jog to mix in dry ingredients and let sponge with the lid on (warmth) for 10 minutes. This takes the place of a second rise later. Then add:

1 1/2 Tb salt
& more flour till bowl begins to clean.

Knead for 5-6 minutes. Place in loaf pans (4 to 5-1 1/2 lb loaf pans or 6-1 lb size pans). Let rise. Bake 30 minutes at 350°.

English Muffin Loaves

2 1/2 cups warm water
1/2 cup powdered milk
1 Tb sugar or honey
1 1/2 Tb instant yeast

Combine with 3 cups of flour. Jog and let rest 5 minutes. Add:

1 tsp baking powder
2 tsp salt
2 cups flour to make a stiff batter.

Spoon into 2 greased (and sprinkled with cornmeal) 8 x 4" pans. (Sprinkle tops with cornmeal.) Cover and let rise. Bake about 25 minutes at 400°.

Sweet Rolls
(Makes 4 dozen)

In mixer bowl mix together:

        2 cups warm water
        2 Tb instant yeast
        1/2-2/3 cup oil
        1/2-2/3 cup honey
        4 eggs
        1 1/2 tsp lemon peel
        1 Tb vanilla
        (1/8 cup pure gluten)
        3 cups whole wheat flour

Let sponge for 10 minutes.
Then add:

        1 Tb salt
        & more flour till sides of bowl begin to clean.

Knead about 5-6 minutes. Shape into desired rolls.

This is the **sweet roll filling** I do the most:
 In a quart glass measuring pitcher melt:

        1/2 cup butter

 Then add:

        1 1/2 cups brown sugar
        2 tsp cinnamon
        3 Tb molasses

Combine all together and add:

        1 1/2 - 2 cups finely chopped nuts

With all the filling in one measuring cup, you can distribute it more evenly amongst the 4 dozen rolls. I roll out a batch of dough real thin (less dough between the filling) and spread the filling. Roll up dough tightly. Roll it about on the oiled counter to even up. Slice with a string or dental floss (slide under dough roll, position, and pull the ends crossing opposite each other to cut nicely without squashing). I always start in the middle and cut portions - to keep even and keep count. Let rise in the pans. (I actually squash my rolls in the pan before letting them rise, much to peoples' horror. I'm not sure why. I think it will help them fill out the pan and touch one another so they will be soft.)

Bake for 20-25 minutes at 375° or 10 minutes at 400°. I used to dump them out immediatly on a rack but so much of the filling remains in the pan. Now I just let them cool in the pan on a rack and remove with a spatula.

Please read the Bread chapter to help understand my bread making techniques.

My baking pans are 11 1/2 x 17" and are stainless steel. The four dozen rolls fit nicely in two of these pans, making fairly big cinnamon rolls (or dinner rolls).

Another variation:
   1/3 cup honey
   1/3 cup molasses
   2 - 3 tsp cinnamon
then add the nuts.
(If you like more filling, double)
1 cup soaked and chopped raisins could be added (easiest done in blender, then strained. Save the water to use in bread.) I partially soak raisins because they tend to draw moisture from bread. I'll often chop by pulsing in the blender because some in our family don't like a "huge ole" raisin.

My mother just spreads some softened butter on the rolled out dough, sprinkles on brown sugar, cinnamon, blueberries, nuts, etc. and rolls up. The filling possibilities are numerous.

Both grandmas frost theirs, which my children like, using a simple, powdered sugar frosting. I don't think I'd frost those I was going to freeze, or they may become soggy when thawed.

Did you know there is a science to cooking eggs? Call it the culinary alchemy of eggs. Now, why? I like to know why, not just follow a recipe. It's fun to be able to use our heads while we cook. Eggs have air pockets at the large end of the egg. Older eggs have more air. In heating, a race begins between the buildup of pressure within the egg and its release of air oozing out the end. If the air pocket is heated faster than the air can escape, the shell cracks. Some have larger pores, some have harder shells, so not all crack. Thus the hole poke. Room temperature starts the egg off in a better position for a better finished product. Egg white, 88% water and 11% protein, cooks very quickly. The cold water insures a gradual temperature rise. The different regions of the egg can expand in unison. Heat drives the protein to bond and form strong links. Salt helps the solitary proteins to break and bond to form an interlocking molecular network; or in other words, the protein cooks faster. If the egg does crack while cooking, the salt keeps it neat - no ugly streamers of white floating about. So I guess salt is a kind of first aid. As proteins warm, a small portion decomposes to form hydrogen sulfide gas. The gas collects in the coolest part of the egg. A good reason for room temp eggs. Yolk contains iron which attracts sulfur. When the gas reaches the surface of the yolk a dark iron-sulfide deposit forms. Overcooking gives more time for dirty work - the dreaded green yolk. So to prevent the majority of this reaction, chill the shell in cold water. The gas is forced to collect there, pulling it away from the yolk. Now wasn't that interesting?! I love it, just like I enjoy root-word meanings, or footnotes and bibliographies.

Eggs

I love a farm-fresh cooked egg with buttered toast. My preference is soft-cooked. Everyone else in this family follows Monte's liking for well-cooked everything. Oh, but the yolk! Its flavor is superb when soft. My mother taught me a wonderful way to make **sunny-side-up** eggs -

> Break eggs into a hot and barely oiled skillet. Pour in a touch of water and put on lid. The steam will cook the top of the egg. And you serve a beautiful egg!

I also like to soft-cook (not boil) eggs in the shell. An egg topper snips off the top of the egg. Europeans eat eggs this way. I have some Danish eggcups and Monte's mom rosemauled (some would call it tole painting, but rosemauling has strict rules and a guild) some wooden eggcups for me. It's fun eating out of the shell with a little baby spoon.

This is how I **hard-** or **soft-cook** eggs:

> eggs at room temperature
> cold water to cover
> a tablespoon of salt (to pint of water)

Make a hole in the large end of each egg with a pin. I actually have a little hole-making device for eggs and don't know if it's still available. Heat till the water comes to a boil and simmer. I'll not give times since all areas differ due to altitude. Cookbooks can help in this. Refrigerated eggs will require longer cooking times by at least 2 minutes. Immediately after cooking let cold water run in pan till eggs are cool to handle.

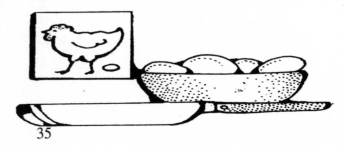

Herbal Eggs and Tofu

> 1 pkg tofu, crumbled
> 2-3 eggs
> 1/4 cup milk
> 2 pinches of herbs:
> (basil, marjoram, rosemary, thyme, or dill . .)
> salt and pepper to taste

Melt 2 Tb butter (I use olive oil) in a skillet. Add tofu and sauté for 3 minutes and then add the herbs. Beat the rest together; add them to the tofu. Scramble to the desired consistency.

Coffee Cake

Preheat oven to 350°.

> 2 cups whole wheat flour
> 3 Tbs baking powder
> 1/8 tsp salt
> 1/3 cup oil
> 1/3 cup honey
> 1 egg
> 1 cup yogurt, plain
> 1 tsp almond extract or vanilla or both
> 3/4 cup raisins
> 1-2 Tb cinnamon

Topping:

> 1/4 melted butter
> 1/4 cup milk
> 3/4 cup pecan halves or pieces
> 2/3-1 cup brown sugar or 1/4-1/2 cup honey
> (your sweet tooth preference)

Mix together dry ingredients. Add liquid ingredients. Add raisins. Pour into greased 8 x 12" baking dish. On top sprinkle the sweetening and nuts. Pour melted butter and milk over mixture. Bake at 350° for 50-60 minutes.

I still remember my sister-in-law, Linda, continuing to snack on this after breakfast. But then of course with Linda, meals can be on-going since we like to drink coffee and talk forever. Linda lives in Wisconsin so we don't get to do this too often.

Sometimes we have this with eggs for lunch. I suppose that's what's known as "brunch."

Milk toast has become a special Papa &
Dawson bedtime snack when Dawson is
absolutely too starving to go to bed.
Luckily this isn't too often. I've told
Dawson I don't know how to make it,
so it remains a Monte thing. In fact, I
asked Dawson how to make it in order
to type this. It's good for breakfast as
well.

These are made very similar to the dry
cereal. Monte invented this recipe.

Some mornings, especially if I've had
headaches, I juice some carrots, an
apple, a small piece of ginger, (I always
keep fresh ginger root in the freezer in a
ziplock bag and break off pieces to grate
or juice.) and a sprig of parsley (keep
this growing on a window sill). You can
juice whatever you like, even cabbage.

As I've said before, not all brands of
tofu are creamy. Some are gritty. The
best brand I've found is Mori-Nu. I
talk more about tofu in the Cooking
Tips chapter.

Milk Toast

Toast and butter slices of bread and break or dice into a
serving bowl, 1 or 2 slices to a bowl. Warm the milk
(about 3/4 cup) in the microwave for a minute. Sprinkle
a little cinnamon on the toast. Pour milk over toast.
Sprinkle with sugar.

Monte's Fiber Crackers

For one of the main ingredients you need to juice something,
because you need the pulp - you know the stuff that you
normally throw away (or we'd put it in the chicken bucket)
after you've juiced.

The best tasting pulp for crackers is from carrots and celery;
a touch of cabbage or anything else is okay, just don't overdo it. Monte looked at the pulp and didn't want to throw it
out, so he mixed it with fresh ground flour, about a 50/50
proportion until it held together and wasn't sticky (I say add
some salt and garlic powder, even some herbs!). Roll it out
as thin as possible on cookie sheets and bake golden brown.
Make sure the center is rolled thin so it bakes evenly. It may
bubble up in places, but we think this improves the texture
and flavor. Then break in pieces and put back in oven to dry,
with the oven off, or put in the dehydrator. Store in a jar on
the counter.

Tofu Shake or Smoothie

In blender combine 1 -10 oz package of tofu, 1/4 cup
honey, 1/4 cup milk powder, and 1 cup water. Blend till
smooth. The rest is up to you. If you like a cold shake,
it's best blended with frozen fruit. For one drink, we
use 2-4 cups frozen peaches and 1/2 tsp vanilla. Add
more water or ice if desired. Another variation we like
adds a pint of frozen berries - strawberries, raspberries,
or blueberries. Apple juice can be used in place of water. Try a banana with a tsp of lemon juice. How about
lemon juice and use ice to replace the water . . . or
orange juice.

The commonest fallacy among women is that simply having children makes them a mother - which is as absurd as believing that having a piano makes one a musician.
Sydney J Harris

The most valuable gift you can give your family is a good example.

You may have tangible wealth untold;
Caskets of jewels and coffers of gold.
Richer than I you can never be -
I had a Mother who read to me.
Strickland Gillilan

Chapter Three
BREADS &
LADIES

Once upon a time the word from which the modern English "lady" came meant "loaf-kneader." It would benefit our families if we homemakers would become "ladies" again. In 1857 Mrs. Sara Hale wrote in her huge cookbook, *Receipts for the Millions*, "To make good bread or to understand the process of making it is the duty of every woman; indeed an art that should never be neglected in the education of a lady. The lady derives her title from 'dividing or distributing bread;' the more perfect the bread the more perfect the lady."

However, perfection in this art, was not easily achieved in the middle nineteenth century, nor today when you use whole grains. If you have never made yeast bread, welcome to the great drama of the kitchen where every ingredient is a character. Yeast is the most important character in making good bread. Yeasts are living organisms and none is exactly like another. They feed on sugars and produce alcohol and carbon dioxide — the "riser" we are after. We could refer to yeast as having souls, because they seem so spirited. The primitive method of bread baking is recorded in Egyptian history as far back as 4000 BC. We know of more recent accounts in the pioneer stories. Have you wondered where pioneers' leavening came from? Have you heard the term "sourdough"? The pioneers' sharing of the bread "starter" was a true act of friendship. My *Alaska Sourdough* cookbook says pioneers often built their cabins around the cook area with a special warm shelf for their starter. They'd as soon spend a year in the hills without their rifles, as to tough it through without their bubbling sourdough pots. A starter could be buried in the center of a transported flour sack.

The initial start for sourdough begins with flour and water mixing to form a dough, which is then kept in a warm place to catch the wild yeast coming from the air. A kitchen can be so sterile or uninitiated (possibly due to no "from scratch" baking going on) that no reaction can occur! Otherwise these organisms are plentiful in the air. For centuries people did not understand what made sourdough starter raise bread. In 1877, Pasteur explained this wonder, and commercial yeasts began to be produced. Sourdough can be started with commercial yeast. Anyway, yeast has a volatile temperament, is productive only within given limits of heat — and resents a drafty room.

Wheat flour is the hero of the drama. It has a secret certain something that makes it elastic and gives body. Rice, rye, oat, corn, soy — no other flour can touch wheat for texture; but wheat flour can share with others, if it remains dominant. One possible problem is the uncertain characteristic of flours. They deviate in their liquid absorbability, and only experience can tell you exactly how much flour to add during the kneading process. There are enzymes in the flour to convert the wheat starch into the sugar on which the yeast feeds. The yeast gases are captured by the rubbery gluten in wheat flour. Like tiny balloons, they cause the bread to rise. Gluten, that secret something, is found in its most complete form in wheat. Gluten can never develop except in the presence of moisture and when the grain is agitated, as in kneading.

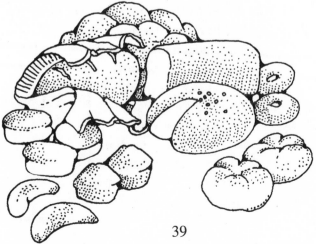

If you've never made yeast bread, you might begin with commercial store-bought unbleached flour. It will produce a fine loaf of bread for you pretty consistently, and you'll learn about the process — how much flour, how much water it will take, and how it reacts to mixing and kneading, and what it looks like in the bowl. Then start adding whole grains; some families need to slowly adjust to whole grains. Let it become an automatic process. People have taken my recipes and say they work well for them, so branch out and explore the world of grains.

Until the twentieth century, the use of white flour was confined to royalty or to the wealthy people who could afford it. In Paris in 1876, the first light, white French rolls were exhibited. The governor of Minnesota was in attendance and he determined that America must have the "benefits" of this discovery and learned how to separate the components of the grain to achieve white flour. In America he developed the steel roller mills which accelerated the grinding of grain to flour. This product contained no wheat germ oil to become rancid. Volumes could be ground and transported nationwide. This new process put all the local stone-grinding mills out of business. White flour became a status symbol and light, white bread became the objective of every home-maker. Few people thought about the bran, germ, wheat oil, and other nutrients that had been eliminated. Illnesses relating to nutrition have become more prevalent, and a major cause has been found to be the removal of the life-giving elements from grains. When the industry was asked to return the flour to its original form, they instead added one mineral, iron, and three B vitamins: niacin, thiamin, and riboflavin to "enrich" the white flour. Commercially ground whole wheat flour contains most of the bran, but the germ of the wheat is still removed to prevent rancidity, prolonging shelf life.

Gluten is often extracted from flour by kneading the flour with water until the dough is rubbery and elastic. The dough is then washed, rinsing away the starch and leaving a rubbery mass of concentrated protein, which is dried and ground into flour. Some people have used gluten to make meat substitutes, but through over-use many end up with gluten intolerance.

Water, milk, potato water, or other liquids are other players to manipulate for an interesting plot. Any one of them lends steam to the production. Liquids should be warm for yeast breads. As for salt and sweetening, they make important but brief entrances, and too much of either inhibits the other characters. Salt is a very important taste factor for me (I talk more about salt below). Sweetening, except for a small amount, I can do without. The sweetening can be honey, molasses, applesauce, fruit juice, or sugar. Fat you can enlist or leave out, though it can give a more tender and lasting appeal. There are quite a few extras you can bring in to give depth and variety, such as seeds, nuts, dried fruit, herbs, spices, or sprouts. Now you know your actors and their qualities. Let the play begin.

BREAD TIPS

The standard 9 x 5-inch pans are too wide for whole-grain breads. Whole grains need narrower walls for support; otherwise they tend to collapse in the center, even with rising bowls. To estimate the pan size and weight of a loaf, follow this simple guideline: One cup of liquid in a recipe makes about one pound of bread.

Pan Size	Bread weight	Cups of Dough
5 3/4 x 3"	3/4-1 pound	1 1/2-2 cups
7 1/2 x 3 1/2"	1 pound	
8 1/2 x 4 1/2"	1 1/2 pounds	3 cups
9 x 5"	2 pounds	

Put most of your ingredients in the bowl having the same amount of flour as warm water. (Except salt. Salt slightly inhibits the yeast growth, but is needed on the whole as a check to rapid bread rise and splitting. Also helps the overall flavor!) Stir until dry ingredients are just mixed, and let sit with lid or a covering (keeps it warm) for about 10 -15 minutes till bubbly. This process is called sponging. *Sponging* makes lighter, fluffier, more flavorful bread and cuts out the need for a second rise (lengthy sponging is the foundation for sour-dough breads). Add your salt and immediately add all but the last cup, which you add till the dough barely begins to clean the bowl of the excess flour. Most of your whole wheat flour needs to be mixed in, *in this first minute after sponging*, when the gluten is developing. Otherwise later additions will just create a dry, crumbly bread. Stop the machine at this point of adding most of your flour, at this barely clean bowl stage, and feel the dough. It should not be sticky but still tacky. Then knead. This tends to be the biggest problem with whole wheat bread making, that of wanting the dough to clean the sides of the bowl like it does with processed flour. Adding too much flour will make a drier, crumbly bread. The kneading time really depends upon the quality of your wheat. White wheat or Prairie Gold (also called Golden 86), only needs about 6 minutes kneading to the elastic stage (it has a very high protein content and is less allergenic, easier on the digestive system. I'm using this grain the most!). (And yes, you can over knead, which is something I just recently learned!) Hard spring and winter wheat require longer kneading time, about 8 -10 minutes (they have high protein too- which means high gluten content and less moisture content). (Soft wheat, called pastry wheat berries, contains less gluten, and is excellent for quick breads, pastries and pastas - not yeast breads.) Some people (in baking classes) like to take a blob of dough at this point and stretch it. If it has been kneaded enough it will stretch elastically when pulled gently and have a thin opaque center, rather than ripping apart with a hole.

The key to a soft whole grain bread is the kneading

I should add a note here about machine versus hand kneading, to address a typical question. I used to make bread by hand when we were first married, but not with fresh ground grain. I researched machines and found that of the American-made, the KitchenAid was the best kneading machine and didn't overheat, so you could do consecutive batches. The KitchenAid will hold around 9 cups of dry ingredients. When checking into grain mills I was exposed to the Bosch. James Beard said it was "the only bread-making machine." It will hold twice as much as the KitchenAid, so I sold it and bought a Bosch figuring I could double my quantity for the same effort. After using many grain grinders, my preference is the Grain Master Whisper Mill. The strong point for machine kneading is that 10 minutes of knead-ing is like 1 hour of hand kneading - and the key to a soft whole grain bread is the kneading. (Another sideline cheer here for machine knead-ing is: I can be cleaning up the kitchen as the work is being done by one of my servants!) As far as bread 'making and baking' machines, if you look at the tiny kneader in the bottom, it is impossible to effectively knead a 100% whole grain bread. You need to add processed flour and gluten to the whole grain flour. But remem-ber, you're only getting one loaf for all that time, to be consumed by most families in one sitting, and none in the freezer!

41

When the dough has been kneaded, dump all the dough onto an *oiled surface using oiled hands* (remember, adding flour will make a dry, crumbly bread!) and cut apart the loaves. Oil the pans with canola oil mixed with a bit of lecithin oil (the lecithin is really important since wholegrains tend to stick with plain oil. I have a little oil well with a cotton applicator and handle that I keep oil in ready.). I like to pat out each dough lump into a rectangle and roll up, pressing as I roll, to remove air bubbles and place seam side down in pans. You can simply form the lump into the right size for the pan. Let the pans sit with a towel over them, out of drafts, till nicely risen — filling out and just barely rounded above the pans. Sometimes this happens quickly and some days it seems to take forever. If it raise too high the bread loses some of its support and will collapse. Bread does rise more in the oven. Gently space the pans in preheated oven to bake. When done, remove from pans immediately to a rack to cool. I lay towels over them and bag up to freeze soon after cleaning so as not to dry out (we've always lived in extremely dry climates). It is not necessary to wash bread pans after each use. Just wipe them clean with a paper towel. I always freeze everything we won't use right away. Never store bread in the refrigerator (except English Muffin bread) as this ruins their consistency and flavor. Instead of keeping bread in plastic bags when out of the freezer, I now keep bread in a metal bread box. Is this nostalgia? Initially yes, but the bread does keep better! A note as to flops: All homemade bread is delicious! Use the bread that's not the greatest sandwich consistency for toast, french toast, bread puddings, croutons, stuffing, etc. I have a bowl that I put unused crusts or pieces of bread in to dry (my basket for serving rolls at the table sits on top of this bowl on my shelf), and then when full and convenient, like before I grind meat or something, I'll grind the dry bread for breadcrumbs. Or some people grate it. The breadcrumbs store freshest in the freezer, but if good and dry I suppose they'd look nice on the shelf in a jar.

Basic Whole Wheat Bread

Place in bowl:

> 6 cups hot water (92- 110 degrees; can be low especially when using the warm fresh ground flour)
>
> 1/3 cup canola or olive oil
>
> 1/3 cup honey
>
> 2 Tb instant yeast (see note on side)
>
> (1/4-1/3 cup pure gluten)
>
> 6 cups whole wheat flour

Mix together. Let sponge for 10-15 minutes till bubbly.
> Add:

> 1 1/2 Tb salt
>
> Enough flour to clean sides of bowl   (I never count. I think this recipe uses around 13 -14 cups of flour in all. Each baking day can be different as far as moisture in the flour or moisture in the air.)

Knead for 5-6 minutes (or 8-10 minutes depending on type of flour used. See previous talk on flour and grain types). Place in 4-5 larger pans or 6 medium (see notes under bread tips). Let raise till double.   Bake 25-30 minutes at 350°.

You can use this dough for pizza using 1 1/2 lbs, or take 2 lbs dough for cinnamon rolls. Roll into a 12 x 18 inch rectangle. Spread with filling of your choice (see actual recipe in Breakfast section). Roll up jelly-roll-style and cut with dental floss. Let rise till double and bake at 350° for 20 minutes. Can glaze with a jam. Or (with 4 lbs of dough) melt in pan: 1/2 cup butter, 1 1/2 cups maple syrup, 1 1/2 cups chopped nuts. Set rolls together in maple glaze. Let rise. Bake at 350° for 20-25 minutes. Remove from oven and let stand in pan for 5 minutes. Turn out of pan to cool on a rack placed over a cookie sheet. Or your filling could be along the lines of pizza toppings but baked in a pan like cinnamon rolls.

Remember I'm using a Bosch so keep in mind the measurements discussed previously. Learn your own machine capacity.

This, along with the Dinner Rolls, is our main bread that I keep the freezer stocked with. Heather is now keeping us in the basics, freeing me up to try new recipes.

I used to use regular active dry yeast (3 Tb). Instant yeast was developed in Europe in the 1960s. Instant yeast is dried at a lower temp than the active dry yeast. The active dry yeast drying temp results in 25% dead cells, whereas the instant yeast has just 5% dead weight. In recipes calling for active dry yeast, decrease the quantity by 25% to account for instant yeasts' strength. Instant yeast is finer, absorbing the water quicker, and has a considerably wider temperature tolerance, between 80-120 degrees.

I also never used to use gluten, but did add 1-2 cups of unbleached flour. Now with the Prairie Gold (formerly Golden 86) white wheat, I could probably get away without the gluten and still have a very soft bread. I get the pure gluten through a co-op, so continue adding it. Most of your grocery store gluten is mixed with highly processed white flour.

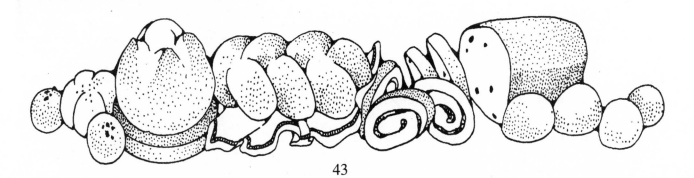

Dinner Rolls
(Hot Dog/Hamburger Buns)

Place in mixer bowl:

> 3 cups warm water
> 2 Tb instant yeast
> 1/3 cup oil
> 1/3 cup honey
> (1/4 cup pure gluten)
> 3 cups whole wheat flour

Mix together and let sponge 10 minutes.
Then add:

> 1 1/2 tsp salt
> 3 eggs, room temp
> & enough flour to clean bowl

Knead for 5-6 minutes (or 8-10 min. See previous bread talk). Having oiled hands and counter top, cut dough into correct proportions- this makes 4 dozen rolls that fit nicely on two 11 1/2 x 17" pans. Shape each into balls for buns and rolls, or into 6" long strips for hot-dog buns.

Bake about 10-15 minutes at 375°.

These are our favorite mainstay dinner rolls. The same dough is used for hot dog or hamburger buns.

I squash all the buns down in the pans when done arranging, then let them rise. I like my rolls to touch when risen and baked so they are soft. Squashing them seems to help them rise so they will touch.

If you like your rolls all around crusty, then you wouldn't want them to touch. I bake french bread dough rolls apart.

Ezekiel Bread

Combine these and mill:

> 7 cups wheat
> 1 cup barley
> 1/4 cup pinto beans
> 1/4 cup soy beans
> 1/4 cup lentils
> 1 cup rye or spelt

In mixer bowl combine:

> 5 cups warm water
> 1/2 cup oil
> 1/2 cup molasses or honey
> 2 Tb scant yeast
> (1/3 cup gluten)
> 5 cups of the above milled flour

Mix together and let sponge 15-30 minutes.
Then add:

> 1 1/2 Tb salt
> 1/3 cup whole millet
> & enough flour to clean bowl

Knead 5-6 minutes. Shape into 4 loaves. Let rise.
Bake 35 minutes at 350°.

Ezekiel 4:9 "Also take for yourself wheat, barley, beans, lentils, millet, and spelt; put them into one vessel, and make bread of them for yourself..."

Spelt is a new grain, actually old, revitalized. It is considered a "warm" grain and is easier to digest than wheat and yet is about the only other grain that contains the gluten for a good bread consistency. Many persons who have allergies or whose bodies are healing, are finding spelt a wonderful grain. The price, though, is not cheap enough to warrant the rest of us to use for everything.

44

I'm calling this Italian bread as well, because we often have "French" bread with "Italian" spaghetti.

French Bread/ Italian
(Bagels & Pretzels)

Place in mixer bowl:

> 6 cups warm water
> 2 1/2 Tb instant yeast
> 2 Tb sugar
> (1/4 cup gluten)
> 6 cups whole wheat flour

Mix together and let sponge 15 minutes. (I think it is in *The Joy of Cooking* that talks about teasing french bread - letting it repeatedly rise and repeatedly kneading down. I don't usually do this, though it shows you the possibilities.)

> Add:
> 1 1/2 Tb salt
> & enough flour to clean the bowl

Knead 5-6 minutes. I have two sizes of french bread pans. With this recipe I make 4 long skinny loaves, 2 long fat loaves, and some bread sticks and sandwich (Hoagie) buns. (Can brush the loaves with egg beaten with 1 Tb water, and slash each loaf diagonally.)
Bake for 20-25 minutes at 450°.

This dough can be used for authentic pretzels or bagels. The step that makes these unique to basic bread is sliding the raised dough forms into boiling water before baking. For forming bagels, use a 7" coil and pinch together ends to form a circle. For pretzels, form a coil rope 16-18" long, with tapered ends and make a pretzel shape. Let rise on a greased baking sheet. Bring 3 quarts water to a boil in a large kettle. Add 1 Tb cream of tartar, 2 Tb baking soda, and 2 Tb honey to the water. Using a slotted spoon, slide each piece into the boiling water, but don't crowd. They will float. For bagels, boil 2 minutes on each side. Remove with slotted spoon, letting drain a bit, and return to baking sheet. They will be slippery. Bake for 20-25 minutes in a 425° oven. For pretzels, boil for about 20 seconds on each side (unless you make them big and thick, then boil longer). Bake about 15 minutes. All of these can be sprinkled with coarse salt or herbs. Bagels can be glazed before baking if you want, using 1 egg yolk mixed with 1 tsp cold water. Coat each bagel and add whatever topping you want. Poppy seeds, chopped onions or garlic, and sesame seeds are some examples. Go to a bagel outlet and see all their varieties.

45

Squaw Bread

In blender put:

        1 cup hot water

        & 1/2 cup raisins

Pulse until finely chopped.

Pour into mixing bowl and add:

        1 cup warm buttermilk

        1 cup rye flour

        2 1/2 cups whole wheat flour

        (1/3 cup gluten)

        1 Tb instant yeast

        1/4 cup oil

        1/4 cup molasses

Mix together and let sponge 10 minutes.

Then add:

        2 scant tsp salt

        & enough flour to clean bowl

Knead 5-6 minutes. Shape into 2 loaves.

Let rise. Bake 35 minutes at 350°.

Vegetable Bread

In blender place:

        1/2 cup canola oil

        3 Tb honey

        2 eggs

        1 - 13 oz canned milk (or water)

        1 stalk celery

        2 large carrots

        1/4 cup parsley

        1 1" wedge cabbage

Liquidize thoroughly.

 In mixing bowl put:

        1/2 cup warm water

        2 Tb scant yeast

Mix and let soften, then add blender mixture and

        3 cups whole wheat flour

        (& 1/4 cup gluten flour)

Mix together and let sponge 15 minutes.

Add:

        1 Tb salt

        & enough flour to clean bowl

Knead 5-6 minutes. Form into 3 loaves.

Let rise. Bake 45 minutes at 350°.

I like to chop raisins this way for any breads I make (don't puree, just barely let the blender pulse, let the raisins settle and barely pulse again). Some of my kids and I, are not partial to huge raisins in most things. The water is excellent in all baked goods. The raisins are moister and won't tend to absorb moisture from the surrounding baked bread.

Mexican Bread

Place in mixer bowl:

        2 cups warm water
        1 cup warmed salsa
        2 Tb oil
        1 Tb honey
        1 Tb instant yeast
        1 Tb Italian/Mexican seasoning
                (1 tsp cumin, 1/2 tsp chili powder,
                1/2 tsp garlic & 1/2 tsp onion powders,
                1/2 tsp oregano)
        (1/4 cup gluten)
        3 cups whole wheat flour

Mix together and let sponge.
Then add:

        1/2 cup mozzarella cheese, grated

Add enough flour to clean the bowl and knead for 5-6 minutes. Make into an exaggerated (tall) round and place on greased pan sprinkled with cornmeal. Let rise. Bake 30 minutes at 375°.

Country Rye Bread

In mixer bowl:

        2 1/4 cups warm potato water
        1 1/2 Tb yeast
        3 Tb canola oil
        1/4 cup honey
        1/4 cup molasses
        (1/4 cup gluten)
        1 cup whole wheat flour
        1 cup rye flour

Mix together and let sponge 15-30 minutes.
Add:

        1 Tb salt
        1/4 cup buckwheat flour
        1/4 cup rolled oats

Mix again. Continue to add flour until mixture barely cleans sides of the bowl. Knead 5-6 minutes. Form into 2 oval shapes. Let rise. Bake 20 minutes at 400°, then 30 minutes at 375°.

In the Dinner or Supper chapter I have a lot of recipes for Mexican foods including salsas. I do have a simple salsa I didn't mention there. I like to add some of my home-canned tomato sauce to a store-bought salsa and add some fresh ground cumin. Chopped green onion is always good to add. Any salsa can be used in this bread.

Remember that all bread recipes can be doubled. Just remember what your machine's capacity is. I've gotten in trouble with quadrupling something and barely fitting it all in the bowl!

47

Swedish Limpa Rye Bread

I really like this bread.

> 1 1/2 cups hot water
> 1 Tb instant yeast
> 2 Tb oil
> 1/4 cup molasses
> 3 Tb honey
> (1/4 cup gluten)
> 1 cup whole wheat flour

Mix the above together and let sponge about 10 minutes.
Add:

> 1 tsp salt
> 1-2 tsp grated orange rind
> 2 1/2 cups rye flour
> 1 1/2 - 2 cups more whole wheat flour

until sides of bowl begin to clean.

Knead 5-6 minutes. Form into two round or oval loaves and place to rise on a greased baking sheet. Bake in 375° oven for 30-35 minutes.

Sky-High Biscuits

> 1 cup unbleached flour
> 2 cups whole wheat flour
> 1 heaping Tb baking powder
> 2 Tb sugar
> 1/2 tsp salt
> 3/4 tsp cream of tartar
> 1/2 cup butter
> 1/4 cup olive oil
> 1 egg
> 1 cup milk

Combine all the dry ingredients. Cut in the butter till a coarse meal. Add liquids. Knead lightly on oiled counter. Roll or pat to 1 inch thickness. Cut into biscuits. Place on greased baking sheet for crusty biscuits, or bake closer together in skillet or 9 x 9" pan. Bake at 450° for 12 to 15 minutes.

Croutons

Croutons are nice in salads. Monte usually makes these so I'll give you his recipe first and then some other options. His first "must" is that the bread be dry. I keep a bowl on the shelf where bread slice stragglers get dumped, those pieces of bread that get left out of the bag, or are on the old side (not moldy). When the bowl is full I make bread crumbs (this is in the Tips section), but Monte will grab the bread and cube it for croutons. He makes enough for one meal and likes to do it in the skillet with some butter or olive oil. Once well heated, coated, and slightly browned, he'll add spices. His favorites are: salt & pepper, garlic & onion powder, basil, parsley, dill, and coriander. Watch that the bread and spices don't burn.

All this can be done in the oven at 300-325°. Cube bread. If not already dry, first dry it in the oven. Melt butter in the baking pan and add salt and garlic powder. For about 4 slices of bread, use 3 Tb butter, and 1/4 tsp garlic powder. Stir occasionally, probably about 15-30 minutes. The bread need not be cubed, but could be crumbled, just not fine or it'll burn easy. Toast and season the crumbles. These are good tossed with cooked pasta as well as salads.

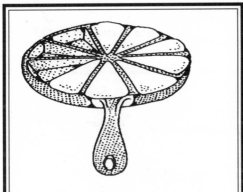

In graduate school, Monte had two kindred geologist friends. This recipe came from one, Phil Anderson, back when we were first married. He's Australian. His mother taught me how to make authentic English tea.

Corn Bread

In blender put:

        3/4 cup wheat kernels (1 cup flour)
        3/4 cup corn kernels (1 cup flour)
        1/4 cup powdered milk
        1 cup water
        1/4 cup oil (or 2 Tb oil & 1/4 cup applesauce)
        3 Tb honey

Blend on high for 4 minutes.
Add:

        4 tsp baking powder
        1/2 tsp salt
        1 egg

Blend (or mix in a bowl). Pour into greased 9 x 9 pan. Bake 20-25 minutes at 425°.

Scones

Preheat oven to 350°

        3 cups whole wheat flour
        1 cup unbleached flour
        1/2 tsp salt
        pinch cream of tartar
        2 tsp baking soda
        1/2 cup butter

Mix the dry ingredients. Cut in butter.
Add liquids:

        1 cup milk
        2 eggs

Work the dough quickly and don't over mix.

        Can add 1/2 cup currants.

Pat the dough into two 1/2" thick circles on baking sheet. Cut the disk into eight wedges. Separate each section from each other. Bake for 20-30 minutes.

Pineapple and Cornmeal Muffins

    4 eggs, separated
    sprinkling cream of tartar
    1 cup unsweetened crushed pineapple
    1/4 cup oil
    2 Tb honey
    1 cup cornmeal
    1 cup whole wheat flour
    2 tsp baking powder
    (1/2 cup chopped pecans)

Whip egg whites with cream of tartar. Beat egg yolks and add the rest of the ingredients. Fold in egg whites. Pour in muffin cups. Fill about 2/3 - 3/4 full. Bake at 350° for 25 minutes.

Blueberry Muffins

Beat in bowl:

    2 eggs

Add:

    4 Tb oil
    3/4 cup milk
    1 3/4 cups whole wheat flour
    3/4 tsp salt
    1/3 cup sugar
    2 tsp baking powder
    1 cup blueberries

You don't need to beat. Just mix until barely moistened. Fill well-greased muffin cups (or paper liners) 2/3 full. Bake at 400° for 20-25 minutes. Chopped cranberries can be used in place of blueberries.

Molasses-Rye Muffins

    1 1/2 cups rye flour
    1/2 tsp baking powder
    1/4 cup oil
    1/4 cup molasses
    1 egg
    6 Tb orange juice
    1/4 cup raisins

Preheat oven to 375°. Prepare 10 muffin cups, greased or lined. Add the liquids to the dry ingredients till just moistened. Bake for 20 minutes.

I always use paper liners because I hate to wash muffin tins. I rarely wash my muffin tins, bread pans, or cookie sheets. I don't scour them shiny clean, ever. Unless they become gooky with something I baked, I just wipe clean with a paper towel. They eventually develop a nice dark look. You could put these in a self-cleaning oven to return to shiny new. My preference (as well as the professionals) is for baking black-ware. It is more expensive, but baked goods bake and brown nicer in the dark metal rather than in the shiny, which reflects the heat. Browned baked goods have the better flavor.

I dislike greasing muffin pans and hate to use the spray oil coatings. I have a little oil well with a cotton-handled applicator for greasing my pans.

These are good with an Orange-Honey Butter: Beat together until fluffy 1/2 cup butter, 1/3 cup oil, 1/4 cup honey, 2 tsp orange juice, and grated rind of 1 orange.

Biscotti

I love Biscotti dipped in coffee, but it's so expensive. What to do? Make your own. When you do, you will find many of the store-bought are bland or texture-less.

I like to add 3/4 cup hazelnuts and 2 Tb anise seeds. Hazelnuts need to be baked in a 350° oven for 8 to 10 minutes to remove their papery skins. While still warm, rub nuts between paper towels to slip the skins. Cool and chop a bit.

I chop nuts by putting them in a plastic bag, like a Ziploc, and hit them with a mallet on the counter.

Some other variations: 3/4 cup pecans, 1 tsp maple flavoring; 1/2-3/4 cup toasted almonds, 2 Tb orange zest (1 cup chopped bittersweet chocolate); 2 tsp cinnamon, 3 Tb unsweetened cocoa; 1 cup dried cranberries, 3/4 cup shelled pistachios, 1 tsp lemon peel. Here again the combinations could be endless. If you want a chocolate glaze, melt 3 oz chocolate chips in double boiler or microwave on medium, checking every 30 seconds. Stir to blend. With a spatula, spread chocolate over one side of biscotti. Biscotti made without butter has a long shelf life. These look so pretty in a special jar - just like those in the gourmet shops.

Remember, I'm making most of these recipes specifying whole wheat flour with the white wheat called Prairie Gold (also Golden 86). If all you have is the hard red spring wheat (darker), you may want to add some unbleached flour. Pastry wheat, oat, rice, and barley flour can be used as well. Families used to all processed flours may need to ease in to all whole grain flours slowly and let your taste buds adjust.

2 1/4 cups whole wheat flour
1 tsp baking soda
1/2 tsp salt
3/4 cup sugar

Mix together.
Add:

3 eggs
1 tsp vanilla
1/4 tsp almond extract

Divide dough in half. If you have trouble handling the dough because of stickiness, do not dust with flour. Try oiling your hands or use a rubber spatula and wax paper. On greased baking sheet form 2 logs about 2" wide and 13" long. Bake 25 minutes at 350°. Cool on a rack for 5-10 minutes. Cut with a serrated knife in diagonal 3/8-1/2" slices. Replace on cookie sheet and cook 10 -15 minutes, turning over once, to dry slightly. Cool completely on a rack before storing.

Whole Wheat Thins

3 cups whole wheat flour
1/3 cup olive oil
Blended well with:
1 cup water
1/2 tsp salt

Mix all ingredients. You could add other spices and herbs. Knead as little as possible to make a smooth dough. Roll very thin on ungreased baking sheets. Cut with pizza cutter (I use a fluted-edged roller) to the size desired. Prick each cracker a couple times with a fork. Bake at 350° for 30-35 minutes or until crisp. I usually remove the outside edges and return the cookie sheet to the oven to let the center brown.

Crackers are very easy to make. Everyone loves them. People just don't think of making crackers, but they're a hit at pot-lucks (pot-blessings), brunches, or anything. Sometimes I bring them along with home-made mustard or a good cheese. Dawson puts peanut butter on them. Serving them with soup is good too.

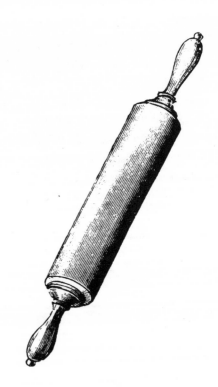

Cheese-Wheat Thins

2 cups whole wheat flour
1/4 tsp baking soda
(1 Tb brown sugar)
1/2 cup butter
1/3 cup milk
1 Tb cider vinegar
1/2 cup grated cheese

Combine milk and vinegar and set aside. This makes a soured milk similar to buttermilk. Combine the rest of the ingredients in mixer with wire whips till it resembles coarse meal. Add milk mixture till just combined. Turn out on oiled counter and knead into a ball. Roll thin on baking sheet and cut into pieces. Prick with a fork. Bake at 375° for about 12-15 minutes.

Look at the end of Breakfast chapter for Monte's Fiber Crackers.

Crackers, tortillas, english muffins, or bread can be turned into little pizzas or open faced sandwiches. Spread the bread with relish, pesto sauce, or chutney. Sprinkle with grated cheese mixed with fresh herbs, and bake. Be creative.

Honey Graham Crackers

1/3 cup honey
1/2 cup butter
1 tsp vanilla
1/2 cup water or milk
3 cups whole wheat flour
1/2 tsp baking soda
1/2 tsp baking powder
pinch of salt
(1 tsp cinnamon)

Cream honey and butter. Add vanilla and milk. Add dry ingredients. Knead gently into a ball. Roll thin on greased baking sheets. Prick with a fork. Bake at 350° for 8-10 minutes. The cooking length will depend on how thin the crackers are.

Wheatless Crackers

1 cup brown rice flour
1 cup oat flour
1 tsp salt
2 tsp baking powder
2 tsp brown sugar
1/2 cup butter
1/3 cup milk (buttermilk, yogurt, or water)

Mix dry ingredients together and cut in the butter. Add the liquid. Dough will seem dry. Roll out on ungreased cookie sheet. Cut and prick with fork. Bake 375° about 10 -12 minutes or until lightly browned.

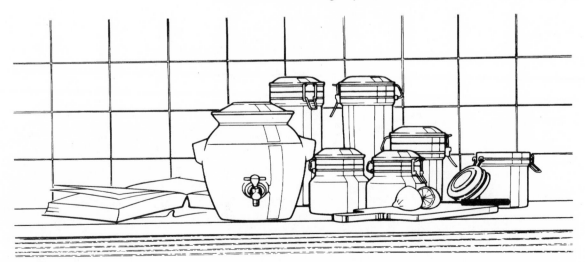

53

Proverbs 31 is not describing women PhDs, women professional athletes, or women CEOs. These are specialists and have done excellently. Proverbs nor I condemn them. Proverbs 31 is describing a woman who has developed all her gifts, not just one, and has developed them in the context of family. She may not be the world's best in any one area but she is the best she can be in all areas of homemaking. Kind of like the female equivalent of the Renaissance man.

Heather Swan

A good woman is hard to find . . . She senses the worth of her work . . .
She's skilled in the crafts of home and hearth, diligent in homemaking."

Proverbs 31
"The Renaissance Woman"

. . . freedom from the responsibility of managing a home and a family,
an equal right with men in business and social careers,
at the expense of home and family . . .
such progress we can only call a progressive deterioration. . .

GK Chesterton
"Brave New Family"

Many of us live publicly with featureless public puppets,
images of the small public abstractions.
It is when we pass our own private gate, and open our own secret door,
that we step into the land of the giants.

Charles Dickens

Chapter Four
DINNER OR SUPPER?

Once upon a time, about eighteen years ago, a young couple called their elderly grandmother and asked if they could come and visit her. "We'll come after dinner." Grandmother anxiously awaited. They finally arrived after dinner. *Their* dinner. *Her* supper. This eighty-two-year-old lady could have taken an afternoon nap.

We never (and I do say never, though some say, "Never say never."), we *never* assume what one's dinner is any more. We ask. Some may still call lunch dinner. Dinner is the iffy one. Supper is *always* supper. We now call dinner, supper.

In the agricultural areas or era, lunch was truly a dinner. They worked hard and lunches were big meals. Lunch time should probably be the biggest meal of the day. Better than going to bed at night soon after a big meal. Some people get home from work so late and literally do go to bed after steak and potatoes. How can our digestive system work when it's supposed to be asleep?

So take your pick. These recipes are family favorites. Eat them for dinner or supper.

Fresh Tomato Spaghetti

       1 lb angel hair pasta
       1 - 1 1/2 lb tomatoes
       1 - 2 Tb dry basil or use fresh (the grocery
            store now carries fresh herbs and I use
            a whole 1 oz package)
       1 - 2 Tb olive oil
       1 tsp salt
       4 garlic cloves, minced

Start water for cooking the pasta. I've learned to omit the salt in the water until I'm ready to drop in the pasta. The salt at this point causes the water to bubble more. While waiting for it to boil, chop the tomatoes into a big serving bowl. Add salt (salt draws the tomatoes' juices out), olive oil, garlic and chopped basil. Stir. Boil the pasta. Angel hair is so fine it doesn't take long. Drain. Add to the tomato mixture and stir, or toss well to coat pasta. Serve with fresh parmesan, Italian bread and a salad.

Many times I'll add chopped green onion, pine nuts, capers, and some pesto sauce . . . It could be endless with pasta.

Regular tomato sauce is easy for a quick meal. I said in the "Bringing In the Harvest" section, I can only the basics, so I use a quart jar of tomato sauce for this. The basic Italian spices are always garlic, onion, basil and oregano. So I just add these to the simmering tomato sauce. Using fresh chopped onion and garlic is always the optimal, but sometimes not the easiest (or is it laziness?). We like the onion and garlic chopped in chunks along with mushrooms. If you want meat, then brown ground meat first. My mom uses Jimmy Dean basic sausage as the meat base. Another taste option, which is done in your *good* restaurants, is to add homemade soup stock. Let this simmer down to eliminate any wateriness, and enrich the flavor. Crushed fennel seeds are a good spice to add as well.

Lasagna can use this same tomato sauce base. If you want a thicker, richer tomato sauce, add a can of tomato paste. The cheesy layer can be made by mixing 2-3 eggs, 1 pint ricotta cheese, 2-3 cups mozzarella cheese, and 1/2 cup parmesan. I put another 1/2 cup parmesan on top. This plus 10 Whole Wheat Lasagna noodles make up a 9x13" baking dish. Bake at 375° for 30-40 minutes.

This recipe, along with the black bean pizza, comes from our friend Bruce. Bruce Cripe lives in Pasadena, California and works for World Vision. He ministers through music all over the world. He is a legend - personally responsible for the sponsoring of nearly 20,000 children! A few years ago Bruce began making our home a regular stop. In fact, we've given him a key to the house and often call the guest room "Bruce's room." Our times together have been fun and inspirational. Bruce produced our album. Bruce's favorite country is Italy and when he's here, he loves to cook Italian. So this dish has become a regular favorite of ours. I'm liking the fresh tomato sauce over the typical cooked/canned heavy tomato sauce.

Bruce always likes a lot of garlic in everything. So do we! Bruce has gotten us hooked on dipping bread in olive oil that has fresh ground pepper and garlic added. This can be better than butter. He loves our fresh-ground grain bread so much, that I'll often find him snacking on it dipped in the oil.

A package of tofu can replace the eggs. I've not tried it yet. I have used cubed or crumbled tofu sautéed with the onion, garlic and spices in spaghetti. This is good.

We met an Italian man who does not like this ricotta/egg addition. He just sprinkles the cheese as a layer. Sometimes he'll even use Swiss cheese.

56

Macaroni and Real Cheese

　　1 12 oz bag of the large elbow pasta, 4 cups
cooked (can be slightly under done since it
will cook more)
　　2 cups grated cheese
　　3 Tb flour
　　1/2 tsp salt
　　1/4 tsp pepper
　　3 cups low-fat milk (when you drain the pasta,
　　　　save the water and mix powdered milk
　　　　into this)

In a greased casserole dish, make three layers of all the ingredients but the milk - 1/3 macaroni, 1/3 cheese, sprinkling of flour, salt and pepper. Pour the milk over all. It should come up to the top macaroni layer but not over because it will bubble up and make a real mess in your oven. Bake about 30 minutes in a 350° oven with a cover on, then uncover and bake till all liquid is absorbed and thickened. I bake it about an hour in all. We like the top to get golden brown. Some like bread crumbs sprinkled over the top.

Chicken Pot Pie

> *When persons are in need of a supper brought to them, I use this dish. I've been asked for the recipe, or told they'd feign illness just to get this pie brought. Monte absolutely loves it. To his amazement, when he is out of town, the kids and I like store-bought pot pies, so you can see I'm not a purist. But there's no question, this is a favorite.*

Line a large pie dish with pastry. (See pie section for crust
　　recipe.)
　　　　Shred 1 pint of chicken in the bottom.
Layer:　　3 potatoes, very thinly sliced　(3 layers)
　　　　2 cups frozen mixed vegetables　(2 layers)
Sprinkle each layer with flour, salt, pepper, garlic & onion
Sprinkle on spices:
　　　　1-2 Tb parsley
　　　　1 tsp chervil
　　　　1/2 tsp coriander, ground
Pour over all:
　　　　1 pint chicken broth

Put on top crust. Bake in 400° oven for 45 min -1 hour.

(You can speed the process up by having vegetables and all warm, and then make a white sauce with the broth and seasonings, and pour over all.)

This type of Macaroni and Cheese has been a favorite in my family for many generations. As kids we often requested it for our Birthday meal. It's always requested for my mom to bring to family reunions. Monte grew up in the dairy state (margarine used to be outlawed and people would go over the border to buy it) and he likes real cheese. We once had someone asking if we had any "real" cheese, referring to Velveeta, which is processed cheese. Having grown up on this dish, there is no way I can eat the Kraft style of Macaroni and Cheese.

I don't have my mom's exact recipe since she does it by feel! I am giving you my variation. My mom probably used cheddar. I use colby. She probably used more. I've cut back.

If you want to speed things up you could make a white sauce (see cooking tips) and mix with the macaroni and cheese and then bake. This way everything begins warm and already thickening. Tuna or any meat could be added. If so, mix in some garlic and onion powder. I've made it in the microwave, but miss the browned flavor.

Chicken Divan

2 -10 oz packages of frozen broccoli or use fresh
2 cups cooked chicken (or turkey) pieces
2 cups chicken broth
3 Tb oil
4 Tb whole wheat flour
1 egg
1 Tb lemon juice
1/4 tsp cinnamon
2 seeds cardamom
3 cloves
3/8 tsp cummin
12 peppercorns
18 coriander seeds
1/8 tsp turmeric
1/4 tsp ground fenugreek
> Probably not in your typical grocery store. This is the spice that really makes the curry flavor.
1 cup shredded cheese
2-3 slices buttered bread

Most people make this using cream of chicken soup and store-bought curry powder. Most I've tried are too salty and not nearly as good. This might not be as easy but try it and compare.

The cinnamon through the fenugreek are the typical spices used in store-bought curry powder. When ground fresh the flavor is superior! Either grind them in a mortar and pestle or in a coffee grinder. Use this coffee grinder primarily for spices and herbs. Need to chop parsley or basil? The coffee grinder works great.

This is one of my favorites. It can be made a day or two ahead and refrigerated till needed.

Arrange broccoli in casserole dish and cook a few minutes in the microwave. Place chicken on top of broccoli. Make the white sauce (oil, flour, and broth) in saucepan until thickened, stirring often. Remove from heat. Grind spices in mortar and pestle or coffee grinder. Mix a bit of the warm white sauce into the egg to prevent cooking the egg. Add egg mixture into the rest of the white sauce. Add the lemon juice and spices. Pour over chicken. Mix bread cubes and cheese together and sprinkle over all. Bake at 350° for 20-30 minutes. We like the top to get browned in the oven.

Baked Chicken

2 chicken fryers in serving pieces or 6 breasts
1 cup wheat germ (or just extra flour)
1 cup whole wheat flour
1 heaping tsp of a seasoning mix:
> (parsley, basil, thyme, powdered garlic and onion, paprika . . .)
1/2 tsp oregano
1/2 tsp salt
1/4 tsp pepper

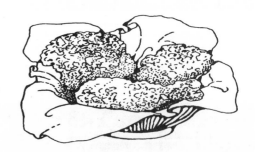

This is very comparable to fried chicken flavor.

Wash and dry chicken pieces. Place dry ingredients and several pieces of chicken in a paper bag. Shake vigorously until well coated. Place in single layer in a greased pan. Bake in a preheated 400° oven about 50 minutes, turning once. Cook until chicken is fork-tender.

When we moved to Colorado and visited a local church (we hadn't actually moved here yet but were looking), we prayed someone would invite us home for dinner. Someone did, and this family has become an extention of our own and vice-versa. Carol Lewis has been a mentor for me. The Bible speaks of older women teaching the younger women and I don't wait for someone to come to me. I see people with something I need to develop in my life and I ask, in a sense, to sit at their feet. Since Carol had grown up on a farm and gardened in this area for thirty years, I learned a lot from her. Hospitality is one of her gifts and Carol is a good cook. This is one of her recipes we love. Bet you can't eat just one!

I use the same marinade with meat pieces, mushrooms, and garlic cloves for kebobs. For the pineapple juice, use the juice from a crushed pineapple can packed in its own juices. Use the crushed pineapple in muffins.

We don't like to do the entire cooking process of meat on the grill. Most meats we pre-cook in a closed dutch oven at 300-350° until tender. They retain a lot of their juiciness and yet get the yummy barbecue flavor. Then grill them turning and basting frequently until the sauce cooks in. Most people never save their game animal ribs, but we do. If cooked fairly soon, they have no game flavor. Game flavor comes from the connecting tissue and fat of the animal. This we carefully cut away when butchering. So to keep the meat on the bone is not good. The fat of elk and deer has a lower pH and is less stable than that of pork or beef. It gets gamey over time, even in the freezer. We'll cook elk ribs along with regular ribs. Pre-cooking chicken for grilling is really a must in our opinion.

Chinese Chicken Wings (or Kebob Marinade)

20-25 chicken wings - cut at joint and discard tips

Combine:

1 cup soy sauce
1/4 cup orange juice
2 Tb sugar
1/4 cup oil
1 tsp chopped garlic
1 tsp ground ginger
1/4 cup pineapple juice

Marinate overnight in the refrigerator. Drain liquid, place on baking sheet, and bake at 375° for 45 minutes. Baste 2 times. If not brown near the end - broil a bit. Most times I put marinade and chicken on the baking sheet and bake longer, letting the juices cook down.

Speaking of barbecue (see side note on kebobs) makes me hungry for my mom's **Sauce-Painted Spareribs**. The recipe actually is her dad's, my Grandpa Magnuson. It's the best barbecue sauce *ever* for any meats.

1 cup catsup
1/4 cup lemon juice (fresh squeezed is best)
2 Tb brown sugar
1 Tb soy sauce
1 Tb Horseradish & Mustard (half of each)
1 Tb grated onion
1 1/2 tsp salt
1/2 tsp pepper
1/4 tsp oregano, marjoram, & / or thyme (I usually do 1/4 of each)
1/4 tsp either tobasco sauce or cayenne pepper
1 clove garlic (minced)

Simmer this over low heat at least 10 minutes. Improves with age so store some for later use.

My mouth is watering just thinking of these!

59

Chicken Spaghetti Casserole

    4 Tb olive oil
    4 Tb whole wheat flour
    3 cups chicken broth
    1 tsp salt
    1/4 tsp pepper
    1/4 tsp nutmeg
    1/4 pound sautéed mushrooms
    (I just crumble in a couple of handfuls
        of my dried mushrooms)
    2 cups cooked chicken pieces
    1/4 cup parmesan cheese
    dash of paprika
    1/2 lb spaghetti, cooked and drained

> *I first tasted this at our friends' house, Dave and Gina, who live in Tucson, Arizona. They lived with us prior to us moving to Colorado. They've built a beautiful, authentic southwestern home in the desert just beyond where we had built our home.*
>
> *Later I looked through my cookbooks and put this recipe together. I almost never use just one recipe, but lay out the books and pick and choose from each. Spaghetti squash could be tried as a substitute for the pasta.*

Make up white sauce with oil, flour, broth and add the spices and mushrooms until thickened. Add chicken. Place the spaghetti in a 9 x 13" baking dish. Top with sauce. Sprinkle with cheese and paprika. Bake at 350° for 20-25 minutes or until bubbly.

Chicken Breadcrust Quiche

    3 cups bread cubes
    1 Tb minced onion
    1 Tb parsley
    1/2 tsp ground sage
    1/2 tsp ground thyme
    1/2 tsp powdered garlic
    1/8 tsp pepper
    2 cups cooked chicken pieces
    4 Tb oil
    4 Tb whole wheat flour
    2 1/2 cups broth
    1 tsp salt
    2 eggs
    1 cup dry bread cubes
    1/4 cup butter, melted

> *This is really a strata. A breakfast strata is made laying the bread slices in the dish and pouring the egg/milk mixture over the top. It usually sits in the refrigerator over night.*
>
> *I like this because the flavorings remind me of Thanksgiving.*

Mix bread cubes with spices and arrange in a greased 9 x 13" baking dish. Top with meat. Make white sauce in saucepan (see previous mention by Macaroni and Cheese and in the Tips section). Remove from heat. Mix a bit of sauce into the eggs. Blend egg mixture slowly into hot mixture. Pour over bread and meat. Mix bread crumbs and butter; sprinkle over casserole. Bake 20-30 minutes at 375°.

Quiche Lorraine

A 9" precooked pie crust
(Bake 6 minutes at 475°. Look in pie section for crust and pre-baking suggestions.)

8 slices bacon, cooked and crumbled
1 cup shredded cheese
(original recipes use Swiss cheese, you can use any)
3 eggs
2 cups milk
1/4 tsp salt
1/8 tsp pepper
1 Tb flour
dash nutmeg

In pre-cooked and slightly cooled crust put cheese and bacon. Pour the other mixed ingredients (custard) over it. Bake at 325° for 35-40 minutes or until the center is set. Let rest about 10 minutes before cutting and serving.

This was my very first quiche and still my favorite.

Anything can really be added to quiche. Tomatoes, spinach, nuts (pine nuts!), onions, chives, or leeks. My other favorite is Cauli-Broc Quiche. To the basic custard ingredients add: 1/4 lb sliced mushrooms, 1-1 1/2 cups each cauliflower and broccoli pieces, all of which have been sautéed in butter or olive oil. Add 1/4 tsp each parsley, basil, tarragon, thyme and 1 Tb soy sauce as extras.

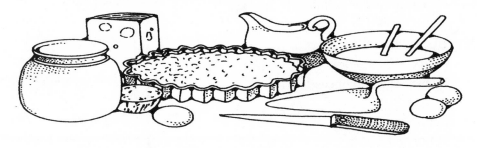

Chicken Tostada Pie

3 Tb oil
3 Tb whole wheat flour
1 1/2 cups broth
1/2 tsp salt
2-3 cups cooked chicken pieces
(or ground beef)
1/2 cup chopped green onions
4 oz chopped mild green chilies
1/2 - 3/4 lb shredded cheese
6 large flour tortillas

Quick fry the tortillas. Make the white sauce till thickened. Add green chilies, onions, and meat. You'll be making layers in a large deep pie dish: tortilla on bottom, thin layer of sauce, cheese, tortilla . . . continue, ending with a tortilla. Press down. Bake at 350° for about 30 minutes. Let set about 10 minutes before serving "pie" pieces.

This was a favorite in my youth and still is. The original recipe calls for a can of cream of chicken soup. I make the white sauce substitute. It's a popular dish to take somewhere. It's even good leftover, cold.

Mild green chilies are called anaheim chilies. They are usually the longest green chilies. We've found three chilies are equivalent to a four-ounce can.

I explain about quick frying tortillas in the Taco recipe. Heat the oil in a skillet till hot. Insert the tortilla to cover, or turn tortilla to get the second side. Remove immediately and place between paper towels. Sometimes I brush both sides with olive oil instead.

61

Tostada Egg

This is a lunch favorite or quickie supper.

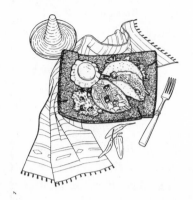

    In a warm, heavy skillet heat one side of a flour tortilla. Remove. Put a bit of oil in the pan and return the tortilla, other side down. Have one egg ready, beaten in a little bowl. Pour the egg on top of the tortilla and spread around. Cover the skillet to help set the egg. Watch the temperature so the bottom does not burn. Once my cast iron skillet is heated, I make most of the tostadas at my number 4 setting. When egg is set, sprinkle about 1 Tb of grated cheese. Fold the tortilla in half like an omelette and remove to a cutting board. Continue making more. We cut these in wedges with a pizza cutter. The kids like them plain. Monte and I like to add chives or green onions, and dip them in salsa. Another method is to place another tortilla on top of the cheese and turn the whole thing over to cook the top tortilla. I only do this if I have fewer eggs and plenty of tortillas. Then the tortillas fill stomachs, rather than eggs. I suppose it's somewhat like a quesadilla with a top.

Chili Relleno Casserole

    1 large can of whole green chilies
    3 cups shredded cheese
    6-7 eggs
    1 cup broth
    1 chopped onion
    1 cup chopped tomato
    1 minced garlic clove
    1/2 tsp salt
    1/2 tsp ground cumin
    1/4 tsp pepper
    1/4 tsp oregano
    4-5 Tb Masa flour
    4 Tb parmesan cheese
    1/2 tsp baking powder
    1/4 tsp salt

This is made in layers, beginning and ending with the opened out green chilies. Cheese goes between. The remainder makes the sauce to pour over the layers. For the sauce, sauté the onion, then add the tomato, then the broth and seasonings; cook while assembling the rest of the ingredients (about 15 minutes). Bake uncovered at 350° about 40 minutes, or until set. I realize while typing this I've probably done it a little bit different from my mom, but still basically the same. (I don't have a recipe card to look at, just added notes in a book.)

Mexican Food

I often use Mexican words for our dishes that have different meanings for some people. I grew up one hour away from the Mexican border in Arizona. Our Tucson flour tortillas were very thin and maybe this was influenced by the many Indian reservations around. When I go back to Tucson I crave "real" tortilla chips. We eat bean burros all the time for lunch and some people call them burritos. Flautas weren't prevalent, nor taquitoes. A quesadilla was larger than any pizza and paper thin. Crisp on the outer edges, soft in the middle where the cheese coated. My favorite Mexican dish is a chimichanga (see Carne Seca meat). Whenever we go to a new Mexican restaurant, I always have to try the chimi. It's my reference point. Fresh tamales were often sold in parking lots and they are a favorite too. Chili rellenos is another. Most are singly made - green chili stuffed with cheese, dipped in batter and fried. Jalepeño poppers are the new craze made in the same way. I like a chili relleno casserole, and so far my mom's outdoes them all. I love to finish off a Mexican meal with a flan.

62

Monte said I had to put this in. Every-one in our family raves over it. The exact recipe he made me write down long ago was a little of this left over and a little of that. We usually do have beans in the 'fridge and Monte's Mexican Meat, so I make these after having Swiss Steak with mashed potatoes. The main message is that enchiladas can be made with leftovers - even chop up and add the leftover vegetables. Gravies and meat drippings always make good bases for Mexican dishes.

We like the white corn tortillas these days. They are so tender. Our green chili sauce is from Hatch, New Mexico, the chili capital of the world.
I buy it by the case from my co-op.

The chilies for the red chili sauce have been hanging around my kitchen awhile, I definitely need to rinse them and at the same time remove the stems and seeds.

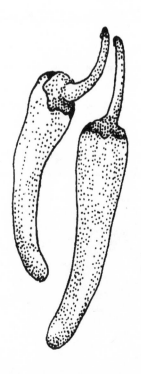

Karey's Enchiladas

In a saucepan heat these proportions:

1/3 of my beans (pg 81) to 2/3 meat

Add leftover:

few Tb each of Swiss Steak gravy, mashed potatoes, and salsa

When heated, add a dollop of mixture across a corn tortilla (these may be leftover from my tacos). Sprinkle with a little grated cheese. Roll and lay side by side in a 7 x 12 baking dish. Spread one can of green chili sauce over all. Bake at 400° about 20 minutes. Broil a few minutes. Serve with finely shredded lettuce or cabbage and chopped tomatoes.

Karey's Favorite Enchiladas

1 1/2 lbs browned meat cubes
cooked with chopped onion and garlic
3/4 cup broth
1/4 cup raisins
1/2 tsp ground cloves
1/4 tsp crushed anise seeds
1/4 cup of red chili sauce

Let this simmer, covered, till tender and the meat can be shredded, about 1 1/2-2 hours.

For the red chili sauce, place about 5 dried anaheim chilies, seeded and stems removed, in a blender with 2 1/2 cups of boiling water; let stand 1 hour. Once soaked, blend until smooth. Transfer to a saucepan and add:

1 clove minced garlic (I add more)
2 Tb tomato paste
1/2 tsp salt
1/2 tsp dried oregano
1/4 tsp ground cumin
1/4 tsp ground coriander

Heat to boiling and simmer for 10 minutes. To assemble the enchiladas, dip 12 corn tortillas in the hot red chili sauce and place about 3 Tb meat mixture in each. Roll and lay side by side in a 9 x 13" baking dish. Cover with the rest of the sauce and bake at 375° degrees until bubbly. Add 1 1/2-2 cups shredded cheese. Serve with sour cream (or substitute with salted plain yogurt) and olives.

Fresh Tomato Salsa

This is a summer sensation. I crave it. When we go to a get-together, I'll often make this right there along with guacamole, and have a big basket of tortilla chips (real chips, not Doritos). Its uniqueness comes from the *fresh* cilantro leaves. Chop tomatoes in small pieces. Plum tomatoes can be used, but sometimes they aren't as flavorful as regular round tomatoes, and I like the regular tomatoes' juiciness. Chop onions and roasted green chilies (canned are fine). Chop lots of cilantro. This herb has seeded itself, like dill, all over my vegetable garden and I don't mind. Add all this together and salt to taste.

Call this **Salsa-a-la-Monte**. He's been doing some work in Mexico and they make salsa right at the table in a stone mortar and pestle made from volcanic rock. Being lava, it is rough and full of holes. He asked to buy this "molcajete" and they sold him the one from the table for four dollars! Monte didn't recognize any of the ingredients. It came out like a paste. This concoction could probably be done in a food processor or blender. He did consult some cookbooks to see some basic varieties and then just went with his instincts. It tastes great. A multi-dimensional fresh flavor. You can create your own sensation with an almost infinite combination of flavors and textures.

Grind seeds before adding the pepper, celery, onion, etc.

    1 tsp coriander seed
    3 tsp basil
    3/4 tsp cumin seed
    3/4 tsp fennel seed
    1 tsp lemon peel
    1 heaping Tb pine nuts
    1/4 of whole red bell pepper, chopped
    1/2 stalk celery, chopped
    5 green onions, chopped
    3 garlic cloves
    1 cup home canned stewed tomatoes
    (1-3 fresh jalapeños)

Guacamole

I guess I have to add my recipe for this as well, since everyone makes it differently. I like them all, but really prefer the basic taste of avocado and tomato together. Rather than mashing the avocado, I just spoon out small chunks, chop a tomato, and mix together. Most times I will just add salt and fresh ground pepper to taste. Or add garlic and onion powder. Other times I will add chopped green onion, garlic, and green chilies. Cottage cheese could be added (don't add extra salt then). Jalepeños would add more spunk. Serve soon or the avocado turns brown. Supposedly putting in the pit slows the browning, but I would add lemon juice if you can't serve it soon.

We have a good friend who gives us this spice mixture. We've called it "Alan's Spices" for years. Since we use it so often in our meat mixtures and sausage, we asked for the recipe -

2 1/2 cups Lawry's Seasoning Salt
1 cup red pepper
2 cups black pepper
1 cup minced dried garlic
1/4 small can cayenne pepper

Carne Seca Meat

The truly authentic shredded Mexican meat, typically used for chimichangas, is called carne seca or dried meat. Monte was at an old-time Mexican restaurant and asked the chef about the meat. He said they rub in and coat the meat with fresh garlic and onion. Beef brisket or flank are the typical cuts of meat. This is then sun-dried in a screened cage for a couple of days (done in a very warm and dry climate). Restaurants have a machine that shreds the dry meat. It is then sautéed and cooked with green chilies, onion, salt and pepper in a cast iron pan. I use Monte's meat mixture for chimis, need to drain off most of the juiciness though. Chimichangas are flour tortillas folded closed over the meat filling and then deep or pan fried till golden and crispy. The oil must be 400° to cook quickly and not absorb the oil. I've brushed the tortillas with olive oil and then baked till crisp. Authentic chimichangas are the ultimate Mexican dish in my opinion. Serve with shredded lettuce, and sour cream.

For Chicken Fajitas, Monte likes to sauté sliced onions. Then add green chili strips and cooked chicken strips and pieces. Though we rarely do it, the best way to pre-cook the chicken is to grill it, basting it well to prevent drying out. Then cut in strips. He spices all this with oregano, summer savory, chervil, parsley, salt and pepper, cumin and nutmeg. Let simmer together a bit. You can eat this mixture as is in a flour tortilla with a bit of cheese, or have a variety of other ingredients like I mention in my taco recipe.

Monte's Mexican Meat

In the past we always used basic ground meat. Monte now makes up a big crockpot full of mainly elk roasts. He'll sometimes add some turkey or pork with bone. A seven-bone, beef roast is a typical meat for the shredded Mexican meats. He claims the secret for superior flavor of any meat is to brown it before baking in the oven in a closed pot or crockpot. I usually do this too, but I tease him that his tastes better because he "babys" it. Sliced onion and celery sautéed in the same pan after the meats adds another flavor burst. He then likes to add some water or cooking wine to pull the browned juices off the bottom of the pan. Mushrooms sautéed following the onions and left in the pan along with the added liquid are good additions. All of these get dumped in the crockpot along with 4 oz of green chilies, and about 4 cups water. Now for the spices: usually ground coriander, garlic, basil, ground pepper, and salt. Then about a teaspoon of "Alan's Spices" (see note on previous page) per 1 1/2 lbs of meat. Monte claims he rubs this in after it's browned. I've just seen him dump it in the pot. Sometimes he'll add some natural meat tenderizer. Some of the spices he leaves whole because he enjoys watching one of us bite down on a coriander, mustard seed, or peppercorn. This is cooked all day. You want the meat to easily shred.

I have another version for Mexican meat. Our friends served an Italian **Porketta** roast and I loved the seasoning so asked for the recipe. They use a pre-made mixture and got the spice breakdown from a relative in Hibbing, Minnesota. I think it's originally done with the spices rubbed into a flat pork roast that is rolled and tied with string. Sometimes I'll do this with an elk flank or brisket. (This meat cut rolled with a bread stuffing is delicious too!) Other times I just cut slits in a big roast, putting the seasoning in the slits. For the spices, grind and mix together one teaspoon each: fennel seed, basil, parsley, celery seed, rosemary, oregano, onion powder, garlic powder, salt and pepper. The only other spice I usually add is a teaspoon of ground cumin seed. Bake the roast in a covered pan at 325° until well done and falling apart. This meat is good served on crispy hard rolls. Served with the meat juices, this makes a superb French Dip.

(Let's see . . . this was my Mexican meat made from an Italian recipe and great for French Dip!)

Flour Tortillas

        2 cups flour
        1/2 tsp salt
        1/4 cup oil
        1/3-1/2 cup water

Mix all together and knead 2-3 minutes. Let rest in plastic wrap at room temp for 30 minutes. If using whole wheat flour, let it sit longer so the flour can absorb the liquids. It will then hold together. Roll pieces into balls and keep covered with plastic wrap to prevent drying. Have a heavy griddle or skillet heating near your work area for cooking as you make each one. Roll each dough ball on a floured surface as thin as possible. Monte says a heavy rolling pin makes this easier. The one he uses is marble. Cook each tortilla on the hot dry griddle until the top is bubbly and the bottom is flecked with brown spots, about 20-30 seconds. Turn and cook other side until speckled. Press down a bit on these with a spatula. Have a large piece of foil ready to enclose them as they're made, stacking tortillas inside. Monte talked with the chef at an authentic restaurant in Tucson, and he makes them this way, omitting the oil. They turn out much more elastic when made without oil.

Corn Tortillas can be made similarly, using 2 cups Masa Harina and 1 - 1 1/4 cups warm water. Dough should be stiff. I have a tortilla press, but Monte thinks rolling is easy. Circles are much easier to achieve when you start out with a ball of dough rather than a uneven glop. If using a press, these are usually made between two pieces of plastic wrap or waxed paper, and can be reused (until destroyed). If dough is too sticky add more Masa Harina, a tablespoon at a time. Cook the same as flour tortillas on an ungreased skillet.
Masa Harina is made from a special process of cooking dried corn (10 cups) with water (10 cups) and lime powder (2 Tb) for a couple of hours until tender, then drain. The corn can then be ground through a meat grinder and used fresh (or freeze) for tamales and corn tortillas. Masa Harina is sold in bags in most grocery stores in the flour section.

I buy flour tortillas by the case and freeze, but for a special treat, Monte will make homemade. Here again, I could make them but . . .
The original recipe makes twelve tortillas from these proportions. You can, of course, make them bigger and, therefore, less of them.

Monica is a Mexican friend of ours and was present one time when Monte was making tortillas. She mentioned "marking" the tortillas, a tradition from her mother. She never turns them when rolling them out. The tortilla is then transferred to the skillet, still without turning. The "marking" is the browning pattern on the bottom as the top bubbles. Turn at this point and cook the other side, but stack them "bottom" down. She then uses them "bottom" down as well. We think this tradition has more to do with orderliness than anything else.

Tacos

I grew up with soft corn tacos my mother always quick fried so they remained soft, and layered between paper towels. Those traditional crisp shells are so hard for kids (and me too) - one bite, it cracks down the middle, and everything falls out!

We hide the bowls of grated cheese, finely chopped tomatoes, shredded lettuce (we often use cabbage since it's a good keeper in the cellar), cooked and warm beans and meat, green onions, sour cream (often times plain, salted yogurt, or yogurt pureed with cottage cheese) and the cooked corn tortillas.

Chicken Curry.

This is wonderful! Little kids don't always care for curry flavoring but they sure like all the condiments.

> 2 onions, sliced
> 2 cloves garlic, minced
> 2 Tb oil
> 1 stick cinnamon
> 1/4 tsp whole cloves
> 1 Tb turmeric
> 1 tsp ginger
> 1 tsp cumin
> 2 Tb coriander
> 1 3-4 lb. chicken (or 1-2 cups already deboned
>   chicken)
> 2 cups tomato juice or sauce
> 1 cup chicken broth

Sauté the onions and garlic in a stock pot. Add the seasonings and sauté together until the onion is transparent. Add the chicken and sauté until well coated with spices. Add the rest of the ingredients and simmer for one or two hours. If desired, thicken with cornstarch dissolved in a little cold water.

Serve with brown rice and separate small bowls of yogurt, coconut, nuts (I like cashews), raisins, cheese, pineapple, bananas, and chutney. Sometimes we use the crunchy chinese noodles. All of this piled together is good. Little kids tend to like everything separate, encircling the curry with little piles of each.

Turkey and Dressing

1 loaf of bread
1/3 cup dried whole sage leaves
3 Tb thyme leaves
1 tsp marjoram
1 large onion, chopped
4-6 celery ribs, chopped
1/4-1/2 cup butter
Turkey with its giblets and all

Homemade bread really makes the best stuffing (Monte made me add this). Dice the bread and let sit in a big bowl all day or overnight to dry. Stir occasionally. Put giblets, heart, liver and maybe even the neck in a pan with about a quart of water and simmer for about one hour, for broth. I don't put these organs into the dressing. I'm sorry, I just don't like them in it.

To begin, melt the butter in a large skillet and sauté the onion and celery. Stir these into the cubed bread with the spices. I put enough of the broth into the bread mixture to moisten it more, but you don't want it soggy. When ready to put the turkey in the oven, stuff both the neck and body cavity. I fill these pretty full. Skewer closed and tie with string. The leftover dressing that doesn't fit in the turkey goes in a covered casserole dish. I'll put more of the broth in this since it's not in the turkey with its juices. This should bake at 350° for about one hour.

The baking of turkey is another thing. I'm going to tell you how I've done it for years. Please check your cookbooks for proper timing. When stuffed it needs five minutes more cooking time per pound. Our turkeys are bigger than 16 pounds so it needs 18-20 minutes per pound. Smaller turkeys need more time per pound (I know this sounds wrong, but look it up!). I cook it breast side up in a closed pan the entire time. (I have done it upside down the whole time, or turned it right side up halfway through, and have even salt-brined the turkey prior to cooking. I don't usually mess with these.) My roasting pan has a rack to keep the bird off the bottom. Begin with a pre-heated 400° oven and then once in, turn down to 325°. I rarely need to baste it because it is enclosed in the pan. A good indication that it's done is the leg easily pulls off, or a fork inserted in the leg and twisted a bit will easily remove meat from the bone. The internal stuffing temperature should be 165°. We don't eat until 4 pm, so I'm not up before dawn.

I'm doing this mainly to give you my stuffing recipe. A friend called this evening asking if my stuffing recipe is going into the book (she also said "to assume we know nothing"). Everyone who has tasted my dressing loves it and says it's the best! My mom deserves the credit and maybe her mom before her. I suppose I should ask. Like her, it's very hard for me to give you exact amounts. In fact, I just dumped water in my mortar and pestle to the level I put my dried (not pulverized yet) sage, just to see the actual measurement.

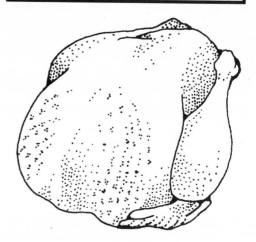

Mashed Potatoes are another favorite I'll mention since I do them differently. Of course they're cooked in plenty of boiling salted water until tender. I never mash them with milk to prevent them from cooling and becoming pasty. If I want milk, I use powdered milk added to the potato water. Don't discard any of this water. Pour it into a canning jar or glass measuring pitcher. Put pats of butter into the potatoes. Use an electric hand beater. With it off, begin the mashing process. Pour a little of the potato water in and begin beating. Keep putting more water in until whipped fluffy and not too wet. Save the remainder of the potato water for the gravy.

1/2 potatoes & 1/2 rutabaga are good mashed together. Once mashed, place dish in oven to melt a sprinkling of cheese on top.

Leftover mashed potatoes are good simply formed into patties and cooked till browned. I do this in my Jet Stream; though could be done on a skillet or in oven.

Cornstarch always needs to mix with cold water. Regular flour doesn't require cold water; any temperature will do.

Don't throw that turkey carcass away! When the meal's over have your husband debone the rest of the turkey. Put the turkey bones back into the roasting pan. Follow the chicken stock recipe in the "Soup" chapter to make broth. Freeze the broth in pint containers, and the leftover turkey in pint containers too.

Gravy can get lumpy, right? When the turkey is removed from the pan, I put the pan on the stove. Mine straddles two burners. For good gravy flavor, you really want to use flour. I only use cornstarch for quick gravies, but not for Thanksgiving. I've seen some people put the flour and some water into a closed glass jar and shake it. I put 1/2 cup flour into a bowl and put a small bit of water in. Stir with a fork to make a paste and remove the lumps. Add a bit more water and stir. Now it's ready to stir into the turkey drippings. Add a couple cups of the potato water into the drippings too. Keep stirring the gravy with it bubbling, to thicken. Taste for saltiness. You may want more potato water too. Once it begins to thicken you can lower the heat and let it simmer, stirring occasionally. With flour thickening it does need to cook to prevent a raw flour taste.

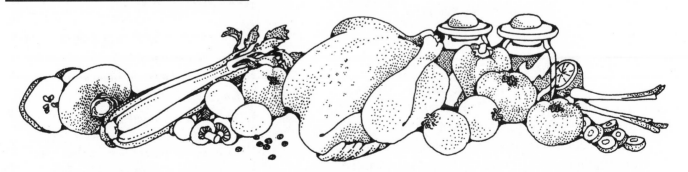

Swiss Steak

When I look at Swiss Steak recipes, they are entirely
different than mine. Maybe mine shouldn't be called
that, but it's what we've always called it. We inherited
the name and recipe from Monte's mom. This is another main meat dish people really like. We use elk or
venison, but it will work with any meat. I slice a roast
thinly, 1/4-1/2" thick across the grain, salt and pepper
one side, and pound whole wheat flour into both sides.
These are browned in an oiled skillet and removed. I
then sauté and brown a thin-sliced onion. Add the meat
back to the skillet with water barely covering. Sometimes we'll add cooking wine. Simmer until the meat
is tender, about an hour or two. I often pressure cook
this. Whenever you coat meat with flour and brown
well, as the meat cooks, it makes its own gravy. Cubed
meat works too (I sprinkle the flour as the meat is browning and I'm stirring) - in fact, over mashed potatoes,
this was Monte's favorite meal as a boy.

Pasty

For the pastry:

> 1 cup butter
> 1 1/4 cups boiling water
> 1 tsp salt
> 4 1/2-5 cups whole wheat flour
> > (or half wheat and white)

Cut up the butter into a bowl and add the boiling water,
stirring till melted. Stir in the salt and flour till forms a ball.
Wrap in plastic wrap and refrigerate while making the filling:

> 1 1/2 lbs meat, cut in 1/4-1/2" cubes
> 4 medium potatoes, peeled and diced
> 1 large onion, finely chopped
> 1 cup chopped carrot
> (1 cup chopped rutabaga,
> > delicious if you have it)
> 1/2 cup chopped celery
> 1 1/2 tsp salt
> 1/2 tsp pepper

Mix together well, especially the salt and pepper. I no longer
chop all this but got a large hole disk for my meat grinder and
grind it all. Divide the chilled dough into 8 (or 16) pieces.
On greased surface, roll a piece of dough into a circle. Place
1 (or 1/2) cup filling in center of each. Crimp to seal. Prick.
Cover baking sheets with foil (can be messy if they leak).
Bake in a preheated 400° oven for 15 minutes, then lower to
375° and continue for 45 minutes to 1 hour, until golden
brown. Sometimes I melt a bit of butter with some water and
brush on in last 5 minutes of baking.

(Pasty is pronounced with a short vowel
"a" sound. Very important!) I originally
learned of this from my sister-in-law
Cindy, who is Finnish, and from the
Upper Peninsula of Michigan. The
miners' wives wanted to make a warm,
whole meal type of sandwich for their
husbands. I've adapted the various
recipes, of course. You can order Pastys
at restaurants in the Upper Peninsula.
Most are served with gravy. One family
we know eats theirs with catsup. I like
them plain. I double this big batch a lot
in the summer or when we're traveling
so we have a "whole meal," easy to grab.
I wrap them individually in foil and
they freeze well.

You have to make them and decide
which size you like. We like the smaller
size which makes 16. The shape is up to
you. Some are folded over like a half
moon. Most I've had in restaurants are
just molded into a ball with the edges
underneath. I make them weird. I just
try to crimp them closed up on top so
they might not leak.

70

Monte learned his fish basics from his mother. I never cared for fish until Monte cooked it for me. I feign igno-rance to this day so I don't have to cook it. I probably wouldn't do it as well anyway. Freshness is the biggest key to good fish. This basic preparation works well with any kind of fish whether frying or baking. Walleye, pike, halibut and perch are particularly good this way. Lay the fish out on a cutting board and trim off all skin, fat, dark meat, membrane, and freezer burn. These typically are strong and fishy in taste (and incidentally, concentrate any chemical pollutants if they are present). Filet or slice the fish 1/4-3/4" thick, and then into 2-4" pieces. Rinse in a bowl of cold water a couple of times. The third time cover the fish with water and add salt and lemon juice. This will draw out and neutralize any fishy taste. If the fish is not fresh this step is particularly important. We do this step even for fresh-caught small trout which we cook whole. Monte's mother does it with smelt. She skins each one! This was one of Monte's all-time favorite meals.

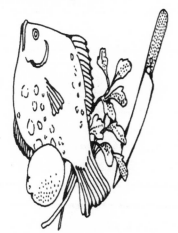

Remember to save the fish scraps. I use them for a broth for potato soup or clam chowder.

Monte's Fish Recipe

As fish soaks, prepare the coating:

1. Put a cup of flour in a bowl
2. Whip 2-3 eggs by hand in another bowl
3. On a bread board, crush saltine crackers with or without bread crumbs. It should be noted that if the bread or crackers are spiced, it will distract from the delicate taste of the fish. (Does that sound like Monte talking or me? 'Tis him.)
4. In a mortar, grind together equal parts dill, dried garlic and basil. Add black pepper and salt to taste. Salt can also be added after the fish is cooked. The spices can be mixed with the crumbs or sprinkled on the fish. Don't overdo it. (Monte's mom usually just uses salt and pepper. With the goodness of fresh fish, this is probably the best way.)
5. Set a metal rack on a baking sheet next to your frying pan or use it to bake your fish on.
6. Drain and rinse fish with cold water, and dry with paper towel.
7. If frying, pour 1/8-1/4" oil into a heavy skillet. Heat to medium-high. If baking, preheat oven to 350°.
8. Coat fish pieces with flour. Shake off loose flour, then dip in eggs and coat completely. Roll in crumbs and set aside until enough is done to fill the pan. If baking, finish coating all and lay on baking rack and bake in the middle of the oven.
9. For pan frying, gently lay fish in hot oil using tongs. Check fish often to see if they are browning properly. Adjust heat as needed. They should gently sizzle and slowly become golden brown. When golden brown, lay on rack and put in warm oven while rest of fish is being fried. Between each batch the old oil should be drained and the pan wiped clean with a paper towel, or the dark brown crumbles will burn and disflavor the next batch. Properly cooked fish will flake to the touch.

Sautéed Fish

Another variation on this recipe is to cut fish in small pieces (catfish trimmings work well for this). Clean the fish well as suggested above. Lay fish on bread board and sprinkle with spices. Sauté until flaky and slightly browned. Add touches of water if the pan is drying out. This fish is excellent on pasta or rice or as a main fish entrée. I do cook this style of fish. In fact, I may have done this before Monte, but it doesn't matter.

Broccoli and Pine Nuts

> 1-2 Tb olive oil
> 2-3 Tb pine nuts or slivered almonds
> 2 Tb lemon juice
> 2 lbs broccoli
> freshly ground pepper to taste

About 10 minutes before meal time, heat oil (or butter) in skillet over medium heat. Add nuts and cook a few minutes, stirring. Add lemon juice and broccoli. Cover and let steam until ready to serve. Stir occasionally.

Hot 'N Hearty (German) Potato Salad

> Scrub 2 lbs potatoes and bake or boil till tender
> (4 strips bacon, cooked and crushed)
> 2 Tb olive oil
> 1/2 cup onion, chopped
> 1/3 cup cider vinegar
> 1/3 cup water
> 1/4 cup chopped parsley or a few tsp dried
> salt and pepper to taste

Sauté the onions until golden. Add vinegar, water and parsley to skillet. Cut the potatoes in chunks and add to skillet. Cook just to heat through. (Add crumbled bacon.) Salt and pepper to taste.

Oven Baked French Fries

> I have a few ways to make these. One came from an Encyclopedia Brown book Travis read. Another from my friend Trish.

Travis brought me this method:

In a bowl have a few Tbs water and 1 Tb olive oil ready. Slice 4-6 potatoes like "french fries," dropping them in the bowl to coat. Stir around and add some salt. Bake in 400° oven, stirring occasionally, till crisp, 45-60 minutes.

Trish's version is identical except she adds 2 egg whites to the bowl. She also suggests lining the baking sheet with foil.

Another version adds a touch of liquid smoke to the bowl along with some parmesan cheese.

72

Vegetables have always been the hardest food item for me to prepare. And my typical thoughts on vegetables have been to at least have one per lunch or supper. Monte's idea is to have at least three at a time! I still struggle with this at times. Some should be cooked, some fresh or raw. Growing up, I hated vegetables. I do like most of them raw. I especially hated cooked spinach and thinking of this reminds me of Popeye. Monte's system does not seem to tolerate most vegetables raw, and yet he hates them cooked too soft. We've found that just barely microwaving, steaming or sautéing has been a good compromise.

I think I should admit that the majority of my life I have not liked tossed green salads either. I've eaten them because I know I should. Now, the last seven years, I'm liking them. I'm not sure why, unless it's just trying to spice them up, either with the extras or trying different lettuce varieties and dressings. I'm sure you know that iceburg has the least amount of nutrients of all the lettuce. Home-grown iceburg isn't like the commercial and has become my favorite. Romaine is another I like to grow, and kale. Then there's spinach, which I love.

We both dislike large chunks of anything in a salad, except for maybe tomato. Because lettuce is thin, I like other vegetables to have a similar look. When peeling a carrot, continue to peel the carrot in shaving curls to add to the salad. Red bell pepper, sliced thin, is sweeter than the green and pretty. Cucumbers, radishes, turnips . . . lend themselves well to slicing thin. My favorite way to prepare the lettuce now is to pile it all on the cutting board and slice through it in very thin strips. If ripped, please have the pieces be bite-sized. Who wants to cut their salad at the table?!

Grilled Vegetables

I have a Jenn-Air stove with a grill. Sometimes my mouth waters for grilled vegetables, especially grilled eggplant. Eggplant is not a favored vegetable. I like it in the Greek dish, Moussaka. Grilled eggplant sandwiches are good. While grilling the 1/4" sliced eggplant, brush with olive oil in which a minced garlic clove has been added. Add thin sliced cheese and basil leaves enclosed in a french bread style roll and you've got a good sandwich. Once I tried this, I started searching the refrigerator for other vegetables to try grilled. These can be saved for further meals, like with pasta. What I really like on grilled or broiled eggplant is pesto sauce.

Pesto Sauce is easy to make in a food processor or blender: 3 cups basil leaves, 1/4 c pine nuts, 1/2 cup olive oil, and 3 garlic cloves. Process till grainy. Fold in 1/2 cup grated parmesan cheese. Try cooking potato slices in pasta pot till almost tender and add pasta to cook near the end. Drain and toss this together with pesto sauce. Good stuff.

Sandwiches are not my first love either. I'd rather eat leftovers for lunch than a typical sandwich. But I've been exploring a variety of things. I like sub sandwiches but they have so much meat and cheese. I think I like the fullness, the large amount of filling to bread. I also don't love mayonnaisey, saucey sandwich spread. I like to spread my bread with Italian dressing, minced garlic, horseradish, pesto sauce . . . something spicy. I'm also trying a variety of thin-sliced veggies. Spicy sprouts are good. If I make a chicken salad, I grind everything in the meat grinder and add carrots, celery, radishes, and almonds. I'm weird. Atypical. Monte says I'm asymmetric.

Roasting Vegetables

This has become a well-liked method of cooking vegetables. Root vegetables are what we usually do. They can be done in a closed container or foil but I prefer them in an open pan. This works best if they are rubbed or coated with oil or a fat. Roasted potatoes have been the favorite with onion. Cut all to uniform sizes and sauté to coat. Add 1 tsp crumbled thyme. Bake in 400° oven until evenly browned, 45-50 minutes. Stir occasionally. You can add garlic to the pan for the last 20 minutes. Crumbled bacon is also tasty. Carrots, turnips, sweet potatoes, shallots, and rutabaga are good. Try combinations of vegetables with other spices or with vinegar. Whole beets can be done this way too. In fact, when beets are done whole, and then peeled and sliced or diced, they won't bleed as much.

Baked Potatoes

I know that most everyone knows about these. I'm just adding a note here so you don't forget about using baked potatoes as a meal with a variety of toppings. Company and kids like to have a variety of condiments, even if they don't put them on the potato. For example, I prefer avocado on the side. I love avocado alone! Many main dish mixtures could be toppers, such as: chili, chili-con-carne, stroganoff, barbecue meat, chunky soups or stews, beans, creamed meat or vegetable sauces (remember the white sauce). Cream sauces can be made with tofu too . . . I'm a sour cream lover, but now I really like salted plain yogurt on a potato. Varieties of chopped vegetables are good extras, and then there's also crumbled bacon and sliced green onions or chives, which I love. Restaurant potatoes are usually baked in foil. They seem so creamy and I wonder if they soak them in water before sealing in foil and baking. The easiest method is to rub down with oil and stick in a 350° oven till tender. Make sure the skin is well scrubbed because some people, like me, eat the skin.

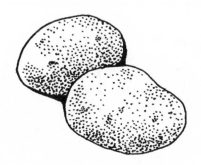

Marinated Cucumber (Tomato) Salad

Thinly slice a cucumber or two.

Mix together:

1/4 cup tarragon-flavored vinegar
3 Tb olive oil
2 tsp oregano
1/8 tsp fresh ground pepper
2 tsp sugar
1/2 tsp dill weed

Pour this over the cucumbers to marinate. It's very pretty with thin sliced tomatoes and / or thin sliced red onions.

Macaroni Salad

This is another childhood favorite of mine. My recipe differs from my mom's, but is similar enough.

3/4 cup mayonnaise
(My mother uses Miracle Whip which is sweeter. I now mix half mayonnaise and half yogurt.)
2 Tb cider vinegar
1 tsp salt
(1 tsp sugar)
1 tsp powdered mustard seed
dash pepper
4 hard-cooked eggs, cooled, peeled and chopped
4 cups cold, cooked and drained, elbow macaroni (12 oz uncooked)
1/2 cup chopped green onions
1/2 cup sliced radishes
3/4 cup diced colby cheese
2 Tb chopped parsley

Combine first six ingredients and mix well. Add remaining ingredients. Cover and refrigerate.

Before slicing, I often take a fork and scrape it down the cucumber's length all around through the green skin. When sliced these lines show up as pretty scallops.

I can think of two persons who come to our house over the holidays who look forward to this dish. With all the other holiday foods and desserts, this tastes so fresh. Vinegar counteracts the sweets. This recipe is part of a Swedish smorgasbord.

Tofu Eggless Mayonnaise
This is a good salad dressing, sandwich spread . . .
2 Tb lemon juice
2 Tb tarragon or cider vinegar
1 clove garlic, minced
1 tsp dijon-style mustard
1/2 cup plain yogurt
1 cup tofu
1-2 tsp soy sauce
2 Tb olive oil
freshly ground pepper
Puree all until smooth in blender.
Use 1 cup of this as a base for other salad dressings: Blue Cheese - add 1 cup buttermilk, 1-2 Tb crumbled blue cheese, 1-3 tsp Worcestershire sauce; Thousand Island - add 2 Tb chili sauce and 2 Tb red pepper relish; Vinaigrette - add 2 more Tb vinegar and 2 Tb lemon juice (can add more mustard).

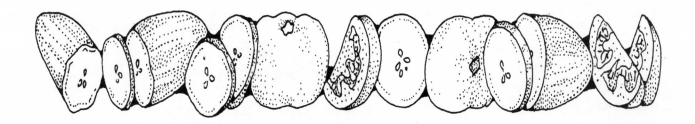

Egg Salad

4 hard cooked eggs
1/3 cup chopped green onions
1/3 cup finely chopped celery
(1/3 cup finely chopped carrot)
1/4 cup yogurt
mayonnaise to moisten
salt and pepper to taste

Mix everything together with a fork. This is typically used as a sandwich filler. I like it with crackers.

Caesar Salad Dressing

Mix in jar and shake.

1/2 cup olive oil
1 crushed garlic clove or more
1 1/2 tsp salt
1/4 tsp dry mustard
generous grating of black pepper
a few drops of soy sauce
juice of one lemon
3 Tb wine or cider vinegar
1 coddled egg or raw egg (For coddling
     simmer egg for 1 1/2 minutes; raw
     eggs may carry salmonella.)
     Mix the egg with a fork in a
     bowl, then add to dressing jar.

Gently tear lettuce into bowl. Sprinkle with 2-3 Tb parmesan cheese and add croutons (see "Bread" section). Pour over the salad and toss well. Serve immediately.

Egg Mustard Dressing and Salad

2 hard cooked eggs,
     yolks and whites separated
1 1/2 tsp yellow mustard
3 Tb cider vinegar
1/8 cup olive oil
2 Tb sugar
16 oz Romaine lettuce or spinach, torn
2 chopped green onions
4 slices bacon cooked and crumbled

Mix yolks, mustard, vinegar, oil, and sugar until smooth. Toss this dressing over the lettuce and add the egg white pieces, green onions and bacon.

Vertue* is harder to begot, than a knowledge of the world;
and if lost in a young person is seldom recovered.

John Locke
"Some Thoughts Concerning Education" 1693

There is a proverb, "As you have made your bed, so you must lie on it;"
which is a lie. If I have made my bed uncomfortable, please God I will make it again.

GK Chesterton
"What's Wrong with the World"

**This is not misspelled. The modern usage of the word virtue has
lost its heart and soul. I feel more comfortable with the original
spelling.*

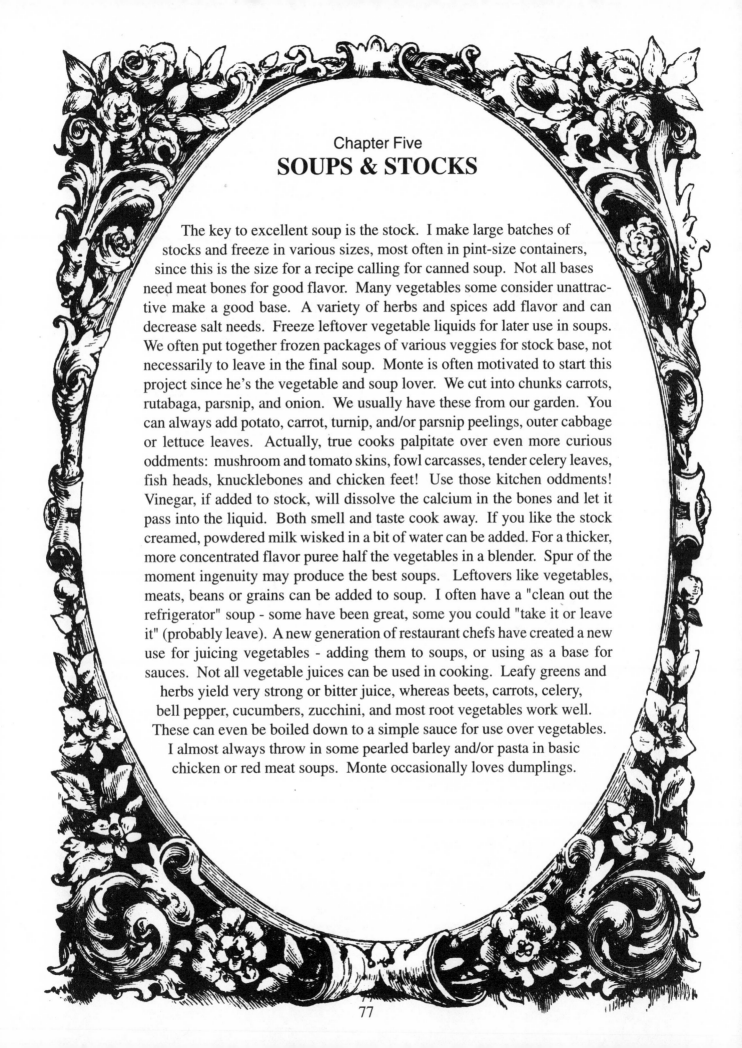

Chapter Five
SOUPS & STOCKS

The key to excellent soup is the stock. I make large batches of stocks and freeze in various sizes, most often in pint-size containers, since this is the size for a recipe calling for canned soup. Not all bases need meat bones for good flavor. Many vegetables some consider unattractive make a good base. A variety of herbs and spices add flavor and can decrease salt needs. Freeze leftover vegetable liquids for later use in soups. We often put together frozen packages of various veggies for stock base, not necessarily to leave in the final soup. Monte is often motivated to start this project since he's the vegetable and soup lover. We cut into chunks carrots, rutabaga, parsnip, and onion. We usually have these from our garden. You can always add potato, carrot, turnip, and/or parsnip peelings, outer cabbage or lettuce leaves. Actually, true cooks palpitate over even more curious oddments: mushroom and tomato skins, fowl carcasses, tender celery leaves, fish heads, knucklebones and chicken feet! Use those kitchen oddments! Vinegar, if added to stock, will dissolve the calcium in the bones and let it pass into the liquid. Both smell and taste cook away. If you like the stock creamed, powdered milk wisked in a bit of water can be added. For a thicker, more concentrated flavor puree half the vegetables in a blender. Spur of the moment ingenuity may produce the best soups. Leftovers like vegetables, meats, beans or grains can be added to soup. I often have a "clean out the refrigerator" soup - some have been great, some you could "take it or leave it" (probably leave). A new generation of restaurant chefs have created a new use for juicing vegetables - adding them to soups, or using as a base for sauces. Not all vegetable juices can be used in cooking. Leafy greens and herbs yield very strong or bitter juice, whereas beets, carrots, celery, bell pepper, cucumbers, zucchini, and most root vegetables work well. These can even be boiled down to a simple sauce for use over vegetables. I almost always throw in some pearled barley and/or pasta in basic chicken or red meat soups. Monte occasionally loves dumplings.

Chicken Stock

          2 pounds bony chicken pieces (backs, necks,
                    and wings)
          3 stalks celery with leaves, cut up
          2 medium carrots, cut up
          1 1/2 tsp salt
          1/4 tsp pepper
          6 cups water
          1 large onion, cut into thirds
          3 whole cloves

Stud the onion with the cloves and put all in the pot. Bring to
boiling. Reduce heat; cover and simmer about an hour until
the chicken falls off the bone. Lift out chicken pieces. Strain
the stock and discard vegetables.

I'll usually make **chicken soup** the night of cooking mass
broth. When the bones are cooled, there's enough meat for
the soup. Strain off some of the broth for your meal and put
in the chicken meat. I always add cubed potatoes, some
barley and maybe some pasta. If I'm in a hurry (tired or
lazy), I'll add frozen mixed vegetables rather than peel and
chop more stuff! Check for saltiness, and flavor to taste.

Here's a **dumpling recipe**:
          1 cup whole wheat flour
          1 Tb baking powder
          1 1/2 tsp salt
          1 egg broken into a 1 cup measure and add
                    milk until the cup is half full.

Beat well and add to the dry ingredients. You can add more
milk but keep the batter as stiff as manageable. Other herbs
can be added but we prefer dumplings plain. 1 - 1 1/2 Tb
butter or oil could replace the egg with 1/2 cup milk, but I
think the egg binds the ingredients together better. To drop
dumpling batter from the spoon easily, dip the spoon into the
soup broth first. Drop the batter from the spoon into the
simmering broth and continue until all the batter is used.
Cover the pot and simmer 5 minutes. Turn them
and cook another 5 minutes. Some recipes
do not turn but cook in the closed
pot for 10 minutes. Serve at once.

*The stock I make the most is chicken.
For years I made this particular recipe
in a 5-quart stockpot or Dutch oven.
Now I have a huge roaster/cooker that
will hold six whole chickens. The more
I can make at a time, utilizing about
the same effort, the better. Then I
don't have to make it as often.*

*I freeze the strained broth and the fat
can be removed later before using it,
otherwise, it's good to make the broth
early so it can be chilled and the
solidified fat lifted off.*

*Dumplings absorb liquid so make sure
you have plenty of broth in your soup.*

*Dumplings can be made alone in a pot
of water. I've not tried this, so don't
know how they'd taste.*

(Warn the kids - dumplings are hot.)

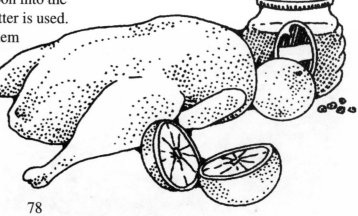

Cream of . . . soup

1/3 cup olive oil (my preference)
1/2 cup whole wheat flour
1 pint chicken broth (can be made with
        water, milk, etc.)
flavorings

Heat oil in a medium saucepan over medium-high heat. Whisk in the flour and cook until foaming, about 1 minute. This is called a Roux. Cooking time can vary from about one minute for white sauce to two to five minutes depending on the toasted brown coloring you want. Whisk in the broth and stir till well blended. Stir occasionally until it becomes thick. Add whatever flavorings you desire. I usually add 1/2-1 tsp salt, 1/2 tsp onion powder, 1/2 tsp garlic powder, and a pinch of pepper. You can grind and add celery seeds. I take a handful of dried mushrooms and pulverize in my hand while letting them sift into the sauce.

Browned Beef Stock

In a large stockpot place:
       6 pounds beef soup bones (neck, shin, shank,
           or marrow bones)
       1 large onion, sliced
       2 medium carrots, cut up

Place these in a 450° oven and let brown evenly for about 30 minutes or till well browned, turning occasionally with tongs. Now on stove top burner, add:
       3 stalks celery with leaves, cut up
       1 large tomato, cut up (optional)
       8 whole black peppercorns
       4 sprigs parsley
       1 bay leaf
       1 clove garlic, halved
       1 Tb salt
       12 cups cold water

Bring to a boil. Reduce heat; cover and simmer for 4 to 5 hours. Remove beef bones and strain stock.

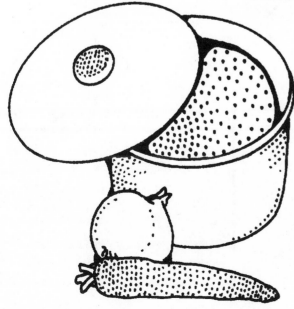

79

Vegetable Stock

2-4 Tb olive oil or butter
3 carrots, chopped
2-4 stocks celery, chopped with the leaves
1-2 large onions, chopped (I've even left the
    skin on; garlic too.)
(12 green beans, 1 potato, 1/2 lb spinach,
    2 leeks)
(1 turnip, rutabaga, and/or parsnip, chopped)
1-2 cloves garlic, halved
1/2 tsp dried thyme, crushed
(2-3 tomatoes, cut up)
1 cup shredded lettuce
2-6 sprigs fresh parsley (or 1 Tb dried)
1 1/2 tsp salt or 3 Tb soy sauce
1/4 tsp pepper or 10 peppercorns
(1 bay leaf, 1 tsp basil)
2-3 quarts water or liquid from cooked
    vegetables

Though I previously mention all sorts of variables for this, here's a basic recipe. Because the vegetables are discarded when the stock is strained, I don't bother with precision chopping. Just chunk. Neither do they need be perfect looking. If you don't have something, don't worry about it. I don't usually waste my good lettuce for this. I'll use the lettuce stems, cores, and not-so-beautiful salad rejects. Since cabbage is in the root cellar, I always use it.

In stockpot heat oil or butter. Add the vegetables up through the thyme. Sauté a bit, cover and cook over low heat about 30 minutes, stirring occasionally. Add remaining ingredients. Bring to a boil, reduce heat, cover and simmer, about 2 hours. Strain and discard the vegetables.

Split Pea Soup

2 cups split peas
(1 ham hock)
10 cups cold water
1 onion, chopped
1 cup celery, chopped
2 cups carrots, chopped
(2 potatoes, cubed, and added later in
    cooking)

Chop the vegetables in some water in the blender and add to the soup pot with peas and rest of water. Cook for 1-2 hours. Season later in cooking. If you used a bone, remove meat from bone and return to the pot. Garnish with fresh chopped parsley.

Many soups we like with corn bread. I talk about food combinations in the "Tips" chapter. Basically, beans and grains, when combined, make for an excellent complete protein meal.

I love the potatoes in this soup. Some split pea recipes do not include them.

These beans are what we use for refried beans.

I usually serve this the first night as soup with the blender corn bread. The rest is pureed in the blender and used for bean burros which we eat a lot of for lunches with homemade or co-op bought (without preservatives) thin tortillas and a touch of cheese. You can leave as is and just mash as you need when heating. In my laziness, we usually eat the burros with unmashed beans. Monte's been mashing them in a hot cast iron skillet as he uses them and adds more green chili or whatever he feels like adding at the time! We often add a touch of "Alan's Spices."

Add salt after cooking is completed because salt toughens the skins.

I made a mistake long ago of making lasagna with unwashed lentils. What a gritty experience.

I have a flat screen strainer I use for everything, but especially for washing beans. I can rinse with water spraying full force and shaking the strainer. Look for rocks. The grit comes from little clay lumps - it's not adhered to the beans!

Monte wanted me to add that this is a favorite. He always eats too much.

Pinto Bean Soup, Chili Beans, Refried Beans

In blender place:

> 2 cups water
> 1 large onion, peeled and quartered
> 1 clove garlic, peeled
> 1 carrot, peeled and cut in chunks

Pulse until vegetables are finely chopped. Place chopped vegetables and the following in a 5-6 quart pan:

> 2 cups water
> 4 cups dry pinto beans, washed and cooked
> 1 Tb cumin, ground
> (sprinkle cayenne pepper)
> 4 oz chopped green chilies
> 1 Tb chili powder
> 1 pint tomato sauce
> (2 Tb chopped fresh cilantro - optional; if not

available, use ground coriander seeds which have a cilantro-like taste.)

Simmer on stove top all day, or pressure cook an hour. (Can be covered and cooked 8 hours or overnight in a 200° oven.) Add 1 tsp salt (or to taste).

Brown Rice and Lentil Soup

In 5 quart pan combine:

> 1 pint stewed tomatoes
> 3 cups water
> 2 cups homemade chicken stock
>> (or one 15 oz can
>> (fattier and not as tasty)
> 2/3 cup lentils (washed!)
> 1/2 cup brown rice
> 1 cup chopped carrots (3-4)
> 1 large onion, chopped
> 2 stalks celery, chopped
> 3-4 cloves garlic, minced
> 1/2 tsp basil
> 1/2 tsp oregano
> 1/2 tsp thyme
> 1 bay leaf
> 1/4 cup minced parsley
> 2 Tb cider vinegar

I usually pulse the vegetables in the blender with some of the water to chop. Bring the soup to a boil on medium high, close lid and pressure cook on low pressure for twenty minutes (otherwise cook a couple of hours). Salt and pepper to taste.

Black Bean Soup

Place in blender:

> 1/2 cup water
> 4 large cloves garlic
> 1 onion, cut in quarters
> 3 green chilies

Blend until chopped and pour into cook pot.
Add:

> 5 1/2 cups water
> 2 cups dry black beans
> 2 bay leaves
> 2-3 tsp cumin
> 1 tsp oregano
> (1 chopped large tomato or small can of
> tomatoes)

Bring to a boil, lower heat, cover and simmer most of the day (or pressure cook an hour).
Add: 1-1 1/2 tsp salt & 1/4 tsp pepper

Cook a bit more and slightly mash the beans.
Serve soup garnished with sliced green onions.

> *Since we buy roasted green chilies from the market and freeze, I figured out that three green chilies, Anaheim, are equivalent to a 4 oz can of chopped.*
>
> *Black beans are delicious. Some localities of Mexican/Spanish peoples serve these daily as a side dish and usually use these as first preference over pinto beans. Black beans also make good refried beans.*

French Onion Soup

> 2 1/2 cups thinly sliced onions
> 4 Tb oil
> 6 cups beef stock
> salt and pepper to taste
> French bread
> parmesan cheese for garnish

Brown onions in oil until a golden-brown. Combine onions and beef stock in soup pot, tightly cover, simmer for about an hour. Season with salt and pepper. Slice the french bread and partially toast until crispy dry. Ladle soup into oven proof serving bowls. Place a french bread slice or two on top of the soup and sprinkle generously with parmesan cheese. Put the bowls on a cookie sheet and place in the oven to broil until the bread and cheese browns. Serve.

> *My mouth is watering thinking of this soup. This is the one soup I probably use beef stock for the most.*
>
> *This is how we usually eat it, but at times I put grated swiss cheese on the top too. The kids aren't partial to swiss cheese, so I don't keep it stocked. I love it.*

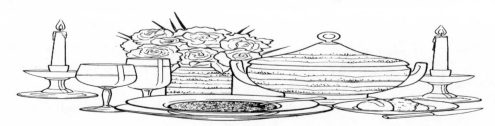

Orange Carrot Soup

1/4 cup butter
1 onion, chopped
4 cups vegetable stock
4-5 carrots, cooked and drained (save the
　　　liquid for vegetable stock)
2 Tb whole wheat flour
4 oz orange juice concentrate
1/4 tsp pepper
1 Tb chopped dried chives

In a skillet, sauté the onion in 2 Tb of the butter. In a blender, place 2 cups of the stock, carrots, and sautéed onion and process until smooth. In a large saucepan, melt the remaining butter and add the flour and cook until bubbly, stirring occasionally. Add the remaining stock and cook until slightly thick. Add the orange juice concentrate, pepper, chives, and carrot mixture; heat thoroughly. At serving time, you could add 1 cup milk and heat but do not boil. You may substitute a spoonful of plain yogurt in each bowl of soup. Garnish each with an orange slice. This is also good served cold.

He is unworthy of life that gives no life to another.
Moroccan Proverb

A teacher, noticing how courteous and polite one of her pupils was,
wished to praise her and teach the class a lesson. She asked, "Who taught you to be so polite?"
The girl laughed and answered, "Really, no one. It just runs in our family."

To bring up a child in the way he should go, travel that way yourself once in a while.
Josh Billings

Children need models more than they need critics.
Joseph Joubert

Do I maintain example . . .
or do I maintain pride?

Chapter Six
BEANS & BURGERS

Possible Therapeutic Benefits of Beans

- Reduce blood cholesterol
- Contain chemicals that inhibit cancer
- Control insulin and blood sugar
- Lower blood pressure
- High fiber for colon and bowel disorders

Bean Arithmetic

- 1 lb beans = 2 cups dry & 6 cups cooked

- 1 lb dry beans, ground to a flour = 5 cups

- 1 cup dry beans + 3 cups water = just right for soaking

- Good cook + Good beans = Good health!

Beans can be ground to a flour and used for instant "cup-a-soups." Simply add to boiling water and let thicken for 3 minutes. The new Grain Master Whisper Mill and the K-Tec are the only mills I'm aware of that will handle all beans easily. Other mills need most beans to be cracked first. Stone mills gum up and must be cleaned after 2 cups of beans. Sort beans and check for rock pieces (or BBs. When you have boys you never know what ends up in the beans or grain!). Place the mill in the sink and if too much dust is being thrown, cover with a kitchen towel. The mill's sponge filter should be shaken clean after each 2-cup batch. Grind beans on a medium setting. Stir the beans where they go into the grinding chamber with the handle of a spoon if they do not feed easily. Only grind dry beans.

Black Bean Pizza

1 large Boboli (salty and fatty, but good!)
pizza crust- or make your own

In skillet sauté:

        A few chopped slices of bacon
        1/2 of each red and green bell pepper, chopped
        onion and a couple of garlic cloves, chopped

Add: 2 cups cooked and drained black beans

Stir to combine all.

Spread crust (if homemade, first spread with some olive oil) with a few Tb tomato sauce. Sprinkle on 1 tsp crushed oregano and a few Tb parmesan cheese, then add bean mixture and some grated monterey jack or mozzarella cheese. We've cut back on the cheese in most recipes to about half. Bake at 400° for about 20 minutes or until done.

This pizza is delicious! I also like to make **Garlic Pizza**. I take some of my dough and make a thin crust, spread it with olive oil and then *lots* of minced garlic. Sprinkle with mozzarella and parmesan and bake. Another one is **Pesto Sauce Pizza**. Rather than tomato sauce on the crust, spread with pesto sauce, then add fresh sliced tomatoes and cheese.

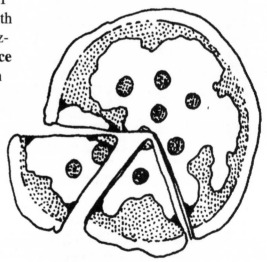

Pinto Bean Squares

       2 cups cooked pinto beans
       1 egg, beaten
       1 cup milk
       1 tsp Worcestershire or Soy Sauce
       1/2 tsp dry mustard (grind those little seeds!)
       1/4 cup onion, chopped fine
       1 cup cooked rice
       1 (or 1 1/2) cup(s) grated cheese

Combine all but 1/4 (1/2) cup cheese for topping. Pour into a well-greased 8-9" square baking dish. Bake at 325° for 45-50 minutes, or until set. Sprinkle with cheese and bake another 5-10 minutes until melted. Allow to set for 10 minutes before serving. Cut into squares.

Burgers and Patties

Most of these do not contain eggs. If you want, you may add an egg to any of the recipes. Eggs bind the ingredients together the best but are not essential. Sometimes letting the ingredients set awhile allows the binding grain to soak in and thicken the mixture. Make sure the beans are well drained.

Bean Burgers

I do all the beans, seeds, and onions through the Bosch meat grinder. You can use whole-grain flour to bind it together rather than just wheat germ.

2 cups cooked beans: kidney or pinto,
              ground or pureed
2/3 cup ground sunflower seeds
1/4 cup finely chopped onion
1/2 tsp chili powder
1 tsp salt
2 Tb oil
3 Tb catsup
1/3 - 1/2 cup wheat germ

Combine all ingredients, adding enough wheat germ so that the mixture will hold its shape. Place on lightly greased baking sheet and bake at 350° for 15-20 minutes. May be cooked on a hot griddle or in Jet Stream or convection oven. If desired, place a slice of cheese on each burger near the end of cooking time.

Rice Burgers

2 cups cooked brown rice
1 small onion
Sage to taste
1/2 tsp celery salt
4 Tb whole wheat flour
3 - 4 Tb milk or water
1/2 cup whole wheat bread crumbs
more bread crumbs for coating

Mix together all ingredients, shape into patties, and coat with more bread crumbs. Place on greased baking pan and bake at 350° until golden or cook on hot griddle.

Soy Burgers

2 cups cooked soybeans or garbanzo beans,
   ground or puréed
1 small onion
(1/2 cup green or red pepper or even green
   chili, chopped fine)
1 tsp garlic powder
1/2 cup tomato sauce (or a little less water or
   broth)
2 stalks celery, chopped
1/2 tsp chili powder
1/2 tsp dry mustard
(I like to add 1/2 tsp marjoram and cumin)
Soy sauce or Braggs (or salt) to taste
Oatmeal, cornmeal, wheat germ, or bread
   crumbs to bind

Combine all ingredients adding enough of the grain to bind
together. (Here again I use the meat grinder.) Shape into
patties and brown on both sides in skillet.

Wheat and Vegetable Patties

2 or 3 cups cooked wheat (or any grain)
1 medium potato
2 medium carrots
1 small onion
1 tsp salt
1/2 tsp garlic powder
1/4 tsp seasoned salt
1 tsp Worcestershire or Soy Sauce
4 to 5 Tb oil

In meat grinder, grind together the grain and vegetables. Add
seasonings and oil. Cook in greased skillet, flattening the
patties with a spatula. May add some cheese.

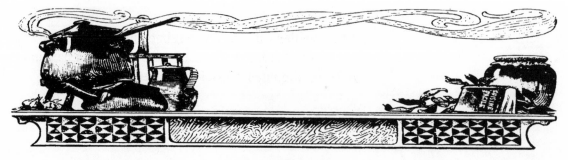

Zucchini Patties

2 cups grated zucchini
2 green onions, chopped
2 Tb oil
1 tsp parsley
1 tsp basil
1/2 tsp salt
1/4 cup ground sunflower seeds
1 cup whole wheat bread crumbs
1/4 cup cooked whole wheat or rice
2 eggs, separated

Sauté onions in oil, then add parsley, zucchini and other ingredients, except the eggs. Add egg yolks to rest of mixture. Beat egg whites and add last. Drop batter on greased hot skillet.

Carrot and Sunflower Patties

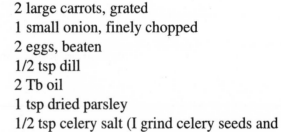

2 large carrots, grated
1 small onion, finely chopped
2 eggs, beaten
1/2 tsp dill
2 Tb oil
1 tsp dried parsley
1/2 tsp celery salt (I grind celery seeds and
        add some salt)
(3/4 cup ground sunflower seeds)

Combine all ingredients and mix well. Chill, then shape into patties. Heat on greased skillet.

Tuna Patties

1 large can (or 2 small) tuna
2 eggs
1/2 small onion, chopped fine
A bit of parsley or herbs of your choice

Mix all ingredients and drop by large spoon into lightly oiled hot skillet. Brown on both sides 4-6 minutes.

Life is uncertain. Eat dessert first.
Christian Nelsen

Art, as far as it is able, follows nature, as a pupil imitates his master;
thus your art must be, as it were, God's grandchild.
Dante

Imagination is the eye of the soul . . .
He who has imagination without learning has wings but no feet.
Joseph Joubert

Imagination is more important than knowledge.
Albert Einstein

Creativity is seeing.

Chapter Seven
PIES & SWEET SOMETHINGS

In many nations, skill in pastry making has been regarded as a
passport to matrimony. I don't know about that, nowadays, but it
may have influenced Monte a bit. While we were courting, we both
attended a student center owned by our church, on the University of Arizona
campus. Every Wednesday evening we had a meal before the Bible study and for
a year I was in charge of overseeing these. I didn't always cook the meals but I
always helped in the planning and preparation since most people aren't used to cooking
for fifty people. How many lettuce heads would you buy?! Anyway, I did sometimes make pies for all those people, and Monte was impressed (as were other guys!).
I made them with Betty Crocker Pie Crust sticks. They turned out well and I
learned the skill of rolling and forming the crust. I went straight from my family's
home to our home. Monte had lived on his own for about seven years, had called
his mama many times (in the course of ruining a good piece of meat), learned
to cook, and taught me things (about meat and vegetables mainly). But
he never learned pastry baking, so when we got married I read whatever I
could get my hands on and taught myself. I was motivated by my
sweet tooth and love of desserts. I can pass up candy any day.
Cakes are not a favorite; but there's no temptation like
pastries and pies.

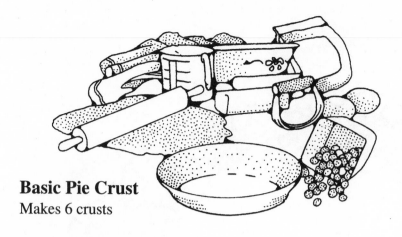

Basic Pie Crust
Makes 6 crusts

5 cups flour
2 tsp salt
1 lb unsalted butter
1/2-1 cup ice water

The flour is tricky. If you need experience in making pie crusts, with ease, then use unbleached flour. I've had great success with half unbleached and half whole wheat. In fact, this is how I've done pie crust for years. I prefer the taste of pie crust made with whole wheat. I sometimes make it with all whole wheat pastry flour, it has a nutty flavor, but . . . it does not always hold together. My pie crusts were all doing fine as 100% whole wheat until the last batch, every single one had to be pieced, and overworking pastry does not make for a flaky crust. It still tastes good, but it can be tough. I am usually asked to bring pies for events. People rave over them. Not to brag, but it means my recipes and techniques must work.

All ingredients should be cold. Cut butter pieces into bowl bottom (prevents wire whips from breaking). Then put the flour and salt in mixer bowl. Process with the whips until the mixture resembles coarse meal (or use food processor or a pastry blender by hand). Add ice water slowly, just until the dough begins to hold together. Do not process long. Most times I'll remove the meal from the bowl and add the water by hand using a pastry blender. Squeeze a bit of dough together. If crumbly, add a bit more water. Turn the dough out onto the counter. Press the dough together. Remember, you do not want to work the dough too much or it will produce a tough rather than flaky pastry. Keeping the dough chilled contributes to a flaky crust, too. At this point I divide the dough into 6ths. Press each section into a flat circle, which makes rolling the cold, hard dough easier. Wrap in plastic wrap and chill for at least an hour. Once rolled out and in the pan refrigerate until ready to use. Remember to keep cold.

There is truly a science to the mixture of flour, fats, and liquids. For pie crust, tenderness and flakiness are musts. The kind of fat and its ratio to flour is very important, as is the preparation technique. Mixing by hand is not necessary. Food processors work very well as long as the ingredients are not over blended. When flour mixes with liquid first, gluten begins to develop. We don't want activated gluten in pie crust. Therefore, the flour needs to be coated with fat. Oil as the fat is simply inferior in texture and taste. Lard today is not always fresh or made from the best "prime" fat. Yes, as there is prime meat, there is prime fat, from around the kidney area. Today marketed lard is made from a variety of fats which produces a stronger permeating flavor. Many people like a mixture of butter and Crisco, 6 to 4 for the flavor of butter and good texture. I avoid shortening, and butter does give good flavor and texture. Oil usually produces tough crusts. Too much water can toughen the crust, as will over processing AND under processing, because the flour is not properly coated with fat.

Bread flour has high protein content and therefore high gluten content. Pastry flour is low in protein, to produce a soft, tender product. I've found that my fresh ground pastry flour works fine in pie crust if it sets a day to settle, and then allow the pie crust to rest awhile, or hold for days refrigerated, to allow an even distribution of the liquid. Baking it till well-browned is another key to superior flavor!

Monte's mother was raised in a very small town hotel and she made many pies each morning before heading off to school. These were baked in a wood cook stove! When you can watch someone form the crust edging it sure simplifies the learning process. More cookbooks these days have beautiful pictures and you can probably figure out a good method to call your own. Martha Stewart's Pies & Tarts book (Monte bought me her books as gifts long before she became the famous TV and magazine domestic goddess) has really advanced my creativity with pie edgings and decorations, not to mention the filling possibilities!

Mystery Pecan Pie

This is always a favorite. I found it in a Tucson realty book.

>1 8 oz pkg cream cheese
>1/3 cup sugar
>1/4 tsp salt
>1 tsp vanilla
>1 egg
>1 1/4 cup chopped pecans

Combine cheese, sugar, salt, vanilla & egg, and blend well. Spread in the bottom of unbaked pastry shell. Sprinkle with pecans.

Combine topping ingredients:
>3 eggs
>1/4 cup sugar
>1 cup light corn syrup
>1 tsp vanilla

Gently pour over pecans. Bake at 375° for 35-40 minutes or till firm.

Squash (Pumpkin) Pie

Blend the following in the blender:
>3 cups squash puree
>3-4 eggs
>1/2 cup honey
>1 tsp salt
>1/4 cup molasses
>1 cup milk
>1/2 tsp ground ginger
>1/2 tsp cinnamon

Cut squash into chunks. If you use pumpkin, make sure it's the small sugar pumpkins. My next preference is butternut, moist; or buttercup, drier. Remove the seeds (don't forget to save the seeds for roasting; see "Cooking Tips" chapter) and steam until fork tender. Let it cool enough to handle. Using a spoon, scrape the pulp from the skin and put in blender and puree.

I use any squash for a "pumpkin" pie. (Though I haven't tried a spaghetti squash!)

Take some of the pie crust dough (like scraps) and cut out leaves, drawing the veins with the back of a knife, and bake on a cookie sheet. Then add these to the top of the pie as a pretty decoration. Or cut out a bunch of leaves and with a little water, attach the leaves to the edge of the crust so that the leaves fall over the edge of the plate. This one must be done before the filling is poured in.

Mix thoroughly but not excessively or it can make finished pie tough. Pour into the pie crust and bake about 1 hour at 375°, until the filling is firm and brown. Let cool before serving.

Rhubarb Custard Pie

Place five cups of 1/2 inch cut rhubarb in an uncooked pastry.

Mix the following and pour over the rhubarb:

> 3 eggs
> 2 Tb whole wheat flour
> 2 Tb tapioca
> 1/3 cup honey
> 1 cup sugar
> 1/2-1 tsp orange peel
> pinch salt

Cover with a top crust and make steam vents. I like to sprinkle a touch of cinnamon and sugar over the crust. Bake for 10 minutes at 400°, then lower temp to 350° and continue baking another 45-60 minutes. We like pie crust well-browned for superior flavor and it gives the bottom crust a chance to thoroughly cook.

Sweet Potato Pecan Pie

> 1 cup cooked sweet potato
> 1/4 cup brown sugar
> 1 egg
> 1 Tb vanilla
> 1/4 tsp salt
> 1/4 tsp cinnamon
> 1/8 tsp allspice
> 1/8 tsp nutmeg

Combine the above in blender until smooth. Spread evenly in the crust-lined pie dish.

> 1/2 cup sugar
> 3/4 cup dark corn syrup
> 2 eggs
> 2 tsp vanilla
> pinch salt
> pinch cinnamon
> 3/4 cup pecans

Combine all except nuts in blender and process until opaque, about 1 min. Stir in nuts and pour over potato filling. Bake at 325° about 1 3/4 hrs or until knife inserted in the center comes out clean. Cool and serve.

This is our family's favorite pie. In fact I'm so familiar with the ingredients that I'm typing it without the recipe in front of me. People who claim they don't like rhubarb or who've never had it, really like my pie.

You can use fresh, frozen or canned rhubarb. I freeze all my rhubarb in 5-cup portions. A canned quart jar would probably be the same amount of fresh rhubarb. Just remember that most canned rhubarb is already sweetened some.

The rhubarb I freeze and can is from our garden. When we moved to this mountain property there were signs of old homestead foundations and the rhubarb had seeded all over the meadow. We transplanted most to the back of our large garden with chokecherries (already there) and an aspen grove behind. Rhubarb makes a great waffle and pancake sauce.

We make Rhubarb Aid from the frozen form of rhubarb. All the frozen bagged rhubarb is measured in a heaping quart measuring pitcher, so I figure it's five cups. After thawing, I put this in the blender with some water and puree it (it won't work with the raw rhubarb). Dilute one cup sugar in warm water. Pour the rhubarb puree into a colander sitting over a large bowl and keep pouring cold water over this, sometimes stirring the rhubarb. In all, use one cup sugar to a gallon of water. With frozen rhubard the drink is very fresh. (It can be made by cooking cut-up rhubarb and straining.) Many people like this beverage and request it when visiting.

Cowboy Pie

> 1 cup cooked, mashed pinto or kidney beans
> 1 cup sugar
> 3 egg yolks
> 1 cup milk
> 1 tsp vanilla
> 1 tsp nutmeg

Combine all and spread in unbaked pie shell. Bake at 350° for 30 minutes or till set. Make a meringue out of the 3 egg whites and 4 Tb sugar. Bake again for 15 minutes or until browned.

Apple Pie or Dutch Apple

> 5-6 cups apples, sliced thin

(If using dried apples, allow 1 lb apples to 1 qt water and soak for several hours or simmer 35-45 minutes.)

Mix with apples:

> 1/2 -2/3 cup brown sugar
> 1/8 tsp salt
> 1-1/2 Tb cornstarch
> (1/4 tsp cinnamon)
> (1/8 tsp nutmeg)
> (1 Tb lemon juice)
> (1/2 tsp lemon rind)
> (1 tsp vanilla)

Stir apples and ingredients gently till coated. Put in unbaked pastry and cover with a top crust. Prick to release steam. I like to take scrap dough and cut out an apple and leaf to decorate the center of the top crust. I sprinkle the crust with cinnamon mixed with sugar. Bake in preheated 450° oven for 10 minutes, then reduce to 350° for another 45 minutes.

For dutch apple pie eliminate the top crust and make this **streusel** topping:

> 1/2 cup white sugar
> 3/4 cup flour
> 5 Tb butter
> (1 tsp cinnamon)

Blend this mixture together with a pastry blender till it is coarse crumbles. Sprinkle on top of the apples. Bake at 350° for 50-60 minutes.

Fresh Strawberry Pie

I suppose I should mention **pre-cooking pie crust**:

> Place rolled dough in pie dish as usual crimping the edges. Prick the dough all over with a fork. Unfilled pie crusts can bubble and heave unless weighted down. I used to keep old rice just for this purpose. Now I have official pie weights. Beans can be used. Pebbles can be used, but, if there's any air pockets, they can explode! Put foil over the crust pressing it gently in place and put in weights. Bake in preheated 450° oven for 10-12 minutes. Remove the foil and the weights a few minutes before done and cook a bit more. If the pie is not to be cooked, make sure the crust is as brown as you want.

This recipe is from a good friend, Jan Glumac, from whom I've learned what true servanthood is, fleshed out in reality.

You will need 1 quart strawberries total
Mash 1 cup berries with 1/3 cup water. Boil for 3 minutes.
 Add:

> 1 cup sugar
> 3 Tb cornstarch
> mixed with 1/3 cup water

(Remember, cornstarch needs to mix with a cold liquid
 before adding to heat.)
Boil this mixture 1 minute.

Spread 3-4 oz cream cheese on a cooked crust (drop chunks on crust while cooling to soften and ease spreading). Place remaining whole (or cut) berries in pie tin and pour sauce over berries. Chill. This can look pretty if the strawberries are uniformly whole and set on the cream cheese with points up.

Chocolate - Walnut Pie

In unbaked pastry put:

> 1 cup chocolate chips
> 1 cup coarse chopped walnuts

Mix and pour over:

> 3 eggs
> 3/4 cup wheat germ
> 1/4 cup oil
> 1/4-1/3 cup honey
> 2 tsp vanilla
> pinch of salt

Bake about 45 minutes at 375°.

This is totally my creation. I've seen some forms of this pie since. Monte always raves about how much he loves it. The first time I made it, I used too much honey. He encouraged me to put the recipe down on paper and into this book.

Bing Cherry Pie

I guess this is totally mine too. All cherry pie recipes I looked up are with sour cherries. I wanted to make one with bing (sweeter) cherries.

6 cups *pitted* bing cherries
1 1/2 cups sugar
4 Tb tapioca

Mix well and put in large pastry-lined pie dish. Add top crust with pastry cherry bunch decoration. Cut vents and sprinkle with cinnamon-sugar mixture. Bake at 450° for 10 minutes, then 350° for almost 1 hour. Let sit awhile to cool and set up.

I like to occasionally use bits of rolled out crust to cut out decorations and set on the top crust before cooking. Like an apple with stem and leaf for an apple pie; cherry cluster for cherry; leaves can be a pumpkin pie edging or bake some leaves on a cookie sheet to be placed on the top of a cooked squash pie. Many overlapping leaves could replace a lattice top.

Blender Impossible Pie

We try and have winter squash a lot. This blender pie is great for the leftovers and tastes like pumpkin pie no matter the squash (except the stringy spaghetti squash!).

1 cup water
1 cup cooked squash (a little extra doesn't
          hurt)
1/3 cup milk powder
4 eggs
1/2 cup whole wheat flour
1/3 cup honey
1 tsp allspice
1 tsp cinnamon

Combine all in the blender and blend. Pour into greased and floured large pie dish. Bake at 350° for about 1 hour or till toothpick or knife comes out clean.

Chocolate Chip Date Cake

I've said before that I'm not a big cake maker. When I do, I don't use cake mixes.

                    2 cups dates cut up
                        (mine are pre-ground from the co-op)
Add: 2 1/2 cups boiling water
                    2 tsp baking soda
Cream: 1/2 cup butter
                    1/3 cup canola oil
        (these replace 1 1/2 cups shortening)
                    3/4 cup honey
        (replaces 2 cups sugar)
                    4 eggs
                    4 tsp unsweetened cocoa
Add to the creamed mixture:
                    3 cups whole wheat flour
                    and date mixture
Spread in large greased 9 x 13" pan.

Sprinkle over top:
                    1/2 cup brown sugar
                    1/2 cup chocolate chips
                    1/2 cup chopped nuts

Bake 45 minutes at 375°

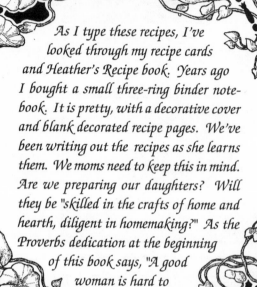

As I type these recipes, I've looked through my recipe cards and Heather's Recipe book. Years ago I bought a small three-ring binder notebook. It is pretty, with a decorative cover and blank decorated recipe pages. We've been writing out the recipes as she learns them. We moms need to keep this in mind. Are we preparing our daughters? Will they be "skilled in the crafts of home and hearth, diligent in homemaking?" As the Proverbs dedication at the beginning of this book says, "A good woman is hard to find!"

Strawberry Angel-food Cake

This recipe is from my mom. It's easy and everyone likes it. It's good for any potluck or get together. You could make your own angel cake (it takes about 10 egg whites), but I don't bother. Actually, at 8000 feet it's rather difficult, sometimes it works and sometimes it's been a big flop. When I think about it, this is an excellent cake to make with the flops!

                    2 small packages of strawberry jello
                    2 cups boiling water
                    2 - 10 oz packages of frozen strawberries
                    1 large frozen whipped topping
                    2 - 1 lb angel food cakes

Mix the jello and water together till dissolved. Add frozen strawberries. Stir occasionally and cool. Break up cakes into pieces. Mix all together. Press into a big cake pan. Keep refrigerated till ready to serve.

Rhubarb Cake

4 cups diced rhubarb, fresh, frozen or canned
3/4 cup sugar (omit if using canned rhubarb)
1/2 cup melted butter
1 1/2 cups sugar
1 egg
1 cup buttermilk
2 cups flour
1 tsp baking soda
1/2 tsp salt
1-2 tsp cinnamon
1 tsp vanilla

Mix rhubarb and sugar, let stand. Cream the butter, sugar and egg. Add buttermilk alternately with combined flour and the rest of the dry ingredients. Mix until smooth; add vanilla. Add rhubarb-sugar mixture. Spread in greased 9x13" pan. Bake at 350° for 45-50 minutes.

If you have no buttermilk or buttermilk powder, put 1 Tb vinegar to a cup of milk (minus the 1 Tb, of course). This creates soured milk and can replace buttermilk in recipes. Yogurt is another cultured milk and can replace buttermilk too. If it's really thick, I just water it down with water or milk.

Upside-Down Skillet Cake

Preheat oven to 350°

Heat large oven-safe (#10 cast iron) skillet and melt:
    1/4 cup butter
Add till dissolved:
    3/4 cup brown sugar
Add 4 cups fruit and simmer to cook down liquids while making the cake.

In mixer whip until stiff:
    4 egg whites
Fold in 1/2-3/4 cup sugar, a bit at a time
Then add:
    4 egg yolks
    1 Tb oil
    1 tsp vanilla
    1 cup whole wheat flour
    1 tsp baking powder

Cover the fruit with the batter. Put the skillet in the oven. Bake about 30 minutes. Immediately reverse onto a serving plate but don't remove pan until brown sugar mixture drains on cake.

You can use canned or frozen peaches, pineapple, apricots or raspberries. If using fresh fruit, do not simmer while making the cake batter. These of course have no liquid as do the canned and frozen.

Hot Fudge Sundae Cake

In a 9 x 9" baking dish, mix all these ingredients:

        1 cup whole wheat flour
        3/4 cup sugar
        2 Tb cocoa
        2 tsp baking powder
        1/4 tsp salt
        1/2 cup milk
        2 Tb oil
        1 tsp vanilla
        1 cup chopped nuts

Sprinkle over this mixture:

        1 cup brown sugar
        1/4 cup cocoa

Pour over all:

        1 3/4 cups hottest tap or boiling water

Bake 40 minutes at 350°. Can serve immediately.
Good alone or with ice cream.

> *This is such a simple and delicious cake. Yes, it can be mixed right in the dish you bake it in!*
>
> *Don't expect a toothpick to come out clean in this one. It bakes the cake part and at the same time develops a creamy hot fudge sauce. And there's not much fat!*

Blooming Dirt Dessert!!

        1/4 cup butter
        8 oz cream cheese
        (1 cup powdered sugar)
        1 - 20 oz pkg of Oreos
        3 1/2 cups milk
        2 - 3 oz pkgs instant vanilla pudding
        1 -12 oz Cool Whip

Cream butter and cream cheese. In separate bowl mix pudding and milk. Add Cool Whip. Crush the Oreos and place 1/3 in a 10" (clean) pot. Add 1/2 filling, 1/3 crumbs, rest of filling, and top with crumbs. Refrigerate overnight. Place a silk flower and gummy worms in the pot.

For another variation, you could use Pecan Sandies and use a pail with shovel.

> *That's the name I was given for this dessert. People who don't know about it sure are surprised. I was. We had invited a family for supper and they offered to bring dessert. They walked in and put a potted plant in the center of the dining room table. Nice, but where's dessert?*
>
> *I'm giving you the actual recipe followed by Heather's from scratch recipe:*
>
> *Heather and I make homemade, cooked vanilla pudding, and chocolate wafer cookies (both of these are in this section). These replace the instant pudding and Oreos. In looking at the ingredients in frozen whipped toppings, I may decide to use real whipped cream.*
>
> *If you take it to someone's house, it might be a nice gesture to leave behind the pot and silk flowers.*

Chocolate Log Roll

> 4 eggs, separated and at room temperature
> 3/4-1 cup sugar
> 1/2 tsp vanilla
> 3 Tb cocoa

Line a 9 x 13" pan with foil and grease it. I began lining the pan with foil because the cake always stuck. Dust wax paper with powdered sugar, large enough to hold inverted baked cake. Whip egg whites. Add sugar. Beat yolks and fold into the whites. Add vanilla and cocoa. Pour and spread to the corners of the pan. Bake at 350° for 20-30 minutes until toothpick tests clean. Let set 5 minutes. Invert onto the powder-sugar paper. May need to use a spatula to help the center come free of the foil. Cool. This rolls around a filling. Vanilla pudding can be used but Travis prefers just whipped cream. Whip 1/2 to whole pint heavy cream with 1/4 cup powdered sugar and 1/2 tsp vanilla. Spread this on the cake and roll, lifting the waxed paper as you go.

Sometimes we serve this with a **Hot Fudge Sauce**.

> To make this, combine in a double boiler: 1/2 cup cocoa, 1 cup sour cream, 1 1/2 cups sugar and 1/2 tsp vanilla. Cook and stir occasionally over boiling water for about 1 hour. This sauce will be thick. It keeps well for a month in a jar in the refrigerator. Great as ice cream topping.

Vanilla Pudding

In saucepan, heat on medium heat:
> 2 cups milk
> 2 Tb cornstarch
> 1/4 cup sugar
> 1/4 tsp salt

When it begins to bubble and thicken, slowly stir some of it into a bowl of 3 beaten eggs. Keep stirring and slowly stir this back into the pan and cook, stirring for 2 minutes. Remove from heat to cool and stir in 1 tsp vanilla extract. Use as is for a dessert or in recipes calling for pudding.

Mexican Flan or Caramel Custard

Heat oven to 325°. Place a 5 1/2-6 cup mold in oven to heat while making **caramelized sugar**.

In a heavy, medium skillet over medium-high heat place 1/2 cup sugar. Stir frequently with a wooden spoon until the sugar is completely melted and deep amber color. Do not burn. (This caramelized sugar is the base for caramel sauce or caramel ice cream.) Immediately pour this into the mold. Holding the mold with a potholder, quickly rotate to coat the bottom.

Wisk together:

> 6 eggs
> 3 cups milk
> 1/2 cup sugar
> 1 tsp vanilla

Pour custard in the mold. Place mold in a large baking pan with 1/2 inch hot water. Place in oven and bake until a knife inserted in center comes out clean, 1 hour+. Remove the mold from the hot water pan and let stand on a rack for 30 minutes. Refrigerate until cold. When ready to serve, loosen inner and outer edges of custard with the tip of a knife. Cover the mold with a serving plate and invert. It might slip out easily or might need some shaking. If it doesn't come out immediately (it usually does), I just let it sit inverted on the serving plate while doing something else.

I use a bundt pan for the flan.

If you want to skip the caramelized sugar step, just place brown sugar in the bottom of the pan and cover with custard. This does not taste as good though. Monte and I did a concert for Valentines Day, and during supper a lady told me this is how she makes it. The brown sugar might cook better if the pan were not in the hot water.

Carmelized sugar solidifies quickly when cool.

Rice Pudding

> 2 cups cooked rice
> 3 eggs
> 1/3-1/2 cup sugar (2-3 Tb honey)
> 1/4 tsp salt
> 2 cups milk
> 1 tsp vanilla

Mix all together. Bake in casserole dish about 50 minutes at 350°. You can sprinkle cinnamon on top.

This is the dish we hide an almond in on Christmas Eve.

I speak of rice pudding in the month of December in the "Art of Life" chapter. This is probably the poor man's version of Ostakaka. Ostakaka must be made with raw milk which is curdled with junket (a natural enzyme in fresh cows' milk). This is the same beginning process for making all cheese. When the whey is drained off, you're left with curds. Curds take the place of the rice in this recipe. I tried to simplify the process using cottage cheese but it wasn't as tasty. Ostakaka is really delicious.

Millet Pudding

    4 cups milk
    1 cup whole millet
    2 eggs
    1/4 cup honey
    1 tsp vanilla

Heat milk and millet in a double boiler, cooking over boiling water for about 1 hour, stirring occasionally. Remove and cool to lukewarm. Add the rest of the ingredients and stir well. Cook about 10 minutes more. Serve warm or cold. Another variation is to replace the honey with 1/3 cup maple syrup and then add 1 tsp cinnamon and 1 cup currants.

Bread Pudding

I've baked this to use up leftover cake, muffins or bread.

    3 eggs
    3 cups milk
    1/3 cup honey
    1 tsp vanilla
    1/4 tsp salt
    1 tsp cinnamon
    1/2 tsp nutmeg
    4-6 cups dry diced bread
    (1/2 cup raisins)

Mix all together. Bake in casserole dish set in pan of hot water for about 1 hour at 350° until a knife inserted comes out clean. It could be baked in a crockpot steamer pan with 1 1/2 cups water in crockpot on high for 3-4 hours. Could add nuts, pineapple . . . try anything.

Rhubarb Bread Pudding

    2 cups diced rhubarb
    3/4 cup sugar (1/3 cup honey)
    2 cups bread cubes
    1 cup milk
    1 egg
    1 tsp lemon or orange peel
    1 1/2 tsp lemon juice

Mix all together and bake in a casserole dish at 375° for about 1 hour.

Cheesecake

Butter a 9-inch spring-form pan and dust with (4) graham
        cracker crumbs.
Whip: 4 egg whites till stiff and blend in:
        1 cup sugar
Combine with 3 - 8 oz packages of cream
        cheese, creamed
Add: 1 tsp vanilla
Bake at 350° for 25 minutes.

For the topping mix together:
        1 pint sour cream
        2 Tb sugar
        1/2 tsp vanilla

Pour topping over baked cheesecake. Bake another 5 minutes at 475°. Chill 2 hours before serving. Monte serves up
tiny slivers. I dole out bigger wedges. This is great with a
raspberry sauce.

When Monte was a hungry college man many people would invite him home for a meal. This recipe came from one of those meals. We love it! We've never tasted a cheesecake that even comes close.

My mom made it using light cream cheese and sour cream. Make sure they do not contain gelatin which will liquify when baked.

Before I had a 9" pan I tried others. A 10" pan does not cook solid enough in the center. An 8" is ideal but I've not found one with high enough sides and I don't want to mess with foil. It cooks nicely in an angel-food cake pan. My pan's bottom removes from the sides.

Cream Cheese Cupcakes

        1 1/2 cups flour
        1/4 cup cocoa
        1 tsp soda
        1/2 tsp salt
        1/3 cup honey (Trish never uses sugar!)
        1 cup water
        1 Tb vinegar
        1/3 cup oil
        1 tsp vanilla
Mix together and fill foil muffin cups 1/3-1/2 full.
Filling:
        8 oz cream cheese
        3 Tb honey
        1 egg
        1/8 tsp salt

This recipe is from my friend Trish Cone. When our families get together, everyone seems to talk at once. Maybe I should re-state that or say, Monte can't figure out how the rest of us can talk all at once and know what each other is saying! The kids are quite busy with their gab at the same time. It's lively. We talk about everything under the sun, including theology. Van Tillian presuppositional apologetics would mix in with herbs for colds along with "how did you make this!"

Cream together and add 1 cup chocolate chips. Add a heaping teaspoon of the filling to the top of each cupcake.
Bake at 350° for 30-35 minutes.

Maple-Yogurt Gingerbread and Lemon Sauce

2 1/4 cups whole wheat flour
2 tsp baking powder
1 tsp baking soda
1 tsp powdered ginger
1/2 tsp cinnamon
1/4 tsp ground cloves
1/3 cup oil
1/2 cup maple syrup
1/2 cup molasses
1/2 cup yogurt
2 eggs

Preheat oven to 350°. Oil a 9x9" baking dish (or 18 muffin tins). Combine all the ingredients until well blended. Pour into the baking pan and bake about 30 minutes. Bake cupcakes for 20-25 minutes. Serve warm with lemon sauce.

Lemon Sauce

2 Tb cornstarch
1 1/2 cups water
1/3 cup honey
1 egg
1/4 cup lemon juice
2 tsp grated lemon rind
1 Tb butter
dash of nutmeg

In a medium sauce pan, mix the cornstarch with a small amount of the water; stir until dissolved. Add the remaining water, honey and egg. Blend well and heat over medium heat, stirring until the mixture comes to a boil. Remove from heat and add the rest of the ingredients. Spoon it generously on servings of gingerbread.

Molasses Ginger Cookies

Cream together:

        1/2 cup butter
        1/4 cup oil
            (these replace 1 cup shortening)
        1 1/2 cups molasses
        1/4 cup sugar (1-2 Tb honey)

Add:

        1 egg
        3 cups whole wheat flour
        1 cup milk powder
        1 1/2 tsp salt
        2 tsp baking soda
        1 tsp cinnamon
        1/2 tsp ginger
        1/4 tsp cloves

Mix well. Chill. Shape into 1 1/4" balls, roll in sugar, and place on greased baking sheet. Bake at 375° about 10 minutes.

Recipes bring up different memories. This one reminds me of Linda Lake, who gave it to me. She and Martin caretake a llama ranch. We used to rent a cabin on one hundred acres above them. This place has the best view in Evergreen: a mountain valley framing Mount Evans, from which flows Bear Creek through our valley.

We love molasses. Sometimes we'll make a brown sugar frosting for them. It's really the leftovers of a boiled brown sugar frosting I make for Dawson's and my Spice birthday cakes.

Raspberry Meringue Kisses

        3 egg whites
        1/8 tsp salt
        1 tsp vinegar
        3 1/2 Tb raspberry jello powder
        3/4 cup sugar
        1 cup chocolate mini-chips

Beat egg whites with salt till foamy. Add jello and sugar gradually. Beat until very stiff. Mix in vinegar; fold in chocolate bits. Drop by teaspoonful onto ungreased cookie sheets covered with brown paper or parchment paper. You can crowd these together to fit on two baking sheets so they can bake at the same time. Bake at 250° for 25 minutes. Turn oven OFF; leave cookies in oven 20 minutes longer. Sometimes I leave them in, forgetting about them until ready to serve.

Heather frequently makes these. The recipe comes from Monte's mom.

Meringue cookies are almost fat free. People really like these. We've tried them with different jellos but they're not as good. One Christmas I tried lime jello so we'd have pink and green. The green browned more and didn't look as appetizing for some reason. We've tried cutting back on the sugar too. A complete flop!

I don't like to use a lot of parchment paper since it is expensive. We've been cutting a brown paper grocery bag to overhang the cookie sheet for years.

Brownie Drop Cookies

8 oz Bakers semi-sweet chocolate
1 Tb butter
3/4 cup sugar
1/4 tsp baking powder
1/8 tsp salt
3/4 cup chopped pecans
2 eggs
1/4 cup flour
1/4 tsp cinnamon
1/2 tsp vanilla

Melt butter and chocolate in double boiler. Beat eggs till foamy. Add sugar 2 Tb at a time. Blend in cooled chocolate. Add remainder of ingredients. Drop on greased cookie sheets by teaspoonful. Bake at 350° for 8-10 minutes. Let cool on baking sheets.

Slice & Bake Chocolate Wafer Cookies

1 cup butter
2/3 cup oil
2 cups sugar
3 eggs
1 Tb vanilla extract
5 cups flour
2 tsp baking soda
1 1/4 cup unsweet cocoa powder

Beat the fats, sugar, eggs, and vanilla. Add the dry ingredients. Divide dough into 4 equal pieces and shape into 8 -10 inch rolls. Wrap in wax paper or plastic wrap. Double wrap and freeze. Each roll makes about 3 dozen cookies.

To bake: Slice partially frozen roll as thin as you can or want. Place 1/2 inch apart on greased baking sheets. Bake at 350° for 8 -10 minutes. Cool on racks.

These are what we use in Blooming Dirt Dessert.

Fruit Soup

Bring to a boil, then simmer for 30 minutes:

        1 12 oz bag pitted prunes, cut up
        1 1/2 cups raisins
        1 cup cut up dried apricots
        2/3 cup dried apples, cut up
        2/3 cup dried pears, cut up
        10 cups water
        2 cinnamon sticks
        2 slices of lemon, peel and all
        6 whole cloves
        2 cans pitted sour cherries

Add: 6 Tb tapioca to
                6 cups grape juice

Let this sit a few minutes then add to the simmering pot. Add another cup of water to rinse out tapioca. Simmer another 30 minutes. Taste for sweetness. I usually add about 3/4 cup sugar. Stir occasionally to keep from sticking. We serve it cold. I like it plain. Monte likes to pour in some cream.

> *When Monte and I were courting, we talked about his family's Christmas traditions. When he said "fruit soup" I was not impressed. It sounded awful! This is now one of my favorite dishes at Christmas. Many of the Scandinavian nationalities have a fruit soup, but with different juices as their base. This is our recipe developed from them all. Most of the fruit is home-dried.*

Maple-Glazed Nuts

I make these every year for the holidays.

        1/2 cup maple syrup
        1 tsp cinnamon
        1 Tb butter
        1/4 tsp salt
        1 1/2 tsp vanilla
        2 cups walnuts

> *I just thought of something . . . This browned mixture would probably be good in place of the caramelized sugar in the Mexican Flan.*

In an iron skillet, stir together all but vanilla and nuts. Cook and stir over medium heat until the mixture becomes brown and thickens. Remove from heat and add the vanilla and nuts. Stir and toss until coated. Let cool on wax paper.

Oven Baked Caramel Popcorn

Pop 1/3-1/2 cup popcorn kernels. In big pan, melt together 1/2 cup butter and 1/2 cup honey. Stir the popped corn into this mixture and bake in a 350° oven. Stir occasionally until crispy. When browned, remove a piece to cool and then taste-test for crispiness.

Crepes

1 cup whole wheat flour
3 eggs
1 1/3 cups milk
2 Tb melted butter or oil
dash salt

Or:
1 1/2 cups oat flour
4 eggs
2 cups milk
2 Tb melted butter or oil
(1 Tb honey)

Have a 6 - 7 inch skillet hot and lightly grease. Very little batter is used at a time - 1 1/2 - 3 Tb (an 8 inch pan uses about 1/4 cup batter). Tilt the pan to coat the bottom. If there's excess batter, just pour it off. Cook until the edges begin to pull away and the top is completely dry, 1-2 minutes. Turn over to cook about 1 minute. Stack on a plate. I usually keep a small plate with some oil in it and a paper towel for oiling the pan. Not all skillets require much oiling. You definitely do not want these to stick and they usually don't. If you plan on freezing them, it's best to put waxed paper between the layers.

You can add 2 Tb honey and 2 Tb cocoa to a basic crepe recipe to make them chocolate. Or add 1/2 cup parmesan cheese for another variation. The crepes can be cut in wedges and baked or fried for "crepe" chips.

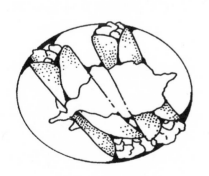

Filling ideas are too numerous to cover here. Bananas sautéed in butter rolled inside with a raspberry sauce is good. Flavored whipped cream (try powdered instant coffee) filling with a chocolate sauce is good. A sweetened cottage and ricotta cheese mixture with chopped nuts is good with a fruit sauce. Fill with ice cream or puddings. Stack crepes with apple or pear sauce spread between layers. Fresh fruits with a portion of the fruit mashed to make a sauce is very good. The Swedish tradition from Wisconsin is with fresh thick cream and blueberries.

In the house of the wise are stores of choice food and oil,
but a foolish man devours all he has.
Proverbs 21:20

Excuses are the cradle that rock man off to sleep.
DL Moody

Chapter Eight
COOKING TIPS & PANTRY STOCKING

This chapter is divided into two parts: cooking tips and lists of basics for stocking your pantry. Cooking tips, along with knowing your ingredients, are my favorite sections in cookbooks. I never miss reading the introductory information at the beginning of each chapter because that's where you learn so much! I'm in no way an expert. My approach to making things is unusual — take dumplings for example — I pull out many cookbooks and compare recipes. That way I see the basics and their proportions and know what I can mess around with, until I formulate my own recipe. The key to my cooking approach is that I "jump in and do." Because I feel free to experiment (including messes) I have expanded my knowledge base.

I don't think I could have a consistent weekly menu, though I do periodically formulate one. It can simplify life. I'm so motivated by creative impulse. We live differently from the usual urban dweller, in that I've been learning over the years to store food. Monte grew up this way. I've taught myself to (cook first) can, freeze, dehydrate, garden, and to use a root cellar. We raise chickens and turkey, and Monte hunts and occasionally fishes. Emu may be our next agricultural adventure. We order a lot of our foods through a health food co-op and often buy in bulk. We don't run to the store very often. Therefore, we must (a self-imposed must, of course) live like farm folk. Sometimes something in the cellar is not keeping well and I must use it up. When it's time to butcher the old chickens, there's a lot of cooking, deboning, and freezing of the meat and broth. Sometimes there aren't enough eggs for something I was planning to make. So what does this paragraph

mean? It means I don't want to run to the store for some one item my monthly menu may have me make for the day. Creativity comes into play as we use what we have available.

Others in our household have specific cravings besides me, so every-so-often, or when I'm in a slump, I ask them what they would like. I always know what Monte's going to say: "Lots of steamed vegetables." He loves vegetables and fruit. I love root vegetables, grains and baked goods. Heather loves yogurt and desserts. Travis loves . . . to consume (especially ice cream). Dawson tries to love everything Papa loves, and spice cake, but can do without oatmeal (which has become quite a joke around the house as a good story line like, "Another adventure of Dawson and the Oatmeal boys," or a song).

I am a mom, not a dietitian or nutritionist (though I read in that area). I strongly believe that everyone is unique - particularly in nutrition and health. That is why it is so difficult for the medical profession to deal with nutrition - every individual is an original. I hope this book does not pigeonhole me into being referred to as "the nutrition, or tips lady." If I always felt good and never had headaches I probably would not have read so much in this area. Monte has helped in nudging me in this direction with his encouragement and enthusiasm. I still have areas to grow and learn in and apply to my life (that's admitting that I'm not the most disciplined, nor fully do I practice what I preach religiously). Our family has fun with life and all God has created and we try to be balanced in our approach to living.

Herbs and spices should be bought in their whole state and ground with a mortar and pestle when needed. This does not take long and the flavor is superior! Since I made mustards from scratch using a coffee grinder, I occasionally use it for grinding spices; it works well for chopping fresh herbs too. Use this grinder for herbs and spices only. I even make curry powder from scratch. Look at the container and read the ingredients. Many informative cookbooks will give you proportions. The main ingredient in curry powder is fenugreek and this seed doesn't grind easily in a mortar (it might in the coffee grinder), so I buy ground fenugreek at a specialty store. Allspice, cloves, and pepper can be ground easily. My favorite spice is coriander. Each year I try growing and drying more and more herbs. They are beautiful plants and many of them are perennials. I grow some on a windowsill, too, to use fresh, like basil, parsley, chives, cilantro, rosemary, and thyme.

Out of an ingredient? Don't run to the store! I look in a cookbook and find a substitute or what that item is made of and "make do." You will learn what is not good in the ingredients and make substitutions (like the bakers chocolate note I have here, or instant puddings and cake mixes, etc). I have some examples within this cookbook. The other day I wanted to make a zucchini pudding and it called for soda crackers. I was out of soda crackers so I looked at a recipe and used those ingredients in the pudding without actually making and crushing the crackers. Once I looked up marshmallows . . . I decided I didn't like the idea of using them! (I've never liked marshmallows anyway!) What you've got to do though is learn what your basic ingredients are and keep them in stock. Always have a shopping list so as to write an item down when getting low. But do get to know your ingredients!

Mock Graham Cracker Pie Crust. Mix in pie pan: 1 cup whole wheat flour, 1 stick (1/2 cup) butter melted (try 1/3 cup oil instead), 1/2 cup finely chopped nuts. Press firmly in pan. Bake at 350° for 12-15 minutes.

Sweetened Condensed Milk. Put 1/3 cup boiling water, 1/3 cup honey and 3 Tb butter or oil in blender. While blending, slowly add 1 cup non-instant milk powder. This recipe equals 1 can.

Non-instant powdered milk is what's suggested for food storage because it is not full of air as is store-bought instant which loses its flavor quickly. Non-instant needs to be blended in the blender. If made the night before, so the foam can settle, it doesn't taste too bad! I use this a lot for breakfast cereals (we don't drink much milk or run to the store all the time to replenish milk) and for making yogurt. I still purchase instant milk from a co-op (much better tasting than the store-bought instant) for use in all my cooking.

Like warm milk or cocoa? Try blending a Tb or so of molasses into a glass of milk and heat. My children even like this.

Simple verses Complex Carbohydrates. Simple, technically "empty," carbohydrates consist of refined sugars and grains. Ingestion of these are factors in many diseases. A meal high in fats and empty carbohydrates will make you feel tired and may even lessen your thinking ability. Complex carbohydrates - fruits, vegetables, beans, and whole grains - give a constant flow of energy, in contrast to the short-lived rush derived from simple carbohydrates. They also provide dietary fiber and bulk to the diet which aid in healthy proper digestion.

Sweeteners. No matter the name, it's still sugar. There is a variety of forms - many highly processed and others closer to the way they occur in nature. Sugar is a type of carbohydrate and is an important source of energy for our bodies. The sugars eaten within a fruit, vegetable, grain, or sugar cane - the whole food - have the accompanying nutrients that aid in proper ingestion. Refined sugars are missing the nutrients that aid in the body's utilization of sugar. When whole foods are eaten with sugar, the food provides nutrients to help the body metabolize the sugar. That's why it's best to consume sweets following a good meal rather than on an empty stomach, causing extreme and dangerous fluctuations in blood sugar levels. If sugar causes a cholesterol problem it could be the company it keeps: cakes, cookies, candy bars, and pies. The liver can only store about 150 grams of glycogen (derived from sugar), and the excess becomes fat globules about the body; you know those things as - "a spare tire," "heavy thighs" and "flabby forearms." We completely avoid the so-called sugar substitutes because they are unnatural and may have potential health effects. I do use white and brown sugar, but also honey, molasses, date sugar, maple syrup, sorghum and sucanat. Molasses is not as sweet as sugar. Honey is more concentrated, so reduce the amount by half or even a third if you're getting your family used to not-so-sweet things. Besides, I like to taste the whole grain flavors. Also, remember to make adjustments in recipes when the sweetener used is a liquid. Date sugar (ground dates) never dissolves but is good in cookies and toppings.

Diastatic Malt is barley (usually) or other grain soaked in water, sprouted, and then dried and ground. It has a sweet taste. The purpose of sugar in breads is to feed the yeast, make the crust brown, and improve the flavor. Diastatic malt, which is widely used in Europe, does all of these things. It is an inexpensive natural sweetener packed with natural nutrients.

Place 1 cup barley (not pearled) or wheat in a quart jar with 2-3 cups warm water. Let set overnight or 24 hours.

Drain well and pour into a sprouter tray or leave in jar with a netting (or piece of womens' nylons) over opening secured with a rubber band. Turn bottle on its side.

Rinse and drain at least twice daily until the sprout is slightly longer than the seed. This takes about 48 hours.

Place sprouted grain on a large baking sheet. Bake at 150° until thoroughly dry, 3-4 hours (make sure they're dry), or dry in a dehydrator.

Place the dried sprouts in a blender and blend on high for 30-45 seconds or until it is of fine meal consistency. Store the malt in a tightly closed glass jar in the refrigerator or freezer. It will keep indefinitely.

Use in any bread recipe. Eliminate or reduce the amount of sweetener in the bread. Use 1 tsp Diastatic Malt for each 2 loaves of bread or each 5 cups of flour.

Use on cereal as a natural sweetener if desired.

Flour. I've discussed this in other sections, but should put a little blurb in here too. You've heard

113

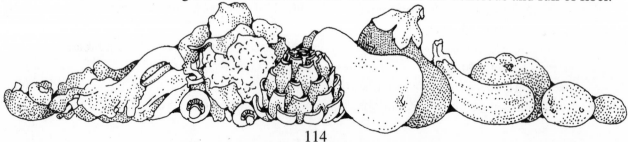

about flour processing elsewhere. Notice the Xs on the flour bag? When people moved from the agricultural centers with local mills, they began getting sick from the rancid and depleted flour. Flour was more-so a main staple, whereas today, we have more food varieties at our fingertips. We may not feel the effects of rancid flour. This bag of flour has more Xs, therefore meeting all the Government enrichment requirements.   I will mention some tips on cooking with fresh-ground flour. I use my home-ground flour in all conventional recipes. If you are just starting out in this area you and your family need to adjust slowly. Start by adding 1/3 to 1/2 whole wheat flour, then gradually add more. Amazingly, after a lifelong diet of processed food, some people require time to handle whole food rich in fiber. For yeast breads, you can use fresh ground, but for all other baked goods, like cookies, cakes, and muffins, I find it best to let the flour settle about a day. There's a lot of air in the fresh ground and so it won't measure the same. Otherwise, if fresh ground, use extra 1/3c per required cup flour. In many recipes I like to add other grain flours since so much of our diet is wheat - but be prepared for some crumbly disasters. Wheat and spelt contain gluten which helps hold things together (see under pie crust section for more detail on this subject). Oat, barley, rice, and millet are good grains for sweet items, but I still add some wheat (you can use the softer pastry wheat). Another hint: when baking with all whole grain flour, let the mixture sit awhile, maybe in the refrigerator, and allow the grain to absorb more liquid. This is required in my whole grain crepe recipe. Don't let this scare you. With using white wheat most of the time I really cook any recipe fairly normal. I haven't bought store flour for years!

Tofu is so versatile it has been referred to as the food of 10,000 flavors and forms. Somewhat bland, it absorbs the flavor of whatever you fix it with and can be used as an ingredient in almost any of your favorite dishes. It cuts down on calories, cholesterol, toxins, and expense. Tofu is low in fat and devoid of any cholesterol. Tofu actually lowers the existing cholesterol level in the body. It's a good source of calcium and other minerals and vitamins, and is also easily digestible. I use it all the time for french toast, replacing the use of a lot of eggs. It can make a good mayonnaise, salad dressing or dip. It's also great as a meat substitute in spaghetti or anything! A warning is in order: just as there are great cookbooks and lousy cookbooks, there is good tofu and not-so-good tofu. I prefer the brand MoriNu because it is creamy, not grainy like some. It stores well in its aseptic box, not requiring refrigeration. I buy this by the case from a co-op. It closely resembles heavy cream and makes wonderful shakes.

Roasted Squash Seeds: Take seeds from any winter squash (fresh or already baked) and put in a small saucepan. Barely cover with water and put in seasonings - such as parmesan cheese, garlic, onion, and salt (about 1 tsp salt/ cup water).   Bring to a boil and nearly simmer dry. Spread on a cookie sheet and dry in the oven. I usually put them in an already-warm oven from our cooked meal, turn off oven and leave in overnight - they will dry. The seasoning will penetrate the seeds and you actually can use less, and not have the mess of stirring the stuff on sheets in the oven. These are delicious and full of fiber.

Our bodies need fats because they carry the fat-soluble vitamins A, D, E, and K. Fats also provide energy, act as an intestinal lubricant, and stay in the digestive tract longer, giving us a full feeling. They soothe and coat the nerves and generate body heat. The right kind of fat is essential for good health. Excess fat is stored in the liver, in arteries, around the heart and in all tissue. One-third of the fats in our diet can be saturated. Current medical thinking is that animal fats do not have adverse effects on cholesterol levels if eaten in conjunction with two-thirds the amount of unsaturated fats.

Monounsaturated fats are found in olive oil, canola oil, avocado, pecans, almonds, and hazelnuts. Canola contains essential fatty acids. Olive oil has the best cholesterol-lowering benefits and helps control high blood pressure and diabetes. It will not become rancid like other oils. Rancidity of oils and nuts is carcinogenic (cancer-causing) as is hydrogenation - overheating and reheating. Rancid animal fats have a strong smell and taste, but rancid vegetable oils may smell and taste normal. "Health food" items need to be fresh; jars sealed. Once opened, refrigerate. Store brand oils have preservatives to keep them from going rancid. Diets high in monounsaturated fats lower the bad LDL cholesterol without lowering good HDL.

Saturated fats are found in all animal products, coconut and palm oils. Pesticides, chemicals and other foreign substances are stored in the fatty tissues of animals. Some call animal fat the "garbage can" of the food chain. The more fatty meat and whole dairy products you consume, the more chemical toxins you ingest. Saturated fat is the "bad boy" of the fat world and works together with LDL cholesterol contributing to circulatory diseases, and can also be linked to a number of cancers. Most margarines and all shortenings, though made from vegetable oils, are saturated due to the **hydrogenation** process. The high heat used in this process forms substances called trans-fatty acids. These unnatural substances have been linked to circulatory problems and cancer. Hydrogenation of good fats such as vegetable oils, and soybean oils, causes these oils to become as saturated as animal fats and are actually worse for your body than the animal fats because they are, in essence, poisons. I heard one instructor of a class make the statement "margarine is just one molecule away from being plastic!" Hydrogenation hardens oils, prolongs shelf life, and causes fried foods and even crackers to be crispier. Hydrogenation also destroys essential fatty acids and is difficult for the body to assimilate. This process can be carcinogenic (cancer-causing). Hydrogenated fats are excessive in margarine, shortening, peanut butter, candy, chocolate and baked store goods. Read the labels!

I use only canola or olive oil. These are monounsaturated fats. Canola is newest on the scene. It's name comes from "Canadian oil" because Canadian scientists are responsible for breeding a form of rapeseed plant from which the oil is pressed. Rapeseed is in the mustard plant family. These are the least saturated of the fats and are less susceptible to the negative effects of light, heat, and oxygen than are the **polyunsaturates** (safflower, sunflower, corn, and soy). Canola oil can be used in cooking with temperatures up to 375°, while olive oil is stable only up to 320°. Since our home-grown meat is low in fat and cholesterol, and we are semi-vegetarian, we do use butter. Margarine, because of its hydrogenation, would be worse for us. For a family that consumes 50% or more fat calories daily, margarine might be a better choice.

In baked goods, **recipes calling for shortening**, I recommend using a mixture. For example: if 1 cup is called for, use 1/2 cup butter and 1/3 cup canola or olive oil. For use at the table, blend together 1/2 cup butter, 1/2 cup canola or olive oil, and 1 tsp powdered lecithin. We have found a margarine spread through the co-op without any hydrogenation.

Chocolate! Yes I love chocolate, and since we eat "Whole"some, I feel it's okay to "have our cake and eat it too." Whenever possible, I bake with the unsweetened cocoa powder because you can choose the sweetener and oil. Baking chocolate contains the saturated fat - coconut oil. One ounce of unsweetened bakers chocolate is equal to 3 Tb cocoa and 1 Tb oil. (Although bad for you, coconut oil is a fascinating oil. Did you know it is what makes the popcorn you buy at a movie theater taste so good? I buy coconut oil by the case for making soap.) Many people think **carob** chips are healthier, but look at their fat source. They usually have coconut oil and/or something hydrogenated. Carob powder needs to be mixed well with water or oil to help it dissolve and not be floury or lumpy. Mixing it with hot water or cooking rids it of a raw taste. I really prefer the flavor of chocolate. For carob to taste similar requires a lot of sweetening, dairy and/or fats. Carob does contain some nutrients, like calcium.

Bread crumbs (and meat grinding): There are often pieces of leftover bread hanging around that I deposit in a bowl on the shelf. I leave these to dry. The Colorado climate is perfect for this. When the bowl is full, run through the meat grinder to make crumbs. I do this when grinding meat or something. Since most of our meat is home butchered we never grind and freeze. Meat stores longer frozen in big pieces. When I grind meat, I do a lot and cook extra: some for hamburgers, the rest for meatloaf, and meatballs. Many of these recipes contain bread crumbs. I grind the onion, or any other vegetable used — so much easier! In fact, you should grind your own meats, even though store purchased. You can buy better cuts, trim off all fat, and know what's in them! Homemade sausage is fun to make. Look for more info on this under Christmas (December, in Art of Life chapter).

Soy Sauce. Read those labels. Almost all but health food brands contain MSG and other garbage. There is something new called Braggs Liquid Aminos. It's still brewed soybeans but has no sodium and yet tastes salty! At least I can't find salt as an ingredient.

MSG is not always labeled as MSG. If you definitely have reactions (I get headaches, some people turn red, or get puffy, have dizziness, or mental confusion. Children can have reactions of hyperactivity or learning disorders) you need to find its other names. These are what I've learned: autolyzed yeast, hydrolyzed vegetable or plant protein or plain ole' hydrolyzed protein - these are found in just about everything, even in "health" foods! Hydrolyzed milk proteins are usually labeled as sodium caseinate or calcium caseinate and are often in your powdered chocolate drinks, coffee creamers and flavorings, and some ice creams and other dairy products (or substitutes).

Soup broths should be homemade. Nothing out of a can or package can be as tasty (they usually have to add more salt &/or MSG). Monte outlawed canned soup early in our marriage and that's when I discovered why I never liked soup before! It's easy to cook chickens or browned soup bones (details under "Soups & Stocks" chapter), strain and let cool so you can remove the fat that comes to the top. Freeze in various sized containers. Most recipes use pint size. Freeze the deboned cooked chicken in small packets ready for sandwiches, pasta or casseroles. Vinegar (Tbs) added to the cooking bones extracts calcium into the liquid and the vinegar taste cooks out. My sister-in-law Chris started me freezing all liquids left over from cooking vegetables for soup, gravy base or sauces.

Yogurt truly is a wonder food. It contains high quality protein, minerals, vitamins, and enzymes. Yogurt contains all the known vitamins, including the hard to get ones, D and B12. It is nutritionally superior to milk. Yogurt is a pre-digested food changed by lactobacillus bulgaris, a "friendly" bacteria. Because of this, it is digested and utilized in the body twice as fast as milk. Homemade is preferable to store bought. Make sure you buy the plain and low fat. The lower the fat the more readily available calcium. Also make sure it reads "active" or "living cultures." Homemade is sweet not tart, unless you leave it to incubate a long time. Check it for signs of setting after 3 hours. It will set up more in the refrigerator. The sooner it sets and is refrigerated the less tart. (A complete recipe is in the "Breakfast" section). The enzymes in yogurt suppress the putrefactive organisms in incompletely digested foods. They literally crowd them out. They help prevent gas and bloating. My grandmother was wise before her time, and before it became fashionable, in that she told my mother to feed me yogurt while I was on antibiotics. Yogurt replenishes the good bacteria that the antibiotics kill off as it's killing the bad. In fact, older yogurt (refrigerated a week) is said to have an antibiotic effect like penicillin. Yogurt's good bacteria aid in the digestion of food and are necessary in the production of certain vitamins, especially the B vitamins. Don't buy the sweetened yogurts when you can add your own flavoring with the purees or jams you like. I use yogurt as a substitute for sour cream. It can be mixed with mayonnaise or blended with cottage cheese in many recipes as a salad dressing or cheese substitute. Yogurt is high in lactose which is needed in the intestines, and remember that milk is the only food we get lactose from. Lactose goes undigested into the large intestine where it is used as food for the beneficial bacteria, acidophilus. Lactose helps in the assimilation of many minerals - chiefly calcium, phosphorous, and magnesium. Many Europeans use a lot of milk in their diets (raw milk) and most of it is a soured form of milk like yogurt. Soured milk is easily assimilated by the body. Milk is mucus-forming and some people may be extra sensitive to mucus-producing foods. Mucus protects our internal membranes and tissues from bacterial attack. What foods produce this internal lubrication? Grains, nuts and milk, as well as vitamins A, C, and E. But, we need mucus; we would shrivel and dry out without it. Moderation and balance, again. Exodus 3:8 "I have come to bring . . . them to a land flowing with milk and honey"

Eggs and cholesterol: When eggs are fertile, meaning one rooster per at least seven hens, and these hens eat worms, bugs, grass, etc, the eggs have more vitamins, more lecithin, and twice as much unsaturated fatty acids as today's eggs. Cholesterol and lecithin are both in the egg yolk. Lecithin neutralizes cholesterol. Fertile eggs have more lecithin. Think about it! When the egg is fertile there is a life-giving germ present that is absent in mass-produced store eggs (produced by chickens in tiny quarters, faked-out by lights so they continue to produce eggs, and are given medications and hormones because of their unhealthy living conditions). Fertile eggs need to be refrigerated and used sooner because they will rot, though unfertile eggs can last in food storage for a long time in the proper conditions. Something is very different between the two. We've had people who normally get sick from eggs buy our eggs and discover they don't affect them negatively. We feel uncomfortable eating eggs from chickens we don't personally know! Whenever we eat anything we need to think whole.

Think whole! Would you sit and eat 10 apples or plums or oranges, or 300 grapes in one sitting?

(You'd end up with the runs! or canker sores.) But you down just that when drinking juice, and you're missing the fiber and pulp. When drinking juice, dilute it. God made the whole and we often take just a part of it, probably leaving some necessary nutrient out. Take store-bought flour, for example. Because long shelf life is needed, most of the known nutrients are stripped out (bleached) and then the flour is enriched with five or six nutrients. Would you feel rich if someone took $26 from you and only gave back $6? Also think of the fruit quantity when eating dried fruits. When I make fruit leather I've kept track of how many apricots, etc. went into each fruit leather sheet — it makes you realize that you shouldn't consume too much!

Sprouts are easy to make at home and one of the best food sources available. They are called "living food" because they are fresh, uncontaminated, power-packed with nutrients, and good for you! You can have a new crop in 3 to 5 days. My favorite mixture is alfalfa, radish, cabbage, and red clover seeds - pizzazz! Seeds need to be untreated. Another good mixture is mung beans, peas, lentils, wheat, barley, and fenugreek. Soak the seeds overnight in a jar. Pour into a sprouter tray, drain and rinse. You could save this first drain water for soups or bread making. For years I sprouted in jars with a nylon piece stretched over the opening with a rubber band; then I got jars with screen lids, and now I have sprout trays. You need to rinse them 3x a day, especially if in jars because they can mold easily, and you don't want them to dry out. Don't expose these to sunlight or they'll roast in the jar. With sprouting trays there's less chance of mold and sometimes I only remember to rinse 2x a day. Extra rinsing keeps them fresh. Grain sprouts are sweetest and best when the sprout is as long as the seed. Beans are best when 1/4 to 1" long. The alfalfa mixture is best from 1-1 1/2"; exposure to light in the end turns them green. Eat sprouts daily! These are our live enzymes when so much of our food is cooked and not fresh. Sprouting concentrates the nutrients. When first married, Monte and I almost went to live in the Australian outback, "dry camping," for his job. We heard fresh produce was rare, so I was prepared to take plenty of sprouting seeds.

Cooked or Raw? Cooking destroys some of the nutritive value of food. Steam cooking, and crock-pot cooking are preferable. Some vegetables contain oxalic acid that needs some cooking for better digestion - like the cabbage family, asparagus, green beans, winter squash, and potatoes. Beans contain another acid that requires cooking for better assimilation - I cook these and drain the water. Grains are usually better cooked, too. Sprouting all of these breaks down the acid as well. There's a lot of controversy on this. Raw foods contain live enzymes needed for healing and many necessary nutrients. People going through a healing process can benefit from juicing their vegetables and fruit. This brings instant nutrition to the body with minimal work, saving energy for healing.

"Warm" grains and beans are considered best for persons going through a healing process. Often people with allergies can better assimilate these. I'm not that knowledgeable on this subject but thought it should be mentioned and you could research further if there is the need. Spelt is considered a warm grain and is replacing wheat in many allergy-prone persons' diets. I think white beans are considered warm. There are others as well. My opinion is the body breaks down over the years through our poor eating habits and ingestion of processed foods. After a healing process and learning to eat right, the body may handle more foods again. Everyone is different, with varying weaknesses and strengths. It is interesting to learn what adversely affects others and ponder whether our apparently stronger bodies might not like it either. Many can eat good nutritious foods, but only if they rotate them. The typical rotation diet is a four-day rotation where grains, nuts, seeds, legumes, and even oils fall on different days. This indicates to me we need to eat in balance and with variety.

Beans are nature's near-perfect food. They are an abundant source of vitamins, minerals, iron, calcium, amino acids and soluble fiber. They are low in calories, sodium, and fat. In fact, beans lower cholesterol levels even in high-fat diets. If you do not eat beans often, you are more likely to bloat after eating. You need to build up a tolerance for beans by eating small amounts and slowly increasing the amount as your body adjusts. Supposedly cooking them with some rice can reduce gas and bloating. I pour off the soak water and continue cooking. By adding the rest of the ingredients in fresh water, you can reduce some of the gas-causing carbohydrates. Gas is a result of raffinose sugars that reach the large intestine without being completely digested. Harmless intestinal bacteria feast on these sugars giving off a gas by-product. The enzymes in yogurt suppress the putrefactive organisms in incompletely digested foods and help prevent gas and bloating. The fiber found in beans is fermented in the colon into a short chain of fatty acids, which is then re-absorbed by the body. These acids may help inhibit the body from making cholesterol. Dietary fiber, which beans are rich in, is believed to protect against cancer. Fiber is more effective when consumed as a natural part of whole food rather than an added fiber in the diet.

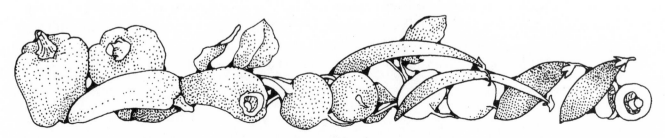

119

Protein. A Dutch chemist gave protein its name from a Greek word meaning "to take first place." Interesting and prophetic! What foods would you say supply protein? "Meat, eggs, and dairy." These protein foods are the most expensive in the budget. Animal proteins contain all the essential amino acid building blocks of protein. Vegetable foods also contain protein-building amino acids, though not in complete proportions. Thus, they've been given a lower status. They can be combined with each other to become high-quality protein. Think of the foods we eat, or various ethnic dishes: Mexican beans and tortillas; Italian pizza's grain, vegetables and cheese; macaroni and cheese; cereal and milk; rice pudding; Spanish rice and beans; peanut butter on whole grain bread . . . What about the

waiter who asks to put parmesan cheese on your salad. Some cookbooks have charts showing protein complements. To sum them up: the amino acids of grains complement those of beans or nuts; the amino acids of beans complement those of nuts or grains; and those of seeds complement grains and beans. Animal proteins added to any of them make for complete protein. If you snack on peanuts (peanuts are legumes you know, not nuts) eat some nuts or seeds. Whole grains, seeds and nuts contain the secret of life - the germ - the spark of life. The best grain protein is in the germ portion.

Some amino acids are made within our bodies, but eight are not and must be supplied by food. The proteins in our body are constantly changing from one form to another, being decomposed and resynthesized from the blood plasma amino acids. Amino acids from old cells are not wasted but recycled in the building of new cells. Thus being overtly conscious of eating high-protein meals all the time is not necessary. Most Americans eat about twice the protein the body needs. Our bodies have a protein limit and once this level is reached, the excess protein is stored as an inferior fuel for energy, fat. New research is showing vegetable proteins to be higher in biological value than animal proteins. Every plant, vegetable, and seed (maybe even fruit) contains some protein. If we eat a good natural, balanced, unrefined diet it is impossible to get inadequate protein. We really don't need to talk about protein or carbohydrates because there really isn't such a breakdown when ALL NATURAL foods contain all the food elements we need, and in higher biological value than in animal products and processed foods.

120

Rice is a grain we like to keep in the refrigerator because it is as handy as beans. In fact, a lunch of rice mixed with beans, especially black beans, and sprinkled with parmesan is a favorite. I keep a box of instant whole grain rice in the pantry for emergencies, but generally use the long-cooking type. I rarely do this on the stove. My favorite no-fuss-method is in the oven. Place 3 cups cold water in an oven-proof dish with a teaspoon of salt and 1 cup rice. Bake 1-1 1/2 hours at 250°. Sometimes I microwave it and other times I pressure cook it for speed.

White Sauce. Rather than make this with a saturated fat, use a good oil. It works great. 1/4 - 1/3 cup oil, 1/2 cup whole wheat flour, 1 pint chicken broth. (In place of the broth, this can be made with water, milk, etc.) This is my "cream of chicken" (mushroom, celery, etc) canned soup substitute. I add spices - powdered garlic & onion, parsley, coriander, and dried crumbled mushrooms, etc. This is also my base for cream of chicken or tuna over toast, and can be a base for scalloped potatoes, chicken divan, or macaroni and cheese (all of which are in the "Dinner or Supper" chapter).

Cookware. The best for your health is stainless steel and glass. The iron you absorb from cast iron cookware is a usable iron in your body. Iron supplements can be unusable or possibly harmful for your body depending on the form of iron. My grandmother told me some iron supplements can damage kidneys. Recent research from Denmark suggests that too much iron may be the primary cause of heart disease in women after menopause and men. Aluminum cookware can be hazardous because aluminum is highly reactive in the presence of oxygen and acidic substances such as tomato sauces or fruit juices. Lasagna left in an aluminum pan will cause discoloration or even pits to form. The reacted aluminum will end up contaminating the Lasagna. Fruit juices also react with aluminum and leach it out of the container. This is the same process which occurs with the more dangerous metal, lead. Stainless steel and glass are non-reactive, as is porcelain, but it easily chips. My bread pans are tin. Cast iron is easy to care for. If new, it needs to be seasoned: heat over low heat on burner (or in a warm oven) and rub oil over inside surface with a paper towel. Repeat several times. Continue oiling after every use until pan is seasoned. Eventually it will develop a nice black finish. Never soak cast iron as it can rust. Never use soap because it is very porous and will absorb the soap. Monte's mom sent me an article years ago on an oldtimer's advice for care of cast iron: never scour hard with a metal scrubby, but use sand or salt. I'll sometimes use the spatula to scrape it clean. The beauty of cast iron is the ease of cleanup when wiped out right away. I usually run it under hot water right away and use my kitchen sink brush to remove food. Allow to dry on a warm burner or oven. It need not be oiled repeatedly once seasoned. The pores, full of oil, heat and bubble when warming up. This kills any possible bacteria. A friend of ours, Gene Swanson, seasons his with a cut potato surface. If a pan is bought used and the black surface looks quite layered with chipping black crust, it can be brought back like new in a self-cleaning oven.

PANTRY STOCKING

" In the house of the wise are stores of choice food and oil,
but a foolish man devours all he has."
Proverbs 21:20

Since I've been asked more than once, "Will you please give me a list of basics I need on my shelf?" I will try compiling one. I've already spoken about the convenience and thrift advantages, but not about security. During financial crossroads or pinches, stored food is like money in the bank. I've even felt God stretching the oil, the grain, the fish, and we were filled. Bad weather, illness or transportation problems could be other crises. More recently, I realize that by not running to the grocery store frequently, I greatly simplify my life. It helps me to stay home and move beyond maintenance into the creative, fun part of life.

Don't continue eating until your pantry (cupboard) is bare. Leave a little and replenish, so that you can have some in store. I tend to double my batches when I cook so there is extra for another meal. Sometimes I plan a week of meals and make a large amount so I can freeze the extra. Years ago I bought some booklets called *Make-a-Mix* and they have been republished together into one book. I prefer mass cooking in this style than doing dozens of meals on one day. Rather than going to the store to get all the ingredients for the mass cooking day, most of my ingredients are in storage.

The best gradual beginning for storage is buying an extra item of something you are currently using each time you go to the store. Food warehouses and co-ops give you many extras. Store what you eat and eat what you store, and replenish regularly. I began this whole lifestyle when living in a townhouse. If there is a will there is a way. We've always looked for more areas and ways to make shelves for both household storage and books! Do you want a well-stocked kitchen, or storage for a year? The year storage plan, especially when you look at pounds required per person, could be overwhelming! We also need to remember, as Jesus says, "Be anxious for nothing . . . do not worry about your life, what you will eat. . . your Father knows that you need these things."

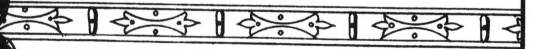

I will look around my kitchen and make lists. Actually I'm looking through my food co-op warehouse catalogue since my cookbooks don't have *my* kitchen type of list.

GRAINS

wheat
rice
oats
barley
rye
millet
corn or popcorn
buckwheat groats
amaranth
quinoa
spelt
kamut
teff

Grains usually come in 25 or 50 lb bags (larger quantities are always cheaper). I keep the bags in the storage room with rodent traps about. If you have a big rodent or bug problem, keep them in buckets. Most restaurant-size (or paint) buckets hold 45 lbs. In my pantry I have pretty colored plastic buckets, like miniature garbage cans with metal wire closures, for easy accessibility. Some of the smaller quantity or lesser used items are stored in Tupperware type buckets and glass jars. Some of my friends use the Rubbermaid big rectangle storage bins. They come in so many pretty colors these days.

Wheat. Hard wheat is what I use most often. It is the high-gluten wheat needed for breads and it has a variety of names: white (Prairie Gold, or Golden 86), red, winter, or spring. Pastry wheat is a softer wheat with less gluten. I believe this is a summer-grown wheat. Though I use the hard wheat for everything, pastry wheat is best for all baking, other than yeast breads.

Rice comes in many varieties. There's long and short grain brown rice. White rice is usually bleached. Wild rice is good, and can be mixed with regular rice. Basmati rice has a nice nutty flavor. I buy a wild rice blend too. I always have a box of instant brown rice for emergencies. Then there's jasmine rice, and "sticky" rice . . .

Oats. I buy oats whole as oat groats. Steel-cut oats are oat groats cut in half, and used for Irish porridge. Then of course thick rolled oats. The cut and rolled oats do eventually go rancid, but after a long time. When we eat hot oat cereal frequently, a bag of these lasts fine.

Barley. I get hulled barley for flour and rolled grain (I have a rolling machine). I keep the pearled for soups.

Corn. I used to buy regular corn, but now only buy popcorn. It can be used for flour and is sweeter than the bigger dried field-corn kernels.

Buckwheat kasha is buckwheat that's been toasted. I've had this in boxes, but usually get raw buckwheat in bulk. Though listed under grains, I believe it's a vegetable.

123

BAKING STAPLES

powdered milk
baking soda
baking powder
cream of tartar
buttermilk powder
cornstarch
cocoa powder
lecithin oil and granules
real vanilla extract
flavorings: almond, anise, etc
tapioca granules
instant yeast
cider vinegar

Powdered milk *is bagged in 10 lb, 25 lb, and 50 lb lots.*

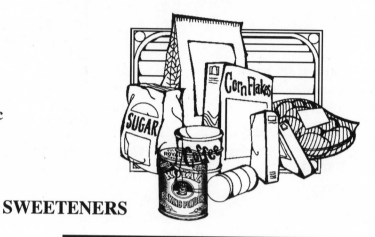

SWEETENERS

honey
maple syrup
molasses
sugar
chocolate chips
sorghum

Molasses. *I stock barbados unsulphered molasses. Blackstrap has more iron, but is overpoweringly strong.*

Sugar. *Both white and brown sugars are in our pantry. Brown sugar is white sugar and molasses.*

Chocolate chips. *Regular chocolate chips and mini-chips are needed in our recipes.*

OILS

olive
canola

All oils except olive need refrigeration to prevent rancidity. I buy these in a 35 lb container. If you cannot keep oils cold, do not buy in large containers but in small sealed jars. I talk about oils in the "Tips" section.

BEANS

pinto
black turtle
lentil
pea, split
small whites
lima, baby
kidney

> These generally come in 25 lb bags. All but the pintos I store in glass jars. I use more pintos so they are in a bucket. Beans are pretty in the jars.

PRODUCE

fruits and vegetables
potatoes
onions
garlic
carrots
celery
lemons
salad makings
squash

SPROUTS

alfalfa seeds
radish seeds
red clover seeds

> I buy these seeds in one pound bags from the co-op. They are my favorite mixture. The other seed-bean mixture I mention under sprouts in this chapter in the "Tips" section, I get from a local health store and do not make them as often.

NUTS

almonds
walnuts
hazelnuts
pecans
cashews
pine nuts

> Nuts need to be kept frozen or they will become rancid and possibly moldy. Moldy nuts are very carcinogenic. This listing is in order from best to worst as far as fat content, but they all contain other qualities that our bodies occasionally need. Here again, I'm just listing the ones I keep stocked.
>
> **Almonds** are a good source of vitamin C.

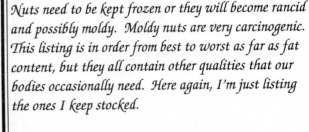

GROCERY

canned fruit
canned tomatoes
peanut butter
condiments
olives
beef and chicken flavoring
salad dressings
tuna
tofu
wheat germ
milks
cereals
jams
tortilla chips
salsa
green chili sauce
pretzels
microwave popcorn

This is how these items are listed in my food warehouse catalogue. Many of my other listed items are in this section too, but in smaller packaging and by the case. The others are listed under Bulk. Some of these I buy and others I can.

Tomato. I stock both sauce and stewed.

Peanut Butter. I don't buy Jiffy or Skippy. Only the natural 100% peanuts for us. The others have sugar and are hydrogenated. The natural needs the oil stirred in before refrigerating!

Condiments consist of catsup, mustard, horseradish, pickle varieties, mayonnaise, and others I'm probably forgetting. Bottled sesame seeds, capers and anchovies.

Beef and Chicken flavorings. I get bouillon flavorings through the health food co-op because hardly anything in the store is free of MSG. Some supposed "healthy" stuff has MSG too. I always read labels. I talk more on this in the "Tips."

Salad Dressings. I buy some basics and still try and make my own.

Tofu. MoriNu is the creamiest tofu I've tried. These come in aseptic packs and don't need to be refrigerated until opened. But don't store in the heat! I use both soft and firm; it doesn't seem to really matter.

Wheat germ. I only get this sealed in jars, then I know it's not rancid. I usually buy the toasted wheat germ because I like it on cereals, yogurt, and ice cream.

Milk My family prefers 1%. Monte, Heather and I use Rice Dream, a milk substitute. It comes in aseptic packs. Evaporated and condensed canned milk are in the pantry too.

Cereals. The basics I keep stocked are Shredded Wheat, Cheerios, Barbara's Shredded Spoonfuls (a healthy variety of Life. Life has yellow dye #5 which once gave me an intense headache when in the hospital.), Kashi, and Puffs-n-Honey.

HERBS AND SPICES

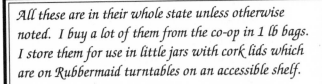

MINT

allspice
anise seed
basil leaf
bay leaf
caraway seed
cardamom pods
celery seed
chili powder
chives
cinnamon
cloves
coriander
cumin seed
dill
fennel seed
flax seed
garlic powder
ginger, ground
juniper berries
lemon peel
marjoram leaf
mustard seed
nutmeg
onion
orange peel
oregano leaf
paprika
parsley leaf
pepper
peppermint leaf
poppy seeds
rosemary
sage leaf
sea salt
sesame seeds
spearmint leaf
thyme leaf
turmeric, ground

ROSEMARY

All these are in their whole state unless otherwise noted. I buy a lot of them from the co-op in 1 lb bags. I store them for use in little jars with cork lids which are on Rubbermaid turntables on an accessible shelf.

Chili powder. *I buy plain chili powder - no other spices are mixed in. I also have the hanging red peppers (anaheims) for use. These, ground, are chili powder.*

Cinnamon *needs to be ground, and then I have the cinnamon sticks. My co-op and the Watkins cinnamon are good quality. If you have the chance to sample the Watkins brand along with the typical store brands, you will taste a definite difference.*

Dill. *Most cooking uses only dill weed. Some things, especially pickles, need the seed.*

Mustard seed. *I use both the brown and yellow.*

Nutmeg. *I buy the ground, but have a nutmeg grinder for the whole.*

Onion. *Both powder and flakes.*

Pepper. *I use the ground a lot, but finally got a clear pepper grinder. I wanted clear so the varied pretty-colored peppercorns could be seen. I'm starting to grind some in the coffee mill each week instead of buying the ground.*

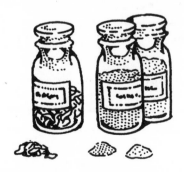

BEVERAGE / TEA HERBS

catnip
comfrey
dandelion root
echinacea
feverfew
hibiscus
hops flowers
jasmine flower
lavender flower
lemongrass
licorice root
many mints
mullein leaf
oregano leaf *(yes in tea!)*
red clover tops
raspberry leaf
rosehips
valerian root

More and more books are coming out with tea recipes utilizing ingredients other than just black tea. Some are for simple enjoyment and others for therapeutic benefits. Though natural, some do contain chemicals of which "more" is not necessarily "better." Here again - moderation, variety and balance. Leafy and flower parts of plants should be made by infusing. Infusion is your basic tea method, boiling water poured over the herb and allowed to steep for about ten minutes. The decoction method is used for roots, barks, twigs, and some berries - simmer for about one hour. As with all my lists, this is not exhaustive. These are what I have around. Many of these are great in potpourris as well.

DRIED FRUIT

apples
apricots
cranberries
currants
date pieces, dry
peach
pears
prunes
raisins
tomatoes
cantaloupe
oranges and grapefruit

Many of these I dry myself and store in sealed bags. Each item has a small jar that I replenish. Some I make fruit leather or roll-ups from and wrap in plastic. I have a small crock for fruit leather that gets replenished. The rest come from a co-op.

Date pieces. I get from the co-op. They look as if they were run through a larger-than-normal holed meat grinder and dusted with flour to keep from sticking together. I use these in hot cereals and in a favorite chocolate chip cake recipe.

DRIED VEGETABLES

mushrooms
broccoli and cauliflower
onions
bell pepper
corn

Over the years I've tried drying many things. And many things sit in jars and never get used. I'll give you the things that get used regularly. If dried vegetables are in accessible jars, your family will often choose a handful as a snack over something else. When dried, the flavors are accentuated and good. Dried mushrooms taste as if they have been sautéed in butter!

Mushrooms. *Whenever button mushrooms are on sale I will dry a bunch. Gourmet books say to never wash mushrooms since they are like little sponges, but to brush the dirt off. I do have a "mushroom" brush, as well as a "potato" brush. These and other kitchen scrubbing brushes stand in a crock by my sink. Oriental mushrooms are better for us than the American button mushrooms. Mushrooms vary greatly in their value as a food.*

Broccoli and Cauliflower *dried are truly great! I use them occasionally in quiche or frittata (like scrambled eggs). People like them for snacks.*

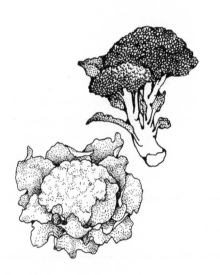

FROZEN

flour tortillas
roasted green chilis
vegetables and fruits
meat
nuts
breads
broth

Flour tortillas. *I buy these by the case - 24/6 pack. They are thin, whole wheat, and without preservatives.*

Roasted green chilis. *The first year I bought these at the farmers market, I bought five bushels! These kept us in chilis for two years. Now I get two bushels. The typical mild canned green chilis are anaheim chilis. These mild chili peppers are the longest of the common fresh peppers. Anaheim chilis are also the kind I get in the decorative hanging red chilies.*

REFRIGERATED

plain yogurt
raw monterey jack or colby cheese
mozzarella
parmesan
cream cheese
butter
margarine
eggs - our own

I regularly keep these in the refrigerator.

Cheese. *I buy raw colby or monterey jack cheese, and parmesan cheese, in bulk, anywhere from 5-10 lbs. If it comes in a big block (once I used the wrong order number and got 40 lbs!), cut it in 1-2 lb pieces and tightly wrap in plastic wrap. If these are wrapped well with no air holes, they will keep in the refrigerator for a month or two. If you have a lot, then freeze. I have no problems with frozen cheese since all we do is grate it. Frozen cheese can sometimes crumble. I use colby/jack cheese for just about all recipes. Mozzarella is for pizza and lasagna. Parmesan is for all Italian dishes and salads. I'm not a cheddar cheese lover. It has a lower moisture (less whey) content by going through a longer heating process, and is aged longer. Remember, this list covers my basics. I still occasionally like blue cheese crumbled on a salad, with oil, vinegar, and herbs. Gorgonzola cheese makes a good sauce with penne pasta and chicken chunks. Ricotta cheese is good with pasta and especially good in lasagna. Ricotta is made from the whey which is the drainings from making all the other cheese from the curds. Whey is low fat and contains most of the milk nutrients. The list of fun cheeses could go on and on.*

Margarine. *Spectrum 100% Canola Oil Spread - I order a case of 12/10 oz tubs and these keep in the back of the 'fridge till we need to order more. There may be other brands coming out now with no hydrogenation. Be sure to check the oil source.*

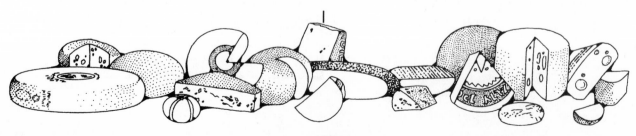

PASTA

long pasta
ribbon egg pasta
tube pasta
special shapes
soup pasta
pasta sheets

At the moment I have quite a variety of beautiful pasta on the counter in ornate jars. Pasta and bean varieties make great gifts bagged in cellophane with colored ribbon ties. I'll list the basics according to their use, or should I say sauce. We frequent a local restaurant run by a native Italian. He always visits with us at our table. Many times all I eat is bread dipped in his fresh pesto sauce and a salad. In Italy meat is never served with pasta but on the side.

Long Pasta. Our preference is angel hair and regular spaghetti pasta. The long pastas are better suited to olive oil and tomato sauces than sauces with large chunks of vegetables or meat. All the ingredients need to cling together when twirled on a fork.

Ribbon egg pasta. Good for absorbing creamy sauces. In sauces where olive oil is prominent, egg pasta absorbs too much oil and becomes sticky and gummy. I sometimes put these in soup.

Tube pasta. One of which is penne, is good with creamy sauces. I use elbow pasta mainly for macaroni and cheese or salads.

Special shapes. Fusilli is my favorite. It is like spaghetti wrapped around a skinny pencil. Special shaped pastas are good with chunky sauces, which cling well to the curves.

Soup pastas. Acini di pepe - very small balls; alphabet; fedelini - basically broken spaghetti.

Pasta sheets are usually lasagna pasta. This dough is what's used for ravioli too.

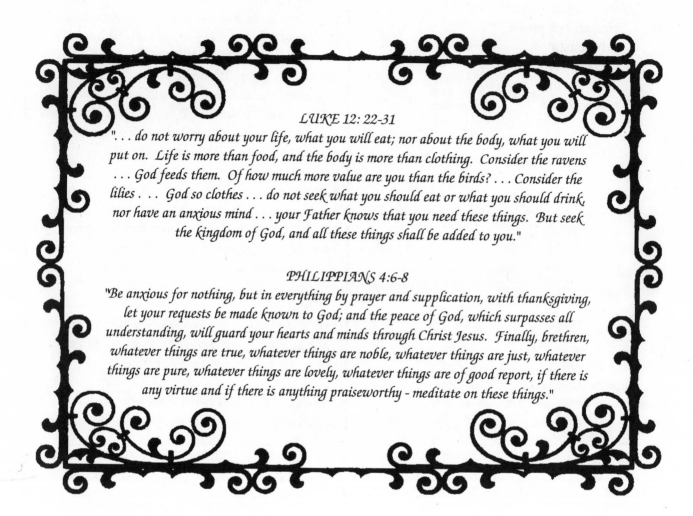

LUKE 12: 22-31

"... do not worry about your life, what you will eat; nor about the body, what you will put on. Life is more than food, and the body is more than clothing. Consider the ravens ... God feeds them. Of how much more value are you than the birds? ... Consider the lilies ... God so clothes ... do not seek what you should eat or what you should drink, nor have an anxious mind ... your Father knows that you need these things. But seek the kingdom of God, and all these things shall be added to you."

PHILIPPIANS 4:6-8

"Be anxious for nothing, but in everything by prayer and supplication, with thanksgiving, let your requests be made known to God; and the peace of God, which surpasses all understanding, will guard your hearts and minds through Christ Jesus. Finally, brethren, whatever things are true, whatever things are noble, whatever things are just, whatever things are pure, whatever things are lovely, whatever things are of good report, if there is any virtue and if there is anything praiseworthy - meditate on these things."

Chapter Nine

COMMON SENSE NUTRITION

Dieters know that losing weight is only half the battle - keeping it off is the real war. What is needed is common-sense eating, not starvation. Do bandaids cover or cure? Most weight control approaches treat the symptoms, not the underlying cause. It seems logical to decrease food intake: quit eating, and consume fewer calories to lose weight. But about 95% will regain their weight plus additional pounds within two years. This kind of eating (or not eating) can actually cause the body to retain fat. Why? Because our bodies are programmed against starvation or restrictive eating. The body cannot tell the difference between starvation and restrictive dieting, but it does know when it isn't getting enough food and nutrients to keep going. When you diet, you are fighting your body. It feels threatened and goes to work to keep you from starving. First, your appetite increases and you are always hungry - may even become obsessed with food. Next, your metabolic rate decreases and you have no energy. You are nervous, irritable, or depressed. After successive diets, your metabolism is so confused that it stays suppressed, even after you quit dieting. The fat level of the body is determined by a weight-regulating mechanism in the brain. There is a weight at which you stabilize when you make no special effort to gain or lose — where your body feels comfortable and tends to maintain. How can you lower this metabolism setpoint? Eat regular wholesome meals, exercise daily, and live positively! As your body adjusts to being fueled and exercised regularly, it will begin to burn more calories. Burning more calories raises your metabolic rate and causes your metabolism to reset at a higher level. If you've been a yo-yo dieter, it may take awhile for your body to readjust and raise your

metabolic rate. You may even have a temporary gain as your body adjusts to normal eating again. Your body no longer needs the fat for survival protection because you are meeting its nutritional needs.

The body seems to take care of first things first! If your body is nutritionally deficient due to poor eating habits, extreme stress, ill health, anorexia, restrictive dieting, or for any other reason, health must be re-established first. If you are using all your daily food intake to provide the necessary energy just to get you through the day, there may be little or none left to repair and rebuild the body and to burn excess fat. Your body deserves the best high-grade fuel available (wholesome foods). As you begin to meet your body's nutritional needs you will probably go through a natural cleansing and healing process.

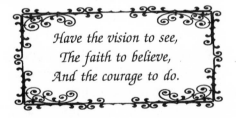

Have the vision to see,
The faith to believe,
And the courage to do.

Temporary changes are what most diets are all about. I'm not talking about a diet, but a lifestyle change — a comfortable, workable, lifestyle change. After the newness, everything will become second nature — from the way you buy your food to the way you prepare and eat it. With patient consistency, you'll become lean and healthy — naturally. Action often comes before motivation. You may not "feel like" giving up fast foods, processed foods, diet pop, and chips, but just do it, and you'll begin to like the way you feel and look. Commit yourself to twenty-one days of true, all-out commitment and dedication to this way of life. Take time now to write down how you feel about yourself. Weigh yourself, and write it down. Take your measurements, and write them down. Changes will come about so naturally that you may forget how the "old you" looked and felt. Changes may need to occur mentally first. Program your subconscious to raise your metabolic rate so you will burn more fat all day. Start visualizing fat cells being gobbled up. Talk back to those inner voices. "I may have a sluggish metabolism, but that will change as I eat fewer fats and sugars and increase my activity." "My genes may make it more difficult, but not impossible!"

Are aches and pains an inevitable aspect of aging? Say no! If you don't use it, you lose it. The more it's used, the better it works. Obesity in children is a growing problem and the major factors are a diet high in fats, sugars, processed foods, and too little activity (TV watching and computer games). Regular exercise helps decrease fat as it increases the resting metabolic rate. Moderate exercise increases this metabolic rate and keeps it high for hours after you stop. You may lose inches faster than pounds because muscle is denser and heavier than fat. Fat floats - muscle sinks. Pound for pound, fat has more volume than muscle. Just remember that an inch loss denotes a fat loss. You want to lose excess fat. Exercise helps build muscle. Muscle curves - fat hangs. Many who diet become littler fat people because when they diet, they often burn muscle, not fat. Our goal is to make our bodies efficient fat-burners.

The body has two sources of fuel: blood sugar and fat. Sugar gives large quantities of energy for short periods of time. Fat is our endurance fuel. You must keep moving to be an efficient fat burner. It requires oxygen over an extended length of time - at least 25-30 minutes without stopping (like a brisk walk). Regular deep breathing can do much to improve your health. A fat-burning exercise should leave you with an energy high, not a feeling of total exhaustion. You may want to sit down for a few minutes, but you should feel invigorated. Otherwise you could be exceeding your aerobic threshold. Stop-and-go activity (sit-ups, leg lifts, weight lifting, etc.) do not put the body in a full fat-burning mode. Exercise is an excellent natural remedy for stress. You'll also develop a calmer, more relaxed attitude toward daily pressures because of the endorphin release from exercise. Endorphins, secreted in the brain as a result of endurance exercise, are nature's tranquilizer!

You are what you eat! Good nutrition includes healthy food and good common-sense eating based on three balanced meals each day. These meals should be high in nutrients and fiber from complex carbohydrates: whole grains, legumes, vegetables and fruits. They are low in cholesterol, fats, and refined carbohydrates: sugar and white flour products; and lower than the norm in sodium. What you eat is more important than how much you eat. Don't be a breakfast skipper. Meal skipping activates the starvation defense I mentioned earlier, and statistics show that meal skippers are fatter than regular eaters. Skipping meals forces the body to store fat for survival and lowers the metabolic rate (calorie burning), leaving you with a "fat metabolism." In the morning you need to break the fast of your body's slow sleep mode, and

speed up the metabolism for the day. When you begin eating breakfasts, you may actually feel hungrier during the day than when you skipped meals. These hunger pangs are simply your body signaling for more of the nutrients and high energy foods it needs to maintain good health and weight control. The hunger response will disappear in a few days as your body adjusts to regular eating. Keep in mind that eating refined carbohydrates (sweets and white flour products) will make you feel hungrier within a short time because of their effect on your blood sugar levels. In contrast, a whole grain breakfast gives high, long-lasting energy.

Eating three meals a day, plus nutritious snacks, helps raise your metabolic rate. Eat something every four to five hours, even if you don't feel hungry. It helps keep your energy high; *food is fuel*. Snack on vegetables if you aren't hungry, and vegetables, grains, beans, and fruits if you are hungry. Your tastes will change as you bypass some of the old high-fat, high-sugar favorites.

Generally, the more food we eat in its natural state, the healthier it will be for us. Whole grains, beans, fresh vegetables, and fruits should make up 65-80% of your total daily food intake. Our meals need to be built around these complex carbohydrates rather than meat which is usually loaded with saturated fat, high in cholesterol, and lacking fiber. Complex carbohydrates are rarely linked to any health risk, and are naturally low in calories and price, and high in nutrition and fiber. Shop the outside perimeter of the grocery store and avoid the center aisles that are full of expensive convenience foods. Your grocery bills will drop dramatically as will your medical bills! You may experience a short period (a week or two) of gas and occa-

sional feelings of fullness, but these are just temporary as your body adjusts to more wholesome foods. Complex carbohydrates promote regular elimination which is vital for good health and fat loss. Whole grains form the cornerstone of good health and weight control. Use them as a crutch at first, and they will help you pass up the tempting sugars and fats. Good whole grain bread is usually less than 20% fat calories. Carry some with you in your purse or vehicle so you'll have the right food available if you get hungry.

Fats pack a lot of fat calories into a very few bites. Not all calories are created equal! Most fat calories eaten are converted to body fat, yet you can eat ample **complex** carbohydrates without a weight gain. There are nine calories in one gram of fat compared to four calories in a gram of protein, sugar, or starch. Alcohol has seven calories per gram. Fats make your mind and body sluggish by slowing circulation and by reducing the oxygen-carrying capacity of the red blood cells. They are being linked to many health problems. A diet high in whole grains, legumes, vegetables and fruits, and low in fats, white flour, and sugars, can help reverse the effects of cholesterol buildup, high triglycerides, and other health problems.

Sugars upset the balance of the body. Your appetite may rage out of control. You are hungry all the time as blood sugar rises, then drops. Your body will rely on them for energy rather than using fat. Artificial sweeteners seem to affect the body in much the same way. A workable plan must have variety and allow for occasional treats, special occasions and favorite foods. Your taste buds will change and the forbidden favorites will have less appeal as you replace them with other tasty foods that are not

high in fats and sugars. Eat a sweet or dessert after a full meal - never on an empty stomach. This helps prevent the blood sugar highs and lows.

White flour is so refined that the body handles it in much the same way as it does sugar. It lacks the nutritional value or the satiety of whole grains. Keep trying whole grains if they aren't your favorite - your taste buds will gradually change. Around 1900 the U.S. food industry started processing whole grain flours into white flour by milling and bleaching (with chlorine!). Once grain has been cracked and milled, oxidation of the oil in it commences rapidly, and the flour becomes rancid within a week. Also many of the grain's nutrients break down and some will even vaporize. It is like the difference between fresh-picked corn and corn that has been at room temperature for a few days. There is no way to know when supermarket-sold flour was milled. Fresh-ground flour needs to be kept in an airtight container in the freezer to keep its nutrients.

Drink six or more glasses of water every day. Keep a full glass of water on your desk or countertop and empty it several times a day. Put a slice of lime or lemon in it if you need a little flavor. You can calculate how much water to daily consume by dividing your weight by two. Divide this figure by eight to get the number of daily glasses. Roughly 70% of body weight is water. We need a steady supply of water to keep our systems functioning at peak performance. It is particularly important for brain function. If you are retaining water, drink! It helps relieve fluid retention. Hungry between meals? Drink water first; you may just be thirsty. Make sure your water is clean!

Don't try to change everything all at once. Gradual changes are easier to adapt to and more likely to be permanent. Don't make an issue of food — just get into good nutrition. Become nutritionally literate. Good health and weight control do require a permanent change. Don't make it a temporary diet but a lifestyle!

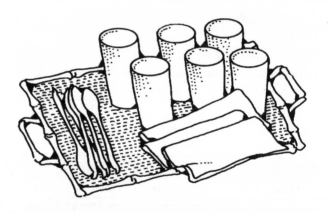

SIX OR *MORE* GLASSES OF WATER A DAY.

More Thoughts on Fat

I have already shown you how to keep your total fat-calories under 30 or 20 percent, but, there is more. There are three types of fats: saturated, polyunsaturated, and monounsaturated. Below is a chemical comparison of the three. It is generally recommended you limit your saturated (bad) fat to one third or less of your total fat intake. A simple guide that will do wonders for your health (and weight) is to limit your saturated fat intake to 10 grams per day. Remember to consider hydrogenated and heated fat (frying) to be saturated (bad) also. This one discipline may be the most important dietary discipline of them all, particularly in regards to the chronic health problems that afflict America.

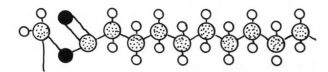

CH₃ (CH₂)₁₆ COOH   Stearic Acid

$CH_3 (CH_2)_{16} COOH$ Stearic Acid
Part of a saturated fat molecule
butter, coconut oil, fatty beef...

● **Carbon**
⊛ **Oxygen**
○ **Hydrogen**

$CH_3 (CH_2)_7 CH=CH (CH_2)_7 COOH$ Oleic Acid
Part of a monounsaturated fat molecule
avocados, olive oil...

$CH_3 (CH_2)_4 CH=CH CH_2 CH=CH (CH_2)_7 COOH$ Linoleic Acid
Part of a polyunsaturated fat molecule
salmon, vegetable oils, safflower oil...

> **Don't diet! Eat regularly! Exercise regularly!**
> **Cut fats, white flour, and sugars!**
> **Live positively!**

The Simple, Common-Sense Lifestyle
A Lifetime Plan

1. Live positively!

2. Exercise at least 30 minutes 3-5x a week. Get adequate rest.

3. Eat 3 meals daily plus wholesome snacks when hungry.

4. Eat more whole grains, legumes, vegetables, and fresh fruits.
   <u>Whole grains</u>: 4 or more servings per day. Eat a variety, not just wheat, but oats, brown rice, barley, rye, millet, buckwheat, quinoa, amaranth, spelt, etc. Use in cereals, breads, pasta, tortillas, side dishes.
   <u>Beans, Peas, Lentils</u>: Eat at least 2-4 cups a week. Eat beans often starting with small portions at first. Add beans to any meal.
   <u>Vegetables</u>: 4 or more servings per day (2-4 cups minimum). Include green and deep yellow vegetables, potatoes, rutabaga, parsnips, cabbage, and squash.
   <u>Fresh fruits</u>: 2-4 servings per day. Eat more in summer when in season.

5. **Drastically Decrease Fats!**
   Fats such as butter, margarine, salad dressing, mayonnaise, cheese, sour cream, whole milk, roasted nuts, chips, peanut butter, shortening, red meats, fried foods, and ice cream.

6. Use lean meat, eggs, and low fat dairy products in moderation.
   <u>Lean meat</u>: 2-4 oz daily if desired.
   Fish and skinned poultry are preferred. Use red meat 2-3 servings per week, mostly as a condiment or seasoning for vegetables and whole grains.
   <u>Low fat dairy</u>: 2 servings daily. Yogurt is the best!

7. Limit or avoid sugars, artificial sweeteners, and white flour products.

8. Avoid or limit alcohol, soft drinks, diet pop, punch, caffeine drinks. Limit juice intake.

9. Use salt sparingly.

10. Drink 6 or more 8-oz. glasses of water daily.

<u>Keep your total daily food intake within these levels:</u>

<u>Complex Carbohydrates</u>	<u>65-80%</u>	<u>Fats</u>	<u>10-20%</u>
<u>Refined Carbohydrates</u>	<u>very low</u>	<u>Proteins</u>	<u>10-15%</u>

-from *Set for Life* by Jane Merrill & Karen Sunderland

- Compute Fat as a Percentage of Calories:

1. Multiply the number of fat grams by 9 to determine the number of fat calories.
2. Divide the number of fat calories by the total number of calories.
3. Multiply the answer in number 2 by 100 to get the percentage of fat.

- A Quick Estimate:

If the calories per serving are close to 100 and the fat grams 3.3, you are getting around 30% fat calories. This is what the FDA recommends. We really should consume less than that amount - 20% is a reasonable amount. To keep daily fat intake at 20% or less, combine small amounts of higher-fat foods with plenty of low-fat grains, beans, vegetables, and fruits each day; then average your total daily food intake. Eating 15-30 grams of fat per day will keep your average under 20% fat if you eat between 1200 and 2600 calories.

> **Count fat grams, not calories!**

- Don't be Fooled by Labels.

When ham or ice cream is advertised as 95% fat free, you are only told the percent of fat by weight. The total fat as a percentage of calories is usually over 60%! Popular 2% milk is 2% fat by weight but 38% fat as a total percentage of calories. The new popular 1% milk is 18% fat and skim is only 3% fat as a total percentage of calories.

- Craving for Something?

Like a Coke Classic or a candy bar? Stop and ask yourself why. Analyze the situation. Are you craving sugar or something as a pacifier? Food addictions are partly emotional — comfort, pleasure, anger, boredom, stress, fatigue, and the like. It may represent the comfort and security of home or your life as a child. Try to identify and control those things that trigger your cravings.

- Plan a Once a Week "Feast Meal".

If you begin to feel deprived of certain foods, you will probably lose motivation as you head toward a long-term health-promoting change. It's not what we eat 5% of the time that'll kill us, but the stuff we feed our bodies the other 95% of the time. So, one meal a week, out of twenty-one should be all right. Those who do this see phase changes. The first phase was passionately anticipating the "feast meal," taking the form of pizzas, chips, french fries, chocolate bars, pastries, pies, and ice cream. That night sleep was miserable, not to mention the next day's headaches, gas pains, skin eruptions, weight gain, foul breath, constipation, and general crabbiness. The next phase comes as healthy eating habits continue to take root. The importance of the "junk out" meal steadily diminishes. Tastes change and attitudes adjust. Even the kids will change. The feast meal continues but without the sense of passionate craving because of incorporating nutritionally correct foods. The goal is to design a strategy that will keep you motivated to move continually toward better eating and optimal health.

What we have to learn to do, we learn by doing.

Aristotle

Chapter Ten
GARDENING
& BRINGING IN THE HARVEST

Gardening is almost a joke, considering where we've lived. We've never been able to simply follow the books. We moved from one extreme - the Arizona desert, to another - the Colorado mountains living at 8,000 feet. I never grew up with gardening, though my paternal grandmother in Tucson always had a garden. My favorite things I remember picking and eating as a child were radishes and onions. That could be all she grew besides strawberries and flowers. Once married, I liked to explore, and of course back then, anything planted had to be edible. It didn't matter where we lived, I planted something. We were the only ones in a townhouse complex with vining string beans as an awning rather than the typical metal or canvas. Also, we were the only ones making furniture in our carport. Monte even hooked up a foot-powered lathe from a picture in a *Foxfire* book and made me a rocking chair with only a handsaw, hunting knife and sandpaper. It truly looks manufactured and I still sit in it today when reading aloud to the kids. Out in the desert, I had a bumper crop of watermelons and tomatoes in January at the base of our porch's south-facing brick wall. When we went back to visit this house, the first we built ourselves, a tomato plant and pepper plant were still in the planter I had planted years ago. They were fairly big plants with woody stems! We even planted a garden in rentals.

Our garden now has a six-foot barbed wire fence with sticks woven in. Why? Elk are pests! They still get in late in the season when the meadow grass browns and the garden green looks so tempting. One year I made fried chicken just when the first green beans were ready to pick. They were fine the day before. This particular year I had planted in companion blocks and the beans were scattered about the garden. The elk had gotten in the night before and ate every green bean bush! Gophers are another nuisance. Most people up here aren't bothered because their ground consists mainly of decomposed and solid rock. We live in a saddle slump* and have beautiful soil. Once while looking at my perfect few-inch-high sweet peas, one disappeared before my eyes, leaving a perfect hole! Just like in a Bugs Bunny cartoon! Another time, I had been picking beautiful beet greens

*See page 146

141

for salad all summer, but when we went to pick the beets at the end of the season, they were hollowed out! I've tried all the tricks in the books. Monte even drove the vehicle to the fence, put the vacuum hose to the exhaust pipe and the other end down a hole. All it did was melt a hole in the hose! I may invest in a ground vibrator which is supposed to work in a 1/4 acre area. Elk used to eat my tulips and other flowers till we put a strawberry black mesh over them. We got a dog to keep them from coming in too close to the house. Eventually we may put an electric fence or alarm around some areas.

I used to plant only edible things, but now I'm into perennials. I plant anything that will come up on its own year after year and provide color throughout the growing season. We built a greenhouse on the back, south side of the house to start most of my plantings early. Our growing season is barely ninety days and our nights cool off slowing down the growth. We also have to water almost daily and our water is *FREEZING* year round. I sympathize with the plants and figure it would be quite a shock treatment and stunt me as well. The cabbage family and salad greens grow best here. The nights are often too cool

for tomatoes to set. We put in another small garden on the back side of the house facing south and the house provides shelter from the wind. Tomatoes planted close to the house grow pretty well. This year was a weird year with snow, rain, and cold into June, so we're excited to see how it works next year.

We sure have the elk stories. Others have enjoyed them, so I'll pass some along to you. I wish we could have photos of all we've seen over the years because it would make an interesting poster accompanied by humorous captions. Monte does have photos of elk fighting, mating, flipping big wheels in the air, licking their chops, and milling around. We may have more photos of elk than kids! But we've missed photos showing all the variety of items caught in their antlers and carted around for awhile. Here's a riddle for you. What goes "crunch, crunch, clang clang, crunch crunch?" An elk eating chokecherries while dragging a clothesline with aluminum poles in its antlers, one moonlit night. An elk butted our kids' big wheel and tossed it 15 feet in the air. That could have been caught. We've seen Christmas lights and garden hoses.

One elk was seen with another bull's head and antlers severed from its body, stuck in its own antlers. That's how wild they fight for supremacy over their harem. Elk are presently milling around and this year we have a volleyball net. So should we take it down or take a chance it will be the next caught item by a passing elk? I remove my hammock each fall because an elk stepped through it. They even like to lick the bird feeder and hummingbird feeder. One elk bedded down for the night below the guest room window and when getting up, its antlers bashed against the wall and scared our guest out of bed! Another year we awakened at three in the morning because the house was shaking. At first I thought someone was playing basketball downstairs. Because of a full moon a bull had seen his reflection in the window, thought it was another bull and was battling it! Monte cracked the window open and said "Boo" which finally scared it away. The funniest part is that our windows are "Hurd" windows and they held up to a herd bull! When we needed additional windows to finish a portion of the house we called "Hurd" thinking they might like to use the idea for an ad *and* give us a break in the cost of more windows. They didn't seem to catch the vision!

The subject of elk may not seem to fit under gardening other than their being a nuisance. But they do fit when discussing bringing in the harvest. Our main meat supply for the past fifteen years has been elk. You are probably thinking, "How horrid." Such thoughts seldom existed until Walt Disney put out "Bambi." Recently I heard on National Public Radio an excerpt read from some written work. The author had stayed at a working cattle ranch and had to participate in the labor, including artificial insemination. She forgot her vegetarian, citified views and said "Bring on the steak!" Oh, concerning a falsehood in Bambi, elk and deer do not mate for life. The males disappear in bachelor herds the majority of the year and only come around in the fall. Then it's a battle for supremacy rule over the biggest harem. Monte hunts with a bow and arrow. He refuses to shoot one in our meadow (though I'm not opposed to it. Once I shot one from the window completely naked but for curlers in my hair!). He hunts on ranches and open lands in our area. Travis now joins him and procured our annual meat supply last year with a bow at 15! If no one gets an elk, I have to buy a gun license and get it. I think I've only had to thrice. It's a finer quality meat than beef. I cook regular beef recipes. No need to mask any "game" flavor. It's just not fatty for flash fry/cooking. We're not real steak eaters anyway. One elk is a lot of meat and lasts us the year. Sometimes we'll get a deer. And we're always finding ways to stock the freezer with fish. Monte doesn't care for the time commitment of fishing unless it is pike or muskies, but others give us fish. With all this going into a freezer besides our chickens and turkeys, and fruits and vegetables, it's often hard to find room for the extra breads Heather and I bake. As a result, we have three freezers.

Where we live, we are "different." There are old ranches about, but the majority of people are professionals, husbands and wives, who commute to Denver. So we are living somewhat of a country life in the midst of suburbia. The closest to country living most subdivisions allow is horses. So our choice in living this way is not because we are surrounded by it. We live in a very fast paced, materialistic, high divorce rate community. The small scale animal husbandry we do has been good for the children to see the cycle of nature. Our kids no longer fret over certain chickens being butchered. They've learned that new ones are born each year and names just get recycled. I think we're on Rocky VII now.

If you don't garden, you can get bulk produce through the farmers at produce stands and markets. I still need to get most of my produce this way. It's fulfilling to hear the canning jar lids go "ping" when sealing, and see the pretty jars on the shelves. Better than wallpaper any day. It's nice to know the fruits and vegetables were at their peak flavor when put up, and it's wonderful to have them handy all winter. If you've not preserved before, evaluate your family's eating habits, and your typical recipes and their ingredients. Think about what you regularly buy within the center isles of the grocery store. Maybe these items are the best starting place. You don't want to put up something that your family never eats or likes.

Begin with the basics and maybe the simplest. I began canning jams. We still make cooked jams but the family prefers some fruit as freezer jam - very fresh! Heather makes these now. Usually strawberry, raspberry and blackberry. This year's new jam was jalapeño. I am going to give some as Christmas basket gifts along with homemade mustard, herb vinegar, knitted washcloth, crocheted kitchen scrubby and soap. Dehydrated vegetables and fruits and their leathers, and herbs are an easy beginning, too. Next I began canning whole or halved fruit. I do everything the easiest way. All canning books say to peel fruits. I've been canning peaches, pears, apricots, and apples with their skins on for almost twenty years and we're all still alive. I never pit cherries when canning, but I do pit for drying or freezing. I never freeze in syrups. I do put them in a bowl of water with lemon juice, citric acid or whatever prevents browning while working with the fruit. Just drain and bag, usually in pie quantities whether it's used for that or not. Many fruits go into cobblers, cakes, muffins, shakes or at the breakfast table still partially frozen. If grapes are cheap at the store, I'll buy extra, freeze on cookie sheets, and bag in ziploc bags. Kids like these "mini popsicles" for snacks. In canning fruits I make a very light sugar syrup - 1 1/4 cups sugar to 10 1/2 cups water. I've always water bathed, but this year bought a pressure canner and am having fun and will probably never water bath again. I did turn my first pressure canned batch of pears to mush though, and learned real fast the impact of just minutes when under pressure. Now I want to can varieties of the dried beans to have handy on the shelf. Another easy beginner is stewed tomatoes, but do cook these down some. I can still see those first year's jars with a few inches of water on the bottom and floating tomato chunks. Now I make tomato sauce as well. With a machine operated berry press, another Bosch attachment, I simply quarter the tomatoes and run them through. The skin and seeds are separated and I get all the pulp. This of course needs to cook down too. A huge roaster/cooker will hold about a bushel of pureed tomatoes for cooking down. Frozen corn was an early first for us. We go directly to the farmer or from a market knowing that it was picked that morning. Most corn turns to starch within the first twenty-four hours, so I never buy it in the store! All the best cobs go immediately into ziplock bags and into

laid-out book *The Busy Person's Guide to Preserving Food* by Janet Chadwick. It's similar to the way I might have laid it out. Not only does it cover each food step-by-step for freezing, drying, and canning, but root cellar storage as well, and includes easy reference charts. My canning has to be adjusted for living at 8,000 feet where water boils around 196° rather than the sea level 212°. This affects canning very much, but not so much with the regular cooking and baking, other than things taking longer to boil. Water bath canning for most fruits is 20 minutes at sea level. For me it takes 46 minutes! The other thing that keeps me from giving canning recipes is the possibility of something

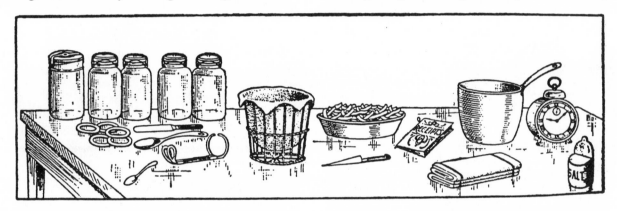

the freezer. I never blanch these. I now leave the husks on for microwave cooking. So much flavor is added with the husks still intact. We also love to soak some in water and grill with the husks on. The imperfect cobs can have the kernels cut off. I have a cob scraper, though cutting over a big bowl with the cob resting on an inverted little bowl in the middle of the big bowl works. Broccoli and green beans need to be blanched before freezing. I found out the "tough" way with a year's worth of tough string beans. Pickles are good for beginners, also.

I've been asked to go into canning in more detail. It is a scary thought. I had no one to show me. I learned from reading books. Ball and Kerr, the canning jar companies, have excellent canning books. My first books were Carla Emery's *An Old Fashioned Recipe Book* and Better Homes and Gardens' *Home Canning Cook Book*. I recently purchased a very well-

going wrong. I would feel responsible because this is much more serious than just having bread flops.

Root cellaring is another fun project that I am still having to learn and improve upon. When we moved to cool Colorado I purchased a great book on root cellaring and was intrigued. It was another "growing in awe of God" step. Many plants do not produce seed until their second year and these usually winter well either left in the ground or in a cold cellar. We don't grow enough for storage but get it from the farmers and markets. We usually take a one-day trip in the fall and pick up everything. A farmer allows us to glean the fields for carrots, onions and cabbage. We stop by a produce stand at another farm and pick up 300 pounds of potatoes, a couple bushels of roasted green chilies (which we freeze), bushels of beets, winter squash, broccoli, tomatoes, and whatever tantalizes us at the moment. The vehicle is packed and smells quite earthy. I get 20-40 pound boxes of fruit from another lady who brings it over from the western slopes of Colorado. Most of the root crops, squash, cabbage and apples will last in the cellar for months. My mom goes to Arizona and brings back boxes of lemons, oranges, and grapefruit after Christmas and these usually last till summer. The cellar also stores bulk maple syrup, molasses, and thirty-five pounds each of olive and canola oils. Monte's family in Wisconsin makes the maple syrup and some years we've gone back to help. I've tried my hand at beekeeping, but at this season of life have chosen to buy fifty-pound buckets of honey which I distribute into jars. I know how to beekeep if ever we want to start up again. We've had bears destroy hives two different years.

Ordering food through co-ops is another great addition to bringing in the harvest. On top of the other mentioned foods, I like to have bulk nuts, cheese, cider vinegar, powdered milk, pastas, herbs and spices, grains and beans on hand. Buying pre-prepared foods is not cost effective, but there are a few regulars I keep in stock such as a few basic cold cereals, tortillas, pesto sauce and occasionally drinks (in the summer), all by the case. Sometimes some of us gals will split cases. This can be fun when wanting to try some new things. Here again, think through your basic ingredients used in making most anything.

If you've not done anything along this line, do not be overwhelmed, but inspired! I did not do it all at once. As a few were mastered, each year I'd try something new. It's been a twenty-year progression. It's not overwhelming at all now to pull out the various supplies and jump in. When we lived in apartments and rentals we lived this way, though on a smaller scale. Remember what I said elsewhere about not waiting for the perfect environment. Maybe we have to be faithful and creative with what we hold in our hands now before we will be entrusted with more.

146

*Monte said I need to explain to you what I mean by saddle slump. Our house is built on a saddle which is a low ridge between two hills. It is also a divide between Bear Creek and Turkey Creek watersheds. Two contrasting micro-climates lie on either side of the saddle. The north slope is alpine with thick rich soil, aspen, blue spruce, douglas fir, mountain maple, springs and deep lush vegetation and snow that stays all winter. On the south slope is high desert/alpine with thin gravelly soil, ponderosa pine, juniper, ball cactus, open meadows, short grass and snow that melts a day or two after it falls. There are more than 200 wildflowers sprinkled throughout the two micro-climates.

The word slump has an interesting history. Monte is a geologist and of course used all his knowl-edge and experience when we positioned the house. It sits on the western shoulder of the saddle so we get east and south sun and are sheltered from the prevailing west wind coming off the mountains. Anyway, there was this flat area — perfect for our house. After a lot of excavation, blasting, and 35 caissons, an embar-rassed geologist (Monte), said we are "building our house on a slump." Apparently a long time ago (hundreds of years?) there was a forest fire in the area. When you dig you can find old charcoal. This was probably followed by heavy snow and/or rain. The back of our house is blasted into bedrock and the front sits on 20' caissons (underground concrete pillars). We built on a bedrock cliff that was the site of a mud slump. The slumping mud moved along a spoon-shaped flat fault about 100' down the bedrock slope and created the flat area. It is really an ideal place for a house once you fasten it to the bedrock — and ours is certainly fastened.

O senseless man, who cannot make a worm, and yet makes gods by dozens.
Montaigne

I can see . . . in what you call the dark, but which to me is golden.
I can see a God-made world, not a man-made world.
Helen Keller

Tell a man there are 300 billion stars in the universe and he'll believe you.
Tell him a bench has wet paint on it and he'll have to touch to be sure.
Jaeger

There is something reassuring and fulfilling about being able to supply yourself with a necessity. Making things for yourself nourishes a more personal and reciprocal relationship between you and the objects around you. Soap can be one of these things. It is made of just two ingredients - fat and lye. Separately these possess dubious reputations, yet combined can make something as noble as soap. Soapmaking requires the learning of a technique or a craft skill. It can be messy, but often things worth doing involve some mess. Fat, lye and water are mixed together at the temperature most favorable for initiating the reaction called saponification. Combined these ingredients turn into a new product, soap and glycerin. In manufactured soap, most of the glycerin is extracted and used in other products such as lotion. Homemade soap retains its natural soothing glycerin. In our dry Colorado climate, many people suffer from dry skin. Homemade soap really helps this condition. The following soap recipes produce excellent quality soap, fine to use on your skin. They are a higher quality than the soaps made in the old days with just grease and wood ash lye. Our bachelor neighbor laughed at soap making — picturing me as Granny from the Beverly Hillbillies. I read in a story book that a barrel of ashes and twelve pounds of hog fat made forty pounds of soap - enough for a year! It was also used for laundry soap. If one moved into a new area they often received soap as gifts since they would not yet have the ingredients to make their own.

The best soaps call for rendered beef fat or tallow. Better yet, suet. Suet is the prime fat. Rather than wait until you stockpile suet you can mix in the muscle fat. Suet may also have an expense, the other being free. I prefer the beef fat soaps and don't mind the rendering process. If you don't want to be bothered with this step you can just buy pre-packaged lard or use Crisco. Lard soap does require scents because it develops a bacon smell. Shortening soaps are harder to saponify, taking more time and usually remain softer. Coconut oil is cheapest through a co-op or from a bakery supplier. Don't expect it to look like oil. It looks more like shortening. Coconut oil provides lather, and is a bit drying to the skin, but still not as much as commercial.

Lye is a constant ingredient in all soaps. It's available among the cleaning supplies in most stores. Read the ingredients because not all drain cleaners are 100% lye. It comes in thirteen-ounce containers which are usually red, white, and blue. It's also referred to as caustic soda. If used with care, it should create no problem. If a bit gets on your skin you will feel a burning, stinging, or itching. Rinse under cold water or with vinegar or lemon juice. In the few years I've made soap, and done it with many people in a class setting, I've never had any severe problems. Do keep it away from children. Sometimes Monte comes in and has me wear safety glasses. All this is just to familiarize you with the cautions and read the label.

Certain equipment is required for making soap. The following recipes use a scale to weigh the ingredients. There are books that have you measure, but I don't like scooping clean the measuring cups, so I prefer weighing. The lye solution is best prepared in a forty-ounce juice jar or five-pound honey jar. This jar will be subject to high and low temperature fluctuations. You'll need its lid as well. The lid needs two holes punched in it on two opposite sides. When pouring the lye you want a steady stream of liquid, somewhat narrower than the

 size of a pencil or straw. You need an enamel or stainless steel pot in which to melt the fats and make the soap. Use a wooden or stainless steel spoon for stirring as other materials corrode. Thermometers are needed to check the temperatures of the lye solution and the fats. It's best to use two thermometers, but one will work. It needs to go down to 90 degrees. The initial lye reaction gives off almost 200 degrees so keep some thermometers away from this until it cools. Rubber gloves and an apron are helpful during the process. Rubber gloves are necessary when cutting and shaping the soap. The mold I use is a department store sweater-size box. Line this with a plastic garbage bag stapled around the upper edges. The last equipment needed will be a flat cardboard cover and a blanket or two on top to keep the soap warm.

To render fat, cut it in chunks or put through a meat grinder. In a big pot put a quart of water and two tablespoons of salt. Dump in the fat and bring to a boil; simmer with lid ajar. Stir occasionally. The process takes about four hours. Four hours gives plenty of usable fat, but cooking longer gives you more. Figure on rendering at least twice as much fat as you need. Strain off the liquid into another container and discard the gushy fat pieces called cracklings. Let the fat cool. Soap is usually a fall project for me and placing it outside (often in snow) overnight solidifies it nicely. Three layers will form: solidified tallow on top, water on the bottom and an intermediary gray and granular layer. Dislodge the fat and scrape clean. Rendered fat can remain refrigerated for two months and frozen indefinitely.

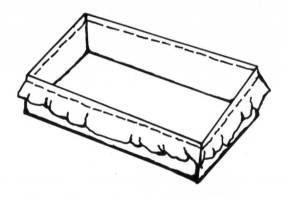

Castile Soap

26 oz olive oil
60 oz tallow

_____

11 oz lye
32 oz water

Copra-Olive Oil Soap

24 oz olive oil
24 oz coconut oil
38 oz tallow

_____

12 oz lye
32 oz water

Palma-Christi Soap

9 oz castor oil
22 oz olive oil
22 oz coconut oil
32 oz lard

_____

11 1/2 oz lye
32 oz water

Vegetable Soap

44 oz olive oil
17 oz coconut oil
24 oz Crisco or any other
    vegetable shortening

_____

10 3/4 oz lye
32 oz water

To make the lye solution, first weigh your jar. Then pour in the correct amount of lye. Slowly add the right weight of water. Remember, this is NOT fluid ounces but ounces by weight! Once measured, remove from scale (be careful, it is hot) and stir using the handle of a wooden spoon until the lye is dissolved (lye not spoon handle - just joking!). Do not let it settle. You can make this up the day before and let it cool. It is easier to bring it up to 95-98° than to bring it down from 200°.

Melt the fats in the soap-making pot over low heat. When three-fourths of the solid fats have melted, remove the pot from the heat and stir occasionally to help finish the melting. When all the fats are melted, fill a sink with cold water and set the pot in it. Immerse a thermometer in the middle of the fats and don't rest it on the bottom of the pot. When the fats read around 105 degrees, fill a basin with hot water and place the lye solution bottle in the hot water with its thermometer. The lye will heat up quickly. Keep juggling the containers and water until they both reach the same temp between 95° and 98°. Cap your lye with its punched holes and have it at hand. (Monte says put on safety glasses!) Start stirring the fats with the wooden spoon. The fats should be in motion before pouring the lye and kept in motion while pouring. You don't need to beat it, just keep the contents moving so the lye will contact and react with as much oily matter as possible. I don't always have, or keep the pan in cold water, but usually do make it in the sink. After it's well mixed I let it sit on the counter, and stir every five to ten minutes. The mixture is ready to pour into your mold when dripped from the spoon it traces across the surface or leaves a trail. It may take from thirty minutes to an hour and a half or even longer before this happens. It depends on which recipe is used. The tallow recipes set up quickly, especially if it was a good quality fat. If it does not appear to be thickening and you can stir no longer, pour it into the mold. I have the box mold sitting on the floor out of the way. Put on its lid and cover with a blanket or two. For the continuing chemical reaction, it's important to let the soap cool slowly.

151

Remove the soap from the mold twenty-four hours later, unless it was a batch that didn't seem to want to trace. Give it another day. Dump it out of the box, peeling away the plastic and save the box for future batches. My table is covered with a plastic table cloth and I wear rubber gloves. Cut it into bars or shapes. The regular soap bars are for our use. For gift giving I usually cut half the slab into shapes with well-made stainless steel cookie cutters and roll the scrap pieces into balls. My favorite shapes are hearts and cowboy boots. This is where the choice of container is important since most cookie cutters are about 1/2" deep. Stack the soap pieces with spaces for air circulation on a rack (mine are stainless steel; I don't know if it makes a difference) for at least two weeks, three to four is even better. The chemical reaction is completed during this time. Aging gives the soap a chance to incorporate any free caustic lye that might be left in your soap, otherwise it will be raw.

Soap embellishments are numerous. Try some after you become confident with soap making. Most additions are added just before pouring into the mold. I usually add a mixture of one ounce each of powdered milk and honey. You can introduce special properties into your soap by making a strong tea of whatever herb, spice, fruit or vegetable and use it to replace part of the water used to dissolve the lye. For scents, use pure oil essences. Try adding 1/2 to 3/4 ounce to the batch, just before pouring into the mold. Natural colorings can also be added. Some teas added to the lye will color the soap. Be forewarned that any substance added directly to lye will have to fight for its life. Natural substances for coloring I've tried and like are cinnamon, turmeric and paprika. Mix a bit of the soap into a tablespoon or ounce of the powder to avoid clumping, then stir back into the batch. I'm going to try adding a teaspoon of candle wax. Liquid bluing works also. We tried marbleizing it, at first it was blue, but before our eyes slowly turned brown. Remember not to add any liquid in large amounts or it will affect the hardening time. If the molds are too small they will cool too quickly which can stop the reaction and result in separation. Liquid soap or soap jelly can be made from soap pieces or shavings: 2 oz shavings to 1 pint boiling water. Keep this in closed container to prevent drying out.

Laundry soap can be produced from these soaps. I read somewhere that the homemade soap does not brighten clothes. Maybe it's just the old style made with wood ash lye. I've not tried using it for laundry soap. If you so desire, it needs to be grated. At this point it could be mixed with some borax. I have found a substitute for laundry though. When taking a quilting class the teacher, who's written quilting books, recommended that fine materials be washed in Orvus WA Paste, a horse soap, because of its non-abrasiveness. The colors remain true without fading. One class member said she uses it for all her laundry. She attributes an almost total remission of her asthma to the use of this paste. Since the class, I've met someone else who said the same thing. Orvus is sodium lauryl sulfate, the most commonly used ingredient in all our soaps and shampoos. Everything else is an additive. If additives are not good for fine materials what about our clothes? What residues are left behind to cause possible allergies? I used it for one year. I stopped last summer when we had so much company and thought they wouldn't appreciate the lack of ease. Orvus is solid when cool, but mixed with warm water in a jar, 1 Tb of it will wash a whole load of laundry. If you have hard water, you may need a bit more. Just check for sudsing when the washer has agitated awhile. Also, it is said that we need to use softeners because of the harshness of additives. I stopped using dryer softeners. Only polyester seems to have problems with static. I'm about to make laundry soap and will tell of it in my next book!

A soap book has just been published that really excites me: *The Complete Soapmaker; Tips, Techniques & Recipes for Luxurious Handmade Soaps*, by Norma Coney. It has similar basic soap recipes to what I've given you but takes them a step further. By making the simple basic soap, the chemical properties of the lye change. She then takes smaller portions and melts them, to which you can then add all sorts of goodies - and her varieties are quite numerous - none of which have to fight for their life with the lye, and can be beautiful colors and shapes.

The hearth is the heart of the home . . . the Victorians were people who had lost the sense of the sacredness of the home. They still believed in the respectability of the home; but that is only another way of saying that they wanted to be respected by other people for reverencing what they did not really reverence . . . They did sometimes quote Horace or Virgil about hearth and altar; but there was never any flame upon their altar . . . the generation in revolt fled from a cold hearth . . .

. . . but a family will really do without rules exactly in proportion as it is a successful family . . .

. . . in order that life should be a story of romance to us, it is necessary that a great part of it, should be settled for us without our permission. If we wish life to be a system, this may be a nuisance; but if we wish it to be a drama, it is an essential. . . A man has control over enough things in his life to be the hero of a novel. But if he had control over everything, there would be so much hero that there would be no novel. And the reason why the lives of the rich are at bottom so tame and uneventful is simply that they can choose the events. They are dull because they are omnipotent. They fail to feel the adventures because they can make the adventures. The thing which keeps life romantic and full of fiery possibilities is the existence of these great plain limitations which force all of us to meet the things we do not like or do not expect . . . To be in a romance is to be in uncongenial surroundings . . .

. . . our fathers, believed in the links of kinship and also in the links of logic. Today our logic consists mostly of missing links; and our family largely of absent members . . .

Today there are fewer places to discover, and the real adventure is to stay home.

GK Chesterton
"Brave New Family"

The real voyage of discovery consists not in seeking new landscapes but in having new eyes.
Marcel Proust

Chapter Twelve
RECIPES FOR LIFE

I feel a soliloquy coming on.

I invite you to pick up your favorite beverage, pull up a chair in a cozy spot and join me in a moment of leisure. Let's sip, ponder and muse.

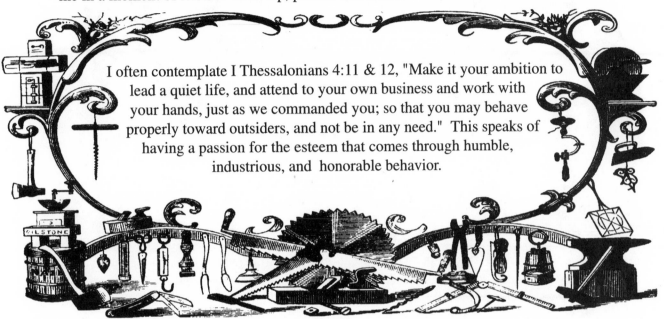

I often contemplate I Thessalonians 4:11 & 12, "Make it your ambition to lead a quiet life, and attend to your own business and work with your hands, just as we commanded you; so that you may behave properly toward outsiders, and not be in any need." This speaks of having a passion for the esteem that comes through humble, industrious, and honorable behavior.

What did Paul mean by a quiet life when he penned this passage long ago? Many are drawn to certain eras of time such as early American country, or Victorian eras. (I'm not drawn to art deco, maybe it's just me, or then again is it the worldview art deco grew out of?) I think of all the past eras as being quiet. And yet Paul in the New Testament is instructing *them* to lead a quiet life. Progress has provided unprecedented affluence, education, technology, and entertainment. We have comforts and conveniences our ancestors could only dream about. If we enjoy so much more material abundance and access to knowledge than our ancestors, why are we not more content and fulfilled? The gentle flow of history has become a flood. Are we playing a different game, by different rules, on a different stage than any other people in the history of the world; "Little House on the Freeway?" Much of the past can be graphically illustrated by an almost horizontal gradual upward line as life slowly unfolded. Life in this century is happening very quickly, and can be pictured as an all-of-a-sudden up-curving line looking like a "J." Physically and mentally we can't keep up. Will this exponential progress continue without a respite? Are we in a transition? If so, to what? Is progress the bad guy? What constitutes progress or success? Good things may be consuming the best things. Maybe in all eras when people turn their backs on God, they cover the emptiness by busily filling their lives. Can we redeem ourselves through our own activity? Maybe we need to begin measuring life by virtue rather than love of money, humility rather than intellectualism, meekness rather than power. Progress has not helped nurture and protect the right relationships: for ourselves, others and God. When I feel nostalgic or pining for a romanticized past, what I'm really longing for is tradition, community, and relationship.

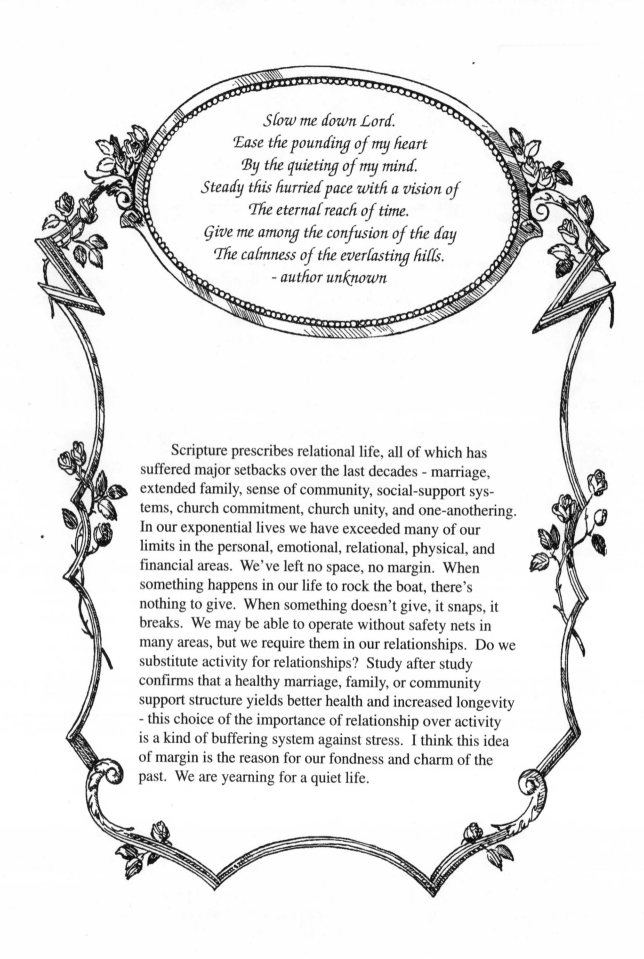

Slow me down Lord.
Ease the pounding of my heart
By the quieting of my mind.
Steady this hurried pace with a vision of
The eternal reach of time.
Give me among the confusion of the day
The calmness of the everlasting hills.
- author unknown

Scripture prescribes relational life, all of which has suffered major setbacks over the last decades - marriage, extended family, sense of community, social-support systems, church commitment, church unity, and one-anothering. In our exponential lives we have exceeded many of our limits in the personal, emotional, relational, physical, and financial areas. We've left no space, no margin. When something happens in our life to rock the boat, there's nothing to give. When something doesn't give, it snaps, it breaks. We may be able to operate without safety nets in many areas, but we require them in our relationships. Do we substitute activity for relationships? Study after study confirms that a healthy marriage, family, or community support structure yields better health and increased longevity - this choice of the importance of relationship over activity is a kind of buffering system against stress. I think this idea of margin is the reason for our fondness and charm of the past. We are yearning for a quiet life.

THOSE WERE THE BEST DAYS

Her work seems to never end, and lately her days run together.
But she knows the page she'll write tonight, will last forever.
She listens for the little boy, who'll soon stand at her knee,
Holding up his story book he'll say, "Mommie will you read to me."

Another day nearly done, he can settle down and read the news.
But then a sweet voice whispers his name, "Daddy, can I read with you."
He puts down his evening paper and draws his treasure near.
With his arm around his little girl, it all becomes perfectly clear.

A home's not a big house on a hill, its not a picture in a magazine.
It's not two strangers with their kids, watchin' strangers on TV.
'Cause homes are built on dreams we share,
And homes are held together with bedtime prayers,
And that old-fashion family love.
And knowin' that Jesus cares.
Mostly knowin' that Jesus cares.

Mamma teaches to the heart, and she's a model of hope and love.
Daddy protects his family with strength from the Lord above.
They know the house will soon be still, then they'll look back with smiles and say,
"Of all the times we spent on earth those were the best days."

A home's not a big house on a hill, its not a picture in a magazine.
It's not two strangers with their kids, watchin' strangers on TV.
'Cause homes are built on dreams we share,
And homes are held together with bedtime prayers,
And that old-fashion family love.
And knowin' that Jesus cares.
Mostly knowin' that Jesus cares.

by Monte Swan, 1991

Life can be fragile. Humans are beautiful but vulnerable, like breakable, lovely, china cups. Yet at the same time we are strong and resilient. Unlike teacups, humans can heal and grow and move beyond disaster. We can reach out to one another in courage and comfort. So what must we do? Pick up the pieces! Have another cup of tea.

"If you are cold, tea will warm you; if you are too heated, it will cool you; if you are depressed, it will cheer you; if you are exhausted, it will calm you."
- William Gladstone

Serenity. Drive by the fast-food window and collect a full foam cup; or zap one in the microwave. Must we always insist upon the instant?! Fast food restaurants and overnight delivery. We expect solutions to problems in thirty minutes. Someone has said, "I believe with all my heart that human beings crave ritual and ceremony (and loveliness) in our lives." People in our society don't like to wait, but you simply cannot hurry a good pot of tea. Preparing and enjoying tea is a ritual, a "ceremony of loveliness." There is nothing in a cup of tea that cannot be found in a cup of coffee or even a cup of cold water served with the right attitude. Tea takes time. Monte and an English geologist worked together on a project. Come mid-afternoon, no matter where (usually out in the middle of the desert), the Englishman would stop for tea. It seemed he lived above the mechanics of life. Monte felt something transcendent in the ritual. The act of making and drinking tea forces us to slow down. Put the kettle on. Wait for the water to boil. Now, things to prepare — pretty things: cups, plates, possibly even doilies, cloth napkins and tablecloth. Maybe some scones. None of these things are necessary, yet its a good part of the ritual, a tradition. Habits, rituals and customs comfort us deep in our spirits. It's like coming home. An old ritual gaining popularity is the use of fountain pens - writing with real ink. Drawing the ink from a bottle, preparing and doodling with the pen, and letting it dry, can be satisfying. Children delight in traditions. I used to have tea parties with my kids when they were younger. Remembering this, I bought two small cups at a thrift store, just for Dawson and me, to carry on the tradition. Dawson informed me he hates tea, but he loves the tradition of the teapot and a special little cup for him. Rituals perform a valuable function of occupying the body and the senses while freeing the mind and spirit. As tea steeps, carry the tray to a comfortable nook and wait in peace. If with friends, maybe even children, this is an excellent time for good conversations. If alone - read, think, or pray. Still more waiting - the boiling liquid must settle into a comfortable warmth, and then, slowly sip. As you sip, your mind can settle out of its habitual rush. Your relationships - even with yourself - are granted space for a leisurely stretch. Enjoying a cup of tea is an island of calm you can easily visit in the course of your busiest day. It's like stopping and smelling the roses. Quietly and without a threat, it calls us out of ourselves and into relationship.

- some phrases from *If Teacups Could Talk*

OLD TRAILS

Old trails that lead to yesterday.
We walk them in our minds.
There's a message in the memories,
That we've tried to find.

Faded photos of our families.
We read it in their eyes.
And hear a melody, that used to be,
The music in our lives.
The music in our lives.

What are the good old days?
What do they mean?
What have we lost?
Lord, what have we gained?
Nostalgic days gone by.
We dream and think we can.
But do we yearn for what we'll never have?
Or do we hold it in our hands?

We decorate Victorian,
Like pictures in magazines.
We've moved out to the country,
Where the air is always clean.

New recipes for the quiet life.
On a porch swing built for two.
Trying to travel back to another time,
When a handshake would do.
A handshake would do.

What are the good old days?
What do they mean?
What have we lost?
Lord, what have we gained?
Nostalgic days gone by.
We dream and think we can.
But do we yearn for what we'll never have?
Or do we hold it in our hands?

by Monte Swan, 1996

159

We do desire domestic order in the chaos of life. When we move to a new house, filling the rooms with our furniture and belongings, we may decorate the various rooms to magazine picture perfection. In decorating, do we expect to create the atmosphere we imagine? When does a house become a home? Monte and I have "lived" in a lot of places (geology travel even includes our vehicle as "home") and I often say "Home is where my heart is; where my family is." Some transitions move smoothly. Some are a major upheaval, usually emotionally. In a new place, walls and rooms are empty. Empty of memories. The richness of experiences permeate the rooms of a lived-in house. Invite people over and begin new memories with fun and conversation. The bottom line is making relationships important. Curl up and read books together. Put together puzzles; play games. And what about the children's rooms? I notice kids tend to drag all the toys out and play underfoot. Maybe their walls are devoid of lived-in memories. I began folding laundry in their rooms, reading, writing, drawing and coloring, sipping a warm beverage . . . anything to simply be there. For a house to become a home it needs joy and grief, laughter and tears, birth and death, life lived to the utmost. Relax in the deep rhythm.

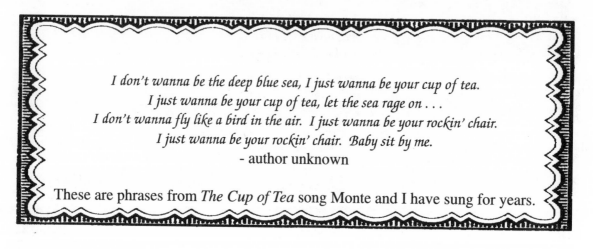

> *I don't wanna be the deep blue sea, I just wanna be your cup of tea.*
> *I just wanna be your cup of tea, let the sea rage on . . .*
> *I don't wanna fly like a bird in the air. I just wanna be your rockin' chair.*
> *I just wanna be your rockin' chair. Baby sit by me.*
> - author unknown
>
> These are phrases from *The Cup of Tea* song Monte and I have sung for years.

Activity has replaced relationships; busyness has replaced intimacy. In the transitoriness of life we can find refuge in the unchangeableness of God. We can turn from being passive objects in a social world that devalues us to being active with God in a new community of love. We are made for a relationship with God, and nothing else can substitute. Quiet living does not mean being a spectator. It can free us, to work from grace, not anxiety. God is. God exists. God is doing things. We can enter into a life with God already in motion. We need to take the time to observe, contemplate and respond to God. "Doing" or busyness can get in the way. Relationship is the fundamental element of life. Just as people choose to live in the rat race, we can choose relationship with God. Over intellectualizing the process can move us away from relationship. The One who calls us into relationship with Himself calls us into a relationship with family, with our children. The family is the oldest and most basic of institutions. Throughout the Bible we see the family as a spiritual unit. We can be in a home ordered by a Father, Son, and Holy Spirit. The trinity is the true metaphor for family. This is relational wholeness.

> *The best way to keep children home is to make the home a pleasant atmosphere - and let the air out of the tires.*
> - Dorothy Parker

God's plan for marriage and families is unsurpassed, and in our society it has been ignored and distorted. Almost everything good can be abused, but that doesn't make the original any less good. God has designed an authentic career for wives and mothers. A pastor's wife, Joy Olender, puts it this way: "The job of wife and mother is a distinctive career, unsurpassed in challenges and advantages. It is emotionally, psychologically and physically demanding. It requires patience, persistence and personal confidence, as well as a noble character, integrity and the ability to love without thought of personal gain. In addition, it requires decision-making and risk-taking and provides the thrill of enduring fulfillment. It is the pursuit of excellence and provides lasting and irreplaceable reward. It is precisely a *real* job!"

WHO WILL BRING THE CHILDREN

Lord restore this mother's heart, make it tender toward her children.
I lay it bruised and broken at Your holy feet.
While my heart is in Your keeping, won't You let me borrow Yours?
Let the children's eyes see Jesus' love in me.

Oh, the world says success never stays at home.
And it's only found in offices and telephones.
Oh, but who will guide the tiny feet,
That can't find their way alone?
Tell me who will bring the children to Your throne?

I come home tired and empty, worn down by the daily grind,
It takes everything I've got just doin' all I can.
When my children run to daddy's arms, won't You let me be the one,
To show the Father's heart of love within a man.

Oh, the world says success never stays at home.
And it's only found in offices and telephones.
Oh, but who will guide the tiny feet,
That can't find their way alone?
Tell me who will bring the children to Your throne?

Bring them to the Father, lead them one by one.
Let the Holy Spirit, draw them through the son.
Show them that He loves them, help them understand.
Bring them to the Father, reaching out Your hand.

Oh, the world says success never stays at home.
And it's only found in offices and telephones.
Oh, but who will guide the tiny feet,
That can't find their way alone?
Tell me who will bring the children to Your throne?

by Kelly Willard and Duncan & Janene MacIvor
(Monte and I sing this song on our album)

Live in such a way
as to intrigue.

I am so thankful for Monte. Thankful for his love and his need for relationship. In our home, I'm actually the one who needs to be more sensitive to the relational needs of *my* husband. He has so many passions and I tend to dump ice water on his fires. Many of my galfriends, we're a group called the Pink Ladies, get together regularly. Sometimes I go and sometimes not. I boldly told them my really best friend is Monte and when something is in conflict, I prefer to be with him. He likes me to be with others too, recognizing girls enjoy girl talk. I seem to enjoy it now, but when a teen, I preferred the guy talk better. I like talking ideas and guys tend to do that more than gals.

Monte and I often go to bed reading books. We drag books to the bathroom and all over the house. We wake with fascinating first words of the morning that carry to the breakfast table and beyond. Sometimes it leaves the kids looking at one another wondering what in the world are we talking about! Both of us have numerous books we're in the midst of. We're growing and streeeeetching during this particular window of time. Everybody has their own windows and timings! It's exciting to think of the rest of our lives and all there is to learn, observe, and contemplate.

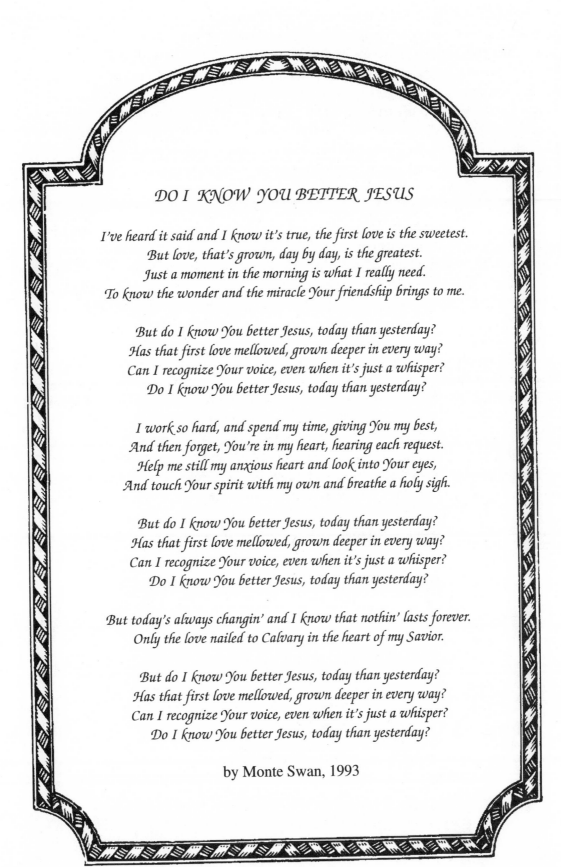

DO I KNOW YOU BETTER JESUS

I've heard it said and I know it's true, the first love is the sweetest.
But love, that's grown, day by day, is the greatest.
Just a moment in the morning is what I really need.
To know the wonder and the miracle Your friendship brings to me.

But do I know You better Jesus, today than yesterday?
Has that first love mellowed, grown deeper in every way?
Can I recognize Your voice, even when it's just a whisper?
Do I know You better Jesus, today than yesterday?

I work so hard, and spend my time, giving You my best,
And then forget, You're in my heart, hearing each request.
Help me still my anxious heart and look into Your eyes,
And touch Your spirit with my own and breathe a holy sigh.

But do I know You better Jesus, today than yesterday?
Has that first love mellowed, grown deeper in every way?
Can I recognize Your voice, even when it's just a whisper?
Do I know You better Jesus, today than yesterday?

But today's always changin' and I know that nothin' lasts forever.
Only the love nailed to Calvary in the heart of my Savior.

But do I know You better Jesus, today than yesterday?
Has that first love mellowed, grown deeper in every way?
Can I recognize Your voice, even when it's just a whisper?
Do I know You better Jesus, today than yesterday?

by Monte Swan, 1993

Monte and I get stimulated from the most prodigious things sometimes. Recently at an out-of-state homeschool conference our thoughts were stimulated concerning external versus internal control. Many speakers and authors are instructing parents on the importance of external control of children. I had pretty much tuned out the speaker that weekend until he started talking about his homeschooled son rebelling. He was 26 and flipping hamburgers as a profession while living in his car. Then, like the prodigal son, he returned. Sounded like a rebellious, non-self-governed son. I believe kids don't need to rebel to "find themselves," or to internalize values. In this day and age, a time period of rebellion seems expected and natural. But is it necessary? What is self? Can we give ourselves a self? This is not a do-it-yourself-*is*-ness.

Once pregnant with my firstborn, I began reading every child-rearing book I got my hands on. I was ready to crush a childish will and let him know who's boss. I began to realize that these babies have personalities. They are persons. Monte and I are naturally optimistic people. We recognize and are drawn to goodness in people and things. It went against our grain to be looking for and focusing on the bad. I thought of the many kids who grow up delinquent - I'm sure out of neglect - but, the attention they were craving probably only came when they did bad. That attention may encourage them to continue down the wrong road. They only want to be noticed. We have a cute story - "There's no such thing as a dragon." So everyone ignored the dragon and he grew bigger and bigger, eventually taking over the house. No matter if he ate all Billy's pancakes and Mom had to lift a tail or something to clean. "There's no such thing as a dragon!" In the end Billy said, while petting the dragon from the upstairs window, "But there *is* a dragon." The dragon began to shrink and returned to cat size. Mom said, "It's not so bad this size. Why did it have to get so big?" Billy said, "I guess it just wanted to be noticed." Children literally don't know which way to go until we reinforce one behavior or another.

This saying used to hang in our house when I was a youth -

"If . . ."
If a child
lives with criticism,
He learns to condemn.
If a child lives with hostility,
He learns to fight.
If a child lives with ridicule,
He learns to be shy.
If a child lives with shame,
He learns to feel guilty.
If a child lives with tolerance,
He learns to be patient.
If a child lives with encouragement,
He learns confidence.

If a child lives with praise,
He learns to appreciate.
If a child lives with fairness,
He learns justice.
If a child lives with security,
He learns to have faith.
If a child lives with approval,
He learns to like himself.
If a child lives with acceptance and friendship,
He learns to find love in the world.
- Dorothy Law Nolte

What should our focus be? Some books have a little more positive focus. Charles Swindoll's *Knowing Your Child* affirms that there is a positive and a negative "bent" to every character trait. We must become students of our children, rather than thinking them an empty vessel that I must fill. They are people with feelings and desires, gifts and talents. In seeking to enter God's plan for my child, I sought to truly know my child. They are made in His image. The will is the power for deciding and determining what one does, and therefore what one is. Children have a mind, with wonderful capacity; a soul, with its wealth of feelings; and a spirit, the moral and religious nature - these are God-given to each of us. My desire is to inspire and guide my children's higher instincts and convictions. John Locke's 1693 *Some Thoughts Concerning Education* addresses this subject as well. As they chose good, I'd praise. We gave much praise when they took their first steps, said their first words, learned to use the toilet, tied their shoes, and rode a bike. As they get older too often we focus on every little misstep they take. Rather we decided to acknowledge and continue focusing on the good skills, behaviors, and attitudes. We almost ignored the bad behavior. I said almost. (I don't mean bad as in the sense of disobeying laws of nature and God's absolutes.) God does not dwell on our sins any more than we as parents should dwell on our children's wrongdoing. Yes, God is a God of justice, but his love and mercy show forth stronger throughout the Bible. His grace should be a strong model for us as we parent. What image of God will our children have as they grow and mature? Surely we begin heaven or hell here in our daily lives with our responses of fear, anger, or love. Surely we experience fear and anger, but we're not meant to remain stuck in them, but turn to God and move on. If I make the choice to do something, I'm more apt to do it and do it well. Thinking of my children as people, treating them with dignity and respect no matter what their age, I wanted to allow them to make choices. I began to believe that training was not telling, not teaching, not commanding, but something far better.

Trample not on any;
there may be some work of grace there,
that thou knowest not of.
The name of God may be written
upon that soul thou treadest on.
- Coleridge

Learning anything is not only telling a child what to do - but showing him, doing it together, modeling, and helping him follow through. This can develop good habits. We continue to praise good choices and soon they begin to do it from preference. Our initial training depended more on forming habits than inculcating rules. The good became the familiar and natural. Remember the saying "Be patient, God isn't finished with me yet."

In order to choose to do right, to make wise decisions, to think for themselves, which was and is our aim, children need to learn the habits connected with principles. If we tell them what to do all the time, how can they ever learn to think for themselves? Rather than "Don't touch." I might say, "I really like that vase, so please take care of it." The first command contains no principle. The second includes the principle of respect for people's property. I turned this around at times when they were little and talked with them about their property and asked which things meant a lot to them, and we talked about things they wanted to share versus things they may not really like to. No one can make a child obey unless he wills to do so. There is no education but self-education. To choose and will for himself what we will, and ultimately what God wills, leads the child onto liberty. Interesting paradox - obedience leading to liberty.

Tell me and I'll forget;
Show me and I may remember;
Involve me and I'll understand.
- Chinese proverb

Another paradox is found in loving our children. They must not be more important than the parents are to each other. The love we give them directly is secondary to the love and security they experience as they witness our love for each other. A close friend, Vicky Goodchild, asked and inspired Monte to write a song around this idea. The song came within minutes, really writing itself - and is one of our favorites.

WHAT THEY NEED EVEN MORE

It comes so naturally, sometimes we just don't see.
How to love the children, the way the Lord meant it to be.
They read between the lines, and they know when our stories rhyme.
They listen to the things we do, they're watchin' us all the time.

And they'll know that we love them, by the way that you love me.
And the way that I love you is what they want to see.
You can't buy it with silver, and words will never do.
All that really matters is, you lovin' me, me lovin' you.

And I'm their gallant knight, turning darkness into light.
And I'm their safe still harbor from the stormy seas at night.
But what they need even more, than just to know, we love them so.
Is for you and me, to let them see, our love for each other grow.

And they'll know that we love them, by the way that you love me.
And the way that I love you is what they want to see.
You can't buy it with silver, and words will never do.
All that really matters is, you lovin' me, me lovin' you.

by Monte Swan, 1992

Monte and I believe it is the heart that gains the heart. In our diligence to find access to their hearts, we believe if our heart and home is filled with God's love and words, our daily living will not be a hindrance but a help in leading their hearts heavenward. Like a courtship - we are romancing their hearts. It would not be set times and formal lectures but spontaneous burstings of the heart. There is a trust element here as well. By making our whole life an attractive example of God's truths, we need to wait for the Holy Spirit who alone can make God's words, and ours,

> *. . man looks to the outside, but the Lord looks at the heart.*
> *- I Samuel 16:7*

"sharp as a two-edged sword" and penetrate deep into the child's heart. When parents live visibly under authority, recognizing the supreme Authority to whom we are subject, children are quick to discern that they too must do the things they should.

> *Just as no one can ever really define love, children still know exactly what it means by how they see you live love - or any of the other gifts you want them to have . . .*

We have anticipated potential problems before they developed. When they were babies and toddlers we did this physically by baby-proofing the house. Monte wanted to pad every corner (I drew the line). Maybe we should be as proactive, or directive, in mental and emotional areas as in the physical. Proactive rather than reactive to more easily reach the heart. When a child is looking at something that they might break or hurt themselves with, we often react in the negative. I felt if I just watched over, asked questions, or even diverted them, their curiosity would be satisfied with no mishap. If we react in the negative they may focus on the "no-no." My mother found me hiding to light matches. I think she chose the right response in suggesting I light matches to my heart's content, but in the kitchen sink. I quickly learned that it was dangerous. Would I have stopped if my mom had simply said "it's dangerous and stay away from them"? With this approach we didn't have a lot of "no-no's." There are so many junctions in life. When we came to a fork in the road in dealing with our children, we had two choices: react angrily or shift our focus to moving forward? We can focus on solutions and what works, what's good in our children's lives, or focus on the problems. We tried to simplify life by making few hard choices. As good behavior continued we would introduce training grounds. We refer to this as preparation. As the child matures, making wise decisions, we broadened the training grounds allowing more prepara-

> *. . . The ability to make smart little choices inevitably leads children to trust themselves to make more important choices about the big issues in life, too.*
> *- Steven W. Vannoy*

tion for life, and lessening our protection. We feel children need to learn to ground themselves in absolutes and principles, and govern themselves internally, not from externalities. Solving conflicts need not be only a win-lose situation. When we continue to acknowledge, praise, and respect them as people, listening to their feelings - many problems resolve themselves. When we limit our telling and commanding, they don't tune us out and stop listening. They like to be a part of the solution.

We really feel our style of education, one of our lifestyle choices, is teaching to the heart. "Living" Books teach to the heart. Stories and modeling teach to the heart. No need for moralizing, sermonettes, and twaddle talk. What occurs in most home's training, when parents are convinced children cannot understand, is that many adults explain and paraphrase to their own heart's content but not the children's. Many believe a child's inborn curiosity for life is to be cultivated, nursed, coddled, and wooed by persuasion. Do we want to feed our children junk food, or natural, whole food for their mind? When we make good literature available as our educational foundation, it is nutritious and satisfying and we don't have to persuade or bribe our children to learn. If you think of it, most educating methodology is such drudgery that it requires more external controls. It degrades these young persons. As there is living food and lifeless food, there are living books and lifeless books. Lifeless books dwell on facts and details. Living books relate to real life, to experience. Children are real people who need to be engaged in real life. Spoon feeding all their lives is not really our mission.

DADDY TAKE ME BACK

Sometimes you'll find us rockin' in a rockin' chair,
Warmin' toes around a woodstove fire.
It really doesn't matter 'cause he doesn't care,
Just as long as we're both there.
Cause when his daddy tells a story, it's pure gold in his little boy's hand.
It touches his heart, and then the visions start, of daddy and his little man.

Daddy take me back, Daddy take me back,
Daddy tell me that story, the one that takes me back,
Daddy take me back, Daddy take me back,
To the days when you were just a boy, Daddy take me back.

So we traveled on back in my memories.
We got lost in boyhood dreams.
Baggy pants and a fishin' hole.
And carefree sunny days.
The child in me and my little boy, became the best of friends.
It's a treasure you see, for him and me, like a story that never ends.

Daddy take me back, Daddy take me back,
Daddy tell me that story, the one that takes me back,
Daddy take me back, Daddy take me back,
To the days when you were just a boy, Daddy take me back.

This old world offers fortune if you're willing to pay,
And if you're lucky it will give you fame.
I'd gladly trade it all for a sunny day,
With my little boy again.
If every single daddy, in the whole wide world could see,
The day it's all said and done, and their race is run,
What a different world this would be.

Daddy take me back, Daddy take me back,
Daddy tell me that story, the one that takes me back,
Daddy take me back, Daddy take me back,
To the days when you were just a boy, Daddy take me back.

by Monte Swan, 1994

169

Charlotte Mason believes that "children come into this world with many relations waiting to be established. Relations with places near and far, with the wide universe, with the past of history, with the present, with the earth they live on and all its offspring of beast and bird, plant, and tree, with their own country and other countries, and above all with that most majestic of human relationships — their relation to God." Where does all this come from? The child comes into this world with an appetite - appetite for wanting to know. Children respond best to knowledge conveyed in literary form. Our part is to feed this appetite with the best books possible, Living Books. Many books and textbooks are reduced to the driest statements of fact . . . almost to the point of starvation; edited till no life is left in them and nothing worth believing in. Actually, someone else had fun reading all the good books, extracted the data, and wrote the "dead" books. Education is an atmosphere. Education is life. "Life is sustained on that which is taken in, not by that which is applied from without," continues Charlotte Mason. "Education is a matter of the spirit," said Lord Haldane, yet we persist in applying training from without. The child is a life to nourish. The life of the mind is nourished by ideas. Our passion is to give our children the great ideas of life - of religion, history, and science. Facts need to be presented within their informing ideas. We can learn about body functions and sex from a textbook, but we can learn about love from *Romeo and Juliet*, I Corinthians 13, or better yet, Gene Stratton Porter's *The Harvester*. "Let information hang upon a principle and be inspired by ideas. The mind is capable of dealing with only one kind of food; it lives, grows, and is nourished upon ideas only. Information solely is to it as a meal of sawdust to the body. We hunger for knowledge, not for information, and must have this 'food' in great abundance

> *Life is sustained on that which is taken in, not by that which is applied from without*
> *- Charlotte Mason.*

and variety and let hang in the halls of his imagination." If we allow our children the freedom of books we are free to be their guide and do not need to force feed them intellectually. Thinking is inseparable from reading. We feed upon the thoughts of others. It is not only a child's intellect we are dealing with, but his heart. Those arrows in our quiver can be turned out sharp as needles, but with no power of contemplation, no common sense. Isn't it more important how and where they are aimed?

170

To strengthen the will is one of the greatest purposes of our training. What is the will? Its function is to choose. With a daily diet of the wise thoughts of great minds, children may gradually and unconsciously get strengthened in their beliefs. Charlotte Mason expands the phrase "'Sow an act, reap a habit. Sow a habit, reap a character.' We must take a step further back and sow the idea or notion which makes the act worthwhile. Entertain the idea which gives birth to the act and the act repeated again and again becomes a habit." With every choice we make we grow in force of character. Right thoughts flow upon the stimulus of an idea and ideas are stored in books and pictures and in the lives of men; these instruct the conscience and stimulate the will, and the man or child chooses. A poet has said, "Our wills are ours we know not how. Our wills are ours to make them Thine." "Choose you this day whom you will serve."

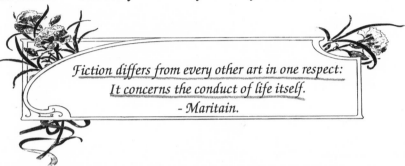

Fiction differs from every other art in one respect:
It concerns the conduct of life itself.
- Maritain.

Living books, fiction, and stories all hold flashes of truth, no matter how simple the story. Great works of imagination are vehicles of truth, but not blueprints. The Ten Commandments are absolutes and they hold fast set against great works of literature. All art - painting, music, and literature - reflects its culture. Great art transcends its culture, perseveres through time, and touches on that which is eternal. Story is often referred to as not true, not real, something made up - or even a waste of time. What a victory for the powers of this world. Our culture has denied its value and produced distortions and fragmentations of real story - with no sense of "home," no resolution, no melody, only drifting despair.

ONCE UPON A TIME

People say that fairy tales don't happen anymore.
That miracles are make believe and the Bible doesn't tell you so.
And 'once upon a time' is a story book line, just some words someone said,
Back when love was forever, families stayed together, and treasures were tucked in bed.

by Monte Swan, 1992

Great literature reflects where we live. Story does not coerce, but inspires. Rather than judging it, let it judge us. John says, "The light shineth in the darkness and the darkness comprehended it not." Story lightens our darkness, guides us. We turn to stories, pictures, and music because they show us who, what, and why we are - and what our relationship is to life and death and the essential. It takes the chaos in which we live and shows us structure and pattern - cosmos in chaos, structure that liberates us - sets us free. God's message is given to us in story. Jesus did very little direct teaching. Rather he taught almost entirely by telling stories.

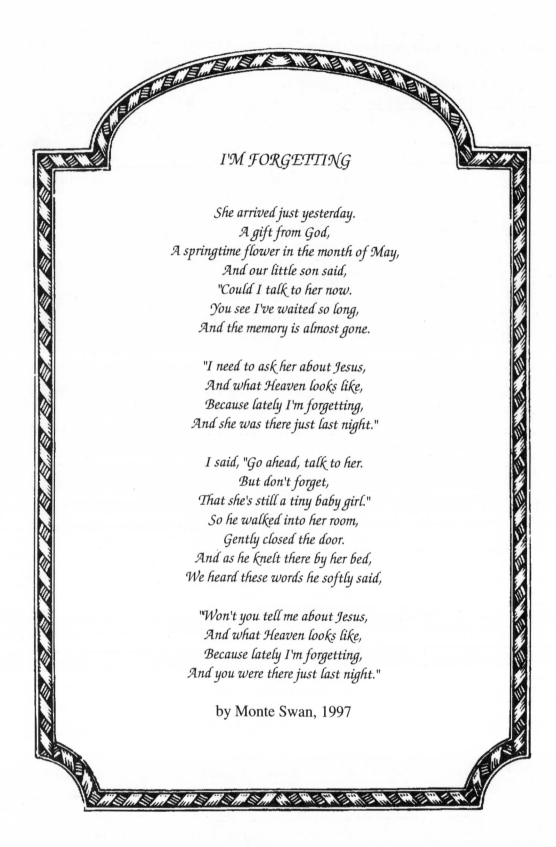

I'M FORGETTING

She arrived just yesterday.
A gift from God,
A springtime flower in the month of May,
And our little son said,
"Could I talk to her now.
You see I've waited so long,
And the memory is almost gone.

"I need to ask her about Jesus,
And what Heaven looks like,
Because lately I'm forgetting,
And she was there just last night."

I said, "Go ahead, talk to her.
But don't forget,
That she's still a tiny baby girl."
So he walked into her room,
Gently closed the door.
And as he knelt there by her bed,
We heard these words he softly said,

"Won't you tell me about Jesus,
And what Heaven looks like,
Because lately I'm forgetting,
And you were there just last night."

by Monte Swan, 1997

172

Life-giving story transcends facts. We are protected by the cultural ideologies of our parents. We develop layers of defensiveness and self protection. Arguing and being rational does not usually break through these defenses. Story, poetry and the arts address ideas indirectly; they sneak up on us. Everytime a story is told well, people get a sense that life has value and meaning, that we are significant. Story gives us a context. All this makes it easier to hear the gospel story and let the Holy Spirit work. We live in story and are co-authors with God in the writing of our own story. We have a beginning and an end. We don't live by facts and information. We accumulate meaning.

Jesus loved children. He said that unless we have the hearts of children, we cannot enter the kingdom of heaven. Children love stories and understand them as truth. Jesus promised that truth would set us free. We've been taught to grow out of our childhood love of story, imagination, creativity, and fun. What does it mean to be adult? Does being adult mean giving up our analogical selves and becoming rational? Jesus spoke in the strong language of mystery, not brute fact. Must we get stuck in a groove of literalism? Literalism and the rational remain in the language of fact. Stories are analogical, passionate, and a search for truth (rather than facts). The Bible is inspiring truth and truth is more important than facts. We don't gain much comfort from facts. We don't need faith for facts. We do need faith for truth. When we become hung up on literalism, we equate truth with fact. Ponder the entire Bible narration such as all of Ezekiel, Elijah, Daniel and his three friends, the Incarnation, the Transfiguration. This is all strong stuff. This moves beyond facts to the redemptive truth of story. Strong story is not meant to be understood in the pale language of provable fact.

Story is affirmation of God's love. In the song, *The Touch of the Master's Hand*, the violin bid was 1, 2, 3 dollars, but from the back of the room a gray-haired man came forward and picked up the old violin and played. The bid changed to 1000, 2000, 3000 dollars. "We do not understand. What changed its worth?" "And many a man with life out of tune, and battered and scarred with sin, is auctioned cheap to a thoughtless crowd, much like the old violin." After dinner in England people gave recitations, sang, or

shared other talents. One famous actor recited the 23rd Psalm. His rendition was magnificent. A little old lady who had been dozing, later recited the 23rd Psalm. Tears were in guests' eyes. When the actor was asked later why the crowd was so moved by a funny, little old lady he replied, "I know the psalm. She knows the shepherd." If we do not truly enjoy our faith, nobody is going to catch the fire of enjoyment from us.

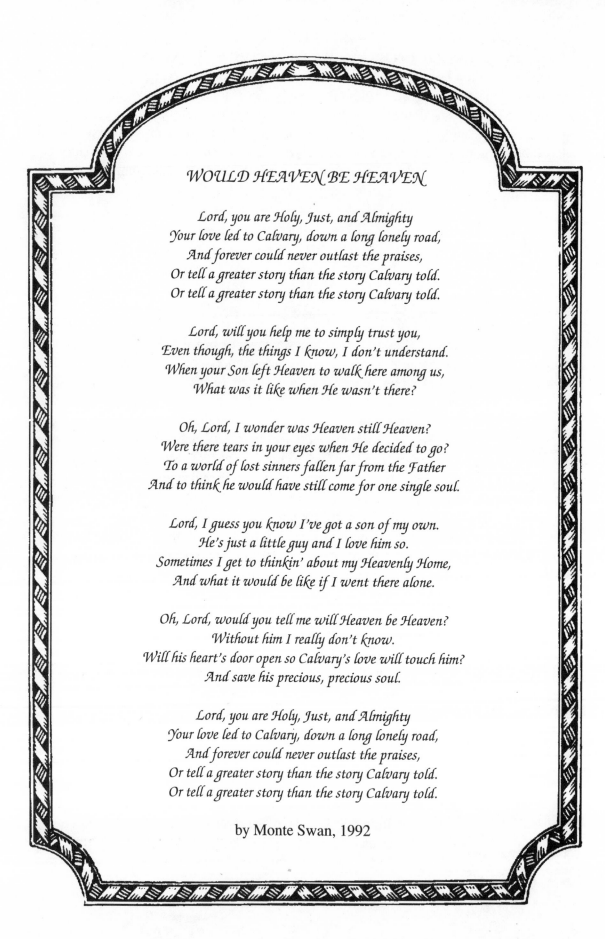

WOULD HEAVEN BE HEAVEN

Lord, you are Holy, Just, and Almighty
Your love led to Calvary, down a long lonely road,
And forever could never outlast the praises,
Or tell a greater story than the story Calvary told.
Or tell a greater story than the story Calvary told.

Lord, will you help me to simply trust you,
Even though, the things I know, I don't understand.
When your Son left Heaven to walk here among us,
What was it like when He wasn't there?

Oh, Lord, I wonder was Heaven still Heaven?
Were there tears in your eyes when He decided to go?
To a world of lost sinners fallen far from the Father
And to think he would have still come for one single soul.

Lord, I guess you know I've got a son of my own.
He's just a little guy and I love him so.
Sometimes I get to thinkin' about my Heavenly Home,
And what it would be like if I went there alone.

Oh, Lord, would you tell me will Heaven be Heaven?
Without him I really don't know.
Will his heart's door open so Calvary's love will touch him?
And save his precious, precious soul.

Lord, you are Holy, Just, and Almighty
Your love led to Calvary, down a long lonely road,
And forever could never outlast the praises,
Or tell a greater story than the story Calvary told.
Or tell a greater story than the story Calvary told.

by Monte Swan, 1992

174

Monte has often been called a "Renaissance man." In the age of the Renaissance it was the highest goal for a man to be painter, architect, goldsmith, and a master of much knowledge. All that he did, he did well and was a part of his daily thought and enjoyment. Today things have changed; the "Renaissance man" is referred to in an uncomplimentary way as a "Jack-of-all-trades." Education today is fragmented and turns out specialists. The whole is lost in the parts. We probably have more knowledge at our fingertips today than ever before and yet are we capable of handling this knowledge creatively? Monte and I love to be stimulated spiritually and scientifically. I think it's all so wonderful! We may never have all the bits and pieces to the picture until we can have Christ put it together in Heaven, but it's all so exciting! The Lord has us meet so many people to help open up new ways of thinking about God and His Word. We are weary of the shallowness of some teaching and we crave more meat than we as a family could maybe chew! Good teaching should keep the *wholeness* of the Bible and not compartmentalize it so, with emphasis on covenants and their building upon one another throughout the Bible. So much of the past century teaching has tended to put God and Christianity in tidy, safe little boxes and produced a defeatist attitude as well. It is indeed a reflection of Enlightenment philosophy. Francis Schaeffer called it the "Evangelical Disaster." Others refer to it as a Rationalistic theology.

> *I believe we must question the traditional religious beliefs continually - not God, not Christ, who are at the center of our lives as believers and creators - but what human beings say about God and about Christ . . .*
> *it is all right to be like a child who constantly asks why . . .*
> *If my religion is true, it will stand up to all my questioning.*
> *- Madeleine L'Engle*

Relationship. Traditions. Community. So much of who and what I am, I attribute to books. Many of the authors are dead or live far away and I could never sit and sip tea with them personally and have great conversations. But, I've grown so through their books filled with great thoughts and ideas. It is almost as good as knowing them personally. But, oh, to sit with George MacDonald or Dorothy Sayers. Our kindred hearts yearn for their friendship. We have grown from the thoughts and ideas that have flowed over our kitchen table. We've tried to focus on relationships throughout our marriage, realizing that's about all we take to Heaven.

> *Anyone who has a library and a garden, wants for nothing.*
> *- Cicero*

We've made an effort to develop traditions, too, and often try to share these with others. Thus, hospitality is important to us. Much of it has been impromptu, which often turns out to be the best. Practicing hospitality builds relationships. Relationships are the basis for community.

Practicing hospitality is Biblical. I think it happened easier in the days without televisions, the days of front porches. As we travel the country I've noticed most front porches closed off. We enter through a back or side door and the front porch is a storage room. Evening walks in previous generations often ended in good conversations on someone's front porch sipping tea, coffee, or lemonade. This is community. I believe God intended our home to be the center and core of our lives, not just a way station. Take a day, once a week, to set aside for hospitality. Sundays are great. That's what the Sabbath is all about - worshipping God first, then rest, family, and community. Plan a meal and attend church not knowing who will come home with you. Children really enjoy this. I believe children are helped in their walk with the Lord when we engage in hospitality. Through this practice they really see and hear us talk of God; hear us evaluate, analyze, and solve problems. Storytelling creates mental pictures that can help in rehearsing or roleplaying hospitality - politeness, etiquette, helpfulness and respect. Hospitality is ministry and when we serve together as a family, our children are more prone to keep in the faith. If no ministry is going on in the home, no ministry can truly go on away from home. Some occasions can be planned, but it's fun to see who the Lord will bring your way. Isn't this education? Real life? "Living each day as it comes" speaks to me of foregoing my wants and goals for the needs of another.

Families who pray together, minister and serve together, stay together. Another aspect of hospitality is mentoring. Mentors in our youths' lives during the teen years is important. Sometimes we can't teach them all things or lead them in all truth. When our children are closely acquainted with other like-minded adults, it affirms the truths we have taught them. They make them their own. Because of our lifestyle choices for our home and family, our kids seem to be avoiding the youth subculture, recognizing it as folly. They are engaged in real life! Mentoring has been an important factor in their lives - one on one through service or work, and hospitality with one-time or long-term guests. We have sought out people with interests similar to those of our kids. We have encouraged interaction between them and our children and discussed our perspective on mentoring. On occasion we have asked them to take our kids along to their workplace or on another activity. We need heroes, people to admire. We can learn from the experience of others, see how others respond in a certain situation, how others solved problems, and see how God can work. Hero images can help with guidance and weapons against evil and manipulation. Many of us tend to live within the comfortable, or within our capacity, and when faced with a choice, will choose the safe way. Children respond to heroes by thinking creatively. Breaking the bounds of darkness and possibly doing the improbable or even impossible. They may in turn become heroes themselves. Is this an age of the anti-hero? Look at this era's popular TV shows and movies. Quality has been sacrificed to profit. I look for people our children can aspire to.

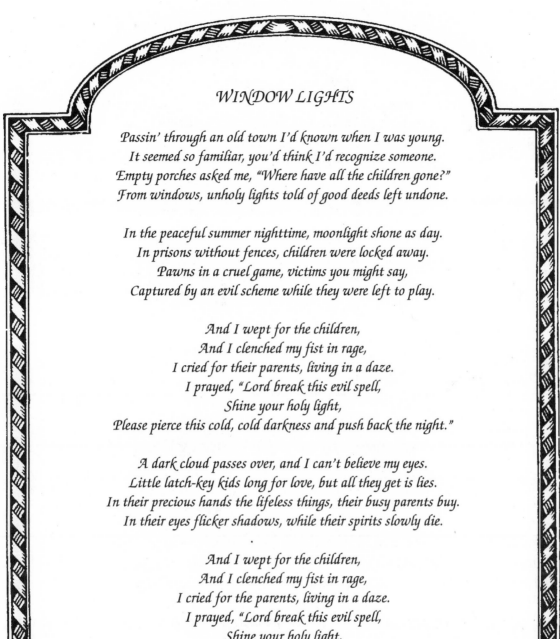

WINDOW LIGHTS

Passin' through an old town I'd known when I was young.
It seemed so familiar, you'd think I'd recognize someone.
Empty porches asked me, "Where have all the children gone?"
From windows, unholy lights told of good deeds left undone.

In the peaceful summer nighttime, moonlight shone as day.
In prisons without fences, children were locked away.
Pawns in a cruel game, victims you might say,
Captured by an evil scheme while they were left to play.

And I wept for the children,
And I clenched my fist in rage,
I cried for their parents, living in a daze.
I prayed, "Lord break this evil spell,
Shine your holy light,
Please pierce this cold, cold darkness and push back the night."

A dark cloud passes over, and I can't believe my eyes.
Little latch-key kids long for love, but all they get is lies.
In their precious hands the lifeless things, their busy parents buy.
In their eyes flicker shadows, while their spirits slowly die.

And I wept for the children,
And I clenched my fist in rage,
I cried for the parents, living in a daze.
I prayed, "Lord break this evil spell,
Shine your holy light,
Please pierce this cold, cold darkness and push back the night."

by Monte Swan, 1993

Can I ramble a bit more? I do want you to know us some. I often refer to books and in reading this book you know literature is very important to us. Our appreciation of literature is the direct result of removing the television from our home for fourteen years when first married. We realized what a time waster it is, a family thief, and a killer of relationships and community. It is rather depressing to drive down a neighborhood street, no one outside, only a blue glow from a front window in just about everyone's home. Our culture's "window lights." It used to be just a few major networks holding us spellbound.

177

Now there are satellites and cable. Many are relinquishing the proper role of parenting and turning it over to strangers. We now have a television, but it is used only one day a week for a special movie (videos) time together as a family (bring out the popcorn!). We still read aloud together, even in the teen years - great books, living books. If we allow our creativity to remain alive, we will never be bored. I say, "To say you are bored means one has no inner reserve." Yes, I said this to little kids. Boredom is a subtle time-waster. When my older two were growing up there was no temptation when a lull hit to turn on the TV. Their creative juices were ongoing; they were never bored or asking me for something to do (and neighbor children were never a temptation either, since we lived out in the country). When I baby-sit I observe the boredom, and the non-ability to play at anything for very long. If our kids are opting out, we have opted out first.

My kids never had nightmares either, not a one. We strove to keep their lives tranquil and as free from moral dilemmas as possible.

> *Let others doubt, but survival without television can be managed.*
> *Ditto for the videocassette recorder and the radio . . .*
> *But, books cannot be done without.*
> *They are, quite simply, the oxygen of intellectual existence.*
>
> *The Man Becomes a Boy Again,*
> *Thanks to Librarian, Philanthropist*
> *by Ben Bleckburn (1990)*

In opening our home in hospitality, we evaluate our season of life, and some long-term guests may not be the best influence on our young family. TV is passive. Reading and play are active. Computer time is limited, too. Kids don't play games anymore, not real games, board games and all. In the old days kids often had discussion groups or clubs, and were also engaged in orations and dramas. This is evident in the *Anne of Green Gables* series or Louisa May Alcott's *Jack and Jill*. We have an old book called *Impromptu*. It contains lists of ideas to throw in a hat and have the young people at get-togethers draw a paper and give a one-minute oration on the subject off the top of the head. Sure develops quick thinking skills and wit. I've collected old books containing children's games. I don't remember all the jump rope, hopscotch, and jacks games because they seemed to disappear along with wearing dresses to school. I never learned marbles. A husband and wife at a "10 Greatest Gifts I Can Give My Children" seminar said, "We're changing from having a 'TV' room to a 'family' room since we know we'll get what we focus on."

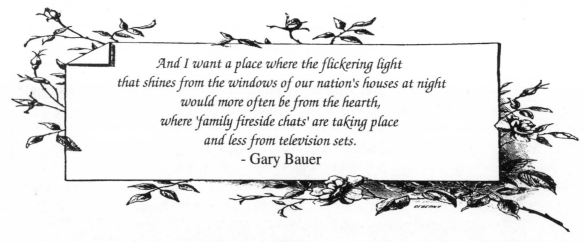

> *And I want a place where the flickering light*
> *that shines from the windows of our nation's houses at night*
> *would more often be from the hearth,*
> *where 'family fireside chats' are taking place*
> *and less from television sets.*
> - Gary Bauer

IS THIS ROMANCE?

When I was just a little girl.
I'd dream of days gone by.
Of dashing prince charmings,
And castles in the sky.
Of a story told untold times,
Romantic words of love.
A haunting strain sung again,
A dance from above.

Could this be Him?
Would He woo us in?
And save us from our sin.
Did He take a chance?
Is this romance?
When love was born again.

All too soon I let my dream,
Fade and slip away.
It left me with empty arms,
And a heart gone astray.
The sorrow and the sadness seemed,
Too much for me to bear,
Till I heard that haunting strain again,
In the words of a prayer.

My dream of everlasting love,
Came true one fair day.
When a brave, pure, honest heart,
Carried me away.
To an enchanted fairy tale,
And a castle in the sky.
Where forever begins today,
And love will never die.

Could this be Him?
Would He woo us in?
And save us from our sin.
Did He take a chance?
Is this romance?
When love was born again.

by Monte Swan, 1997

We know our God is creative. But did you ever imagine God as creating romance or the ultimate romanticist? Does this seem a sacrilege to you? Oh, but it's true. I just read an inspiring true story. For years we have talked with our kids about God's having a plan for their lives. He's created this world and us and knows us better than we know ourselves. Shouldn't it be easy to simply trust him with our lives? We often get anxious wanting to take things into our own hands. If you are to marry, doesn't it seem possible that God would know to whom? Somewhere out in this world is a person for Heather, Travis and Dawson. It would seem the best thing to do would be to focus on being whom God would desire us to be, and to preserve and prepare ourselves for this future mate. We also pray that this person is preserving and preparing themself. Practically speaking, our young adults realize they are not ready for marriage. Therefore, all relationships with the opposite sex are respectful, as with a sister or brother.

In the homeschool arena the phrase "emotional promiscuity" is being discussed. Home educators have commonly pushed beyond cultural norms in courageous, creative ways. This is a good example. Could the giving of one's heart - in puppy love, going steady, boyfriend-girlfriend relationships, and then breaking up - over and over again, be a stepping stone to, and practical training for divorce in later life? Throughout these relationships are we able to preserve a beautiful whole share to give to the one we will spend the rest of our life with?!

Skills for marriage include: learning the practicalities of taking care of a home - financially, homemaking skills, spiritually, emotionally and finally, once married, the physical. Yes, it's the ideal, yet it *is* reachable and real. It helps when we can see it in nitty-gritty, flesh and blood. It's been done, folks. In the book, *His Perfect Faithfulness*, Eric and Leslie Ludy tell "The Story of Our Courtship." In this story we parents as well as our teens can see "the story of God's love and faithfulness toward anyone who will let Him be God . . . and that to allow God to manage their relationships (is anything but) boring, restrictive, unfulfilling, and socially devastating." Leslie says, "Our friendship, engagement, and marriage have been laden with romance unlike any novel has ever portrayed. I simply gave the area of relationship to God and determined to walk in purity, not knowing how He would bless me in return. As a result, I learned firsthand that God's way is the only way to experience pure romance!"

Our boys sing the following song with us.

DADDY WHAT IS HER NAME

He walked 'cross the room, and he stood at my knee,
Then proceeded to tune my guitar.
He looked up at me with those big brown eyes.
Then he strummed me his first little tune.

Daddy, what is her name? Daddy, where does she live?
Does she know Jesus just like I do?
I heard you praying with Mommie to our Father above.
Tell me, Daddy, does she love Jesus too,
Oh, Daddy, does she love Jesus too?

He walked 'cross the room, looked me straight in the eye.
He was wonderin' what girls were about.
I told him the same things my daddy told me.
But I know he still had a few doubts.

Dad, what is her name? Dad, where does she live?
Does she know Jesus just like I do?
I heard you praying with Mom to our Father above.
Tell me, Dad, does she love Jesus too,
Oh, Dad, does she love Jesus too?

He walked 'cross the room and I looked up at him.
He said, Dad, I know she's the one.
But it's funny it seems like we've always been friends,
Even though, we've only first begun.

Dad, I know her name, Dad, I know where she lives,
And she knows Jesus just like I do.
I want to thank you and Mom for the prayers you all said,
'Cause, Dad, she really loves Jesus too,
Oh, Dad, she really loves Jesus too.

It seems like just yesterday he stood at my knee.
His little fingers tuned my guitar.
He looked up at me with those big brown eyes,
And he strummed me his first little tune.
He strummed me his first little tune.

by Monte Swan, 1992

181

Let me finish this chapter with the last three paragraphs of an article entitled "Say 'No' to Busyness" by Phil Lancaster out of his September / October 1995 PATRIARCH Magazine -

Remember how Martha was bustling around with her preparations while Mary sat at Jesus' feet. Martha was an activist. Mary was more concerned for relationships. Here is what Jesus said to Martha when she asked Jesus to make Mary help her: "Martha, Martha, you are worried and upset about many things, but only one thing is needed. Mary has chosen what is better, and it will not be taken away from her" (Lk 10:41,42).

Let's choose relationships over activities. Let this be a picture of your life as a family: sitting together at the feet of Jesus, spending time with him and with each other.

Our Shepherd does not lead us in a rat race, he leads us beside quiet waters and restores our souls. Let's return to a life of quietness and rest in the presence of our Savior. Say "No" to busyness.

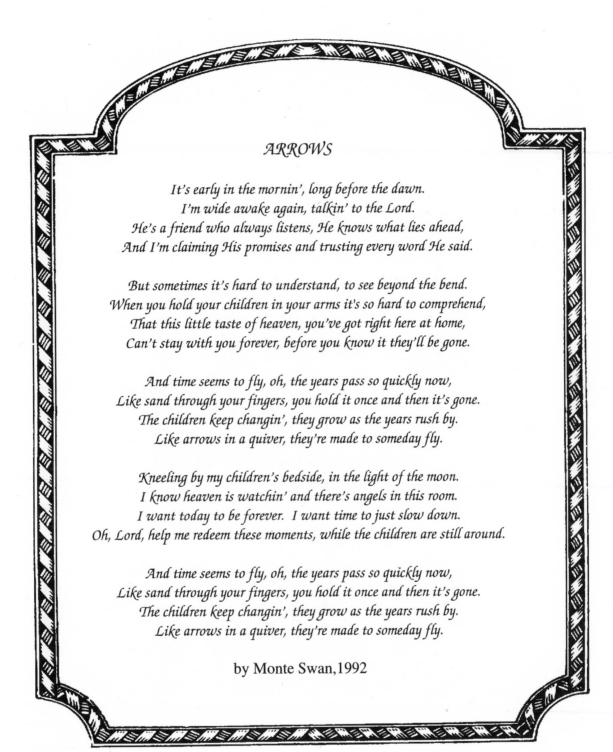

ARROWS

It's early in the mornin', long before the dawn.
I'm wide awake again, talkin' to the Lord.
He's a friend who always listens, He knows what lies ahead,
And I'm claiming His promises and trusting every word He said.

But sometimes it's hard to understand, to see beyond the bend.
When you hold your children in your arms it's so hard to comprehend,
That this little taste of heaven, you've got right here at home,
Can't stay with you forever, before you know it they'll be gone.

And time seems to fly, oh, the years pass so quickly now,
Like sand through your fingers, you hold it once and then it's gone.
The children keep changin', they grow as the years rush by.
Like arrows in a quiver, they're made to someday fly.

Kneeling by my children's bedside, in the light of the moon.
I know heaven is watchin' and there's angels in this room.
I want today to be forever. I want time to just slow down.
Oh, Lord, help me redeem these moments, while the children are still around.

And time seems to fly, oh, the years pass so quickly now,
Like sand through your fingers, you hold it once and then it's gone.
The children keep changin', they grow as the years rush by.
Like arrows in a quiver, they're made to someday fly.

by Monte Swan, 1992

And this our life . . .
Finds tongues in trees, books in the running brooks,
Sermons in stones, and good in everything.
William Shakespeare

We do not want merely to see beauty, though, God Knows, even that is bounty enough.
We want something else which can hardly be put into words -
to be united with the beauty we see, to pass into it,
to receive it into ourselves, to bathe in it, to become part of it.
CS Lewis

I am certain of nothing but the holiness of the heart's affections, and the truth of imagination.
What the imagination seizes as beauty must be truth - whether it existed before or not . . .
The imagination may be compared to Adam's dream - he awoke and found it truth.
John Keats

No one asserts that creativity is the source of life,
but most will claim that they are unique expressions of divine imagination.
Miles P. Callahan

Art enables us to find ourselves and lose ourselves at the same time.
Thomas Merton

Chapter Thirteen
THE ART OF LIFE

"He who would inspire a heart
Must he himself glow."
These words are carved in stone,
on a lintel at the University of Northern Colorado.

Listen children to my Truth,
With your ears, hear My Word.
I will tell you the Eternal Story — the Creation Epic,
Written for the hearts of all generations.
And told from generation to generation.
Your fathers will reveal it,
Telling their children and
Grandchildren the Lord's praises,
His almighty power and the works of His Hands.
For God established a relationship with His people
Based on grace alone.
He gave them laws to live by
That they would show their thanksgiving to Him.
He commanded them to share
His grace with their children,
So the children to come,
Will know the Truth and tell the stories,
To future generations.
That they will put their trust and hope in God,
Remembering His blessed works,
And keeping His commandments.

Paraphrase fo PSALM 78: 1-7
by Monte Swan, 1999

I am a torch bearer passing my light to the next as I have received it from the last. Parents who know God can show His praise, His strength, His wonderful works to their children. Psalm 145:4 speaks of "one generation shall praise thy works to another." If the reader feels you have missed this heritage, take steps to begin a generational cohesiveness. Let us enter into His plans, set our hope on Him, co-create with Him in the poetry of life.

Each of us is a precious gem stone - raw, uncut. Ephesians 2:10 says we are God's workmanship. Workmanship is *poiema* in Greek.   The root word *poieo*, means "to make or do." Another *poieo* word is *poietes* and it means "doer, or poet." *Poietes* (poet) is used several times in the New Testament, and is usually in the context of obedience. So literally, we are to be poets of God's word - "doers of the word." God is the ultimate poet. Genesis tells us we are made in the image of God. As raw gem stones, the artist of our souls can finely sculpt a brilliant diamond. God chisels facets that can reflect the light of eternal values, of truth, of love. In contrast, much of today's society and world system insists upon grinding these stones smooth in such a way that each one is uniformly similar to the other; like marbles rolling 'round together reflecting nothing. The beginning of art can be found in the act of creation itself.

> √ *The imagination of man*
> *is made in the image*
> *of the imagination of God.*
> *- George MacDonald*

> *For every man is primitively planned to be a self,*
> *appointed to be a self, and while it is true that every self as such is angular,*
> *the logical consequence of this merely is that it has to be polished;*
> *not that it has to be ground smooth.*
> *- Soren Kierkegaard*

ANGELS IN DISGUISE

He caught a glimpse of Heaven in a little smile.
As the crowds pressed in around Him, He knelt by the child,
And holdin' him he would say, "Of such is the kingdom of God."
He caught a glimpse of Heaven in one little smile.

Did He say? "Dear little ones, let them come,
Oh, let them come.
They are the only things down here,
That remind me of Home.
This old world's gone crazy.
And its heart's turned to stone.
Let the little ones come, Let the little ones come.
They remind me, they remind me of Home."

Well, I've heard that they are angels in disguise.
If you want to find a treasure just look in their eyes.
And the touch of tiny fingers will make the foolish wise.
So watch for these angels in disguise.

Did He say? "Dear little ones, let them come,
Oh, let them come.
They are the only things down here,
That remind me of Home.
This old world's gone crazy.
And its heart's turned to stone.
Let the little ones come, Let the little ones come.
They remind me, they remind me of Home."

And the touch of tiny fingers will make the foolish wise.
So watch for these angels of God in disguise.

by Monte Swan, 1995

The art or craft of poetry consists of three basic skills: image, rhythm, and voice. Good poetry is usually image-driven, rather than agenda-driven. It paints mental pictures. It will inspire and show, not twaddle or tell. As God's poetry we are to provide others with a picture of the character and nature of God. Creation expresses rhythm: the four seasons, sunrise and sunset. Our lives have their own seasons, sunrises and sunsets. We express rhythm in our living and proclaiming Christ. With rhythm it's not so much what is said, but how it's said. Rhythm within our lives grows slowly as we seek to live the poetic, Christ-like, lifestyle. When I think of rhythm, I think of time. Greek has two words for time: *chronos* and *kairos*. *Chronos* is the measurable passage of time, it is our earth's wristwatch, alarm clock time. *Kairos* is out-of-earthly time and not measurable. It is God's time, real time. In poetry the element of voice, when considering us as poets of God's word, is a paradox. In and of ourselves we have something to say, a voice, but what *are* we apart from God? Isn't it in our passionate pursuit of Him, that we *become* ourselves? Didn't Jesus say, "Whoever wants to save his life will lose it; but whoever loses his life for Me will find it"? *Kairos* can sometimes penetrate, break through *chronos* - like a child at play, or the artist's work. We too often let *kairos* fall asleep, get dull and blunt. In *kairos* we are unselfconscious,

and yet we are far more real. We become what we are called to be, co-creators with God, touching on the wonder of creation.

In the play *Our Town* by Thornton Wilder, it is asked, "Do any human beings ever realize life while they live it?" "No. The saints and poets, maybe. They do some." Saints and poets. Freud put them together as well, saying they are the two classes of human beings who challenge all his psychological categorizing. We are Christ's poem, metaphors. We are called to offer ourselves as a pictorial representation of Him, to invite the world to discover the layers of meaning about Him. God is constantly creating in us, through us, with us; and to create with God is our calling. We were created to observe and contemplate.

Is Your Imagination of God Starved?

"Lift up your eyes on high, and behold who hath created these things." Isaiah 40:26

The people of God in Isaiah's day had starved their imagination by looking on the face of idols, and Isaiah made them look up at the heavens, that is, he made them begin to use their imagination aright. Nature to a saint is sacramental. If we are children of God, we have a tremendous treasure in Nature. In every wind that blows, in every night and day of the year, in every sign of the sky, in every blossoming and in every withering of the earth, there is a real coming of God to us if we will simply use our starved imagination to realize it.

The test of spiritual concentration is bringing the imagination into captivity. Is your imagination looking on the face of an idol? Is the idol yourself? Your work? Your conception of what a worker should be? Your experience of salvation and sanctification? Then your imagination of God is starved, and when you are up against difficulties you have no power, you can only endure in darkness. If your imagination is starved, do not look back to your own experience; it is God Whom you need. Go right out of yourself, away from the face of your idols, away from everything that has been starving your imagination. Rouse yourself, take the gibe that Isaiah gave the people, and deliberately turn your imagination to God.

One of the reasons of stultification in prayer is that there is no imagination, no power of putting ourselves deliberately before God. We have to learn how to be broken bread and poured out wine on the line of intercession more than on the line of personal contact. Imagination is the power God gives a saint to posit himself out of himself into relationships he never was in.

> *It is God who gives thee thy mirror of imagination, and if thou keep it clean, it will give thee back no shadow but of the truth.*
> — George MacDonald

> *. . . in finding out the works of God, the Intellect must labour, workman-like, under the direction of the architect, Imagination.*
> — George MacDonald

Is Your Hope In God Faint and Dying?

"Thou wilt keep him in perfect peace whose imagination is stayed on Thee." Isaiah 26:3

Is your imagination stayed on God or is it starved? The starvation of the imagination is one of the most fruitful sources of exhaustion and sapping in a worker's life. If you have never used your imagination to put yourself before God, begin to do it now. It is no use waiting for God to come; you must put your imagination away from the face of idols and look unto Him and be saved. Imagination is the greatest gift God has given us and it ought to be devoted entirely to Him. If you have been bringing every thought into captivity to the obedience of Christ, it will be one of the greatest assets to faith when the time of trial comes because your faith and the Spirit of God will work together. Learn to associate ideas worthy of God with all that happens in Nature - the sunrises and the sunsets, the sun and the stars, the changing seasons, and your imagination will never be at the mercy of your impulses, but will always be at the service of God.

"We have sinned with our fathers; . . . and have forgotten" - then put a stiletto in the place where you have gone to sleep. "God is not talking to me just now," but He ought to be. Remember Whose you are and Whom you serve. Provoke yourself by recollection, and your affection for God will increase tenfold; your imagination will not be starved any longer, but will be quick and enthusiastic, and your hope will be inexpressibly bright.

- Oswald Chambers
My Utmost For His Highest

Our creative, poet Father, the Supreme artist, in whose image we were made, speaks throughout the Bible of the need for traditions and memories. *Zakar* is the Hebrew root word for "remember" and "memorial." Another meaning from this root is "one who remembers" or "remembering ones." This refers to carrying on the story. Traditions and memories incorporated into our rhythm of life are a testimony, a remembrance of the wonderful faithfulness of God; not just for us individually, but for our children, for future generations. In Joshua 4, the people had miraculously crossed the Jordan River. God had them take up twelve stones. Why? So that when your children ask, "What do these stones mean to you?" you may tell of God's faithfulness and promises. "These stones shall be for a memorial . . . that all the peoples of the earth may know the hand of the Lord, that it is mighty, that you may fear the Lord your God forever." The fear or reverence, and knowledge of his grace. Exodus 3: 14, 15 states, "Thus you shall say to the children . . . this is My name forever, and this is My memorial to all generations." Deuteronomy 8:11 says, "Beware that you do not forget the Lord your God ... lest - when you have eaten and are full, and have built houses . . . and all that you have is multiplied, when your heart is lifted up, and you forget the Lord your God who brought you out. . . of bondage - you say in your heart, 'My power and the might of my hand have gained me this wealth.'"

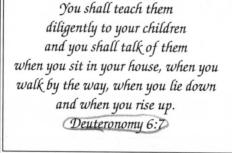

When your children shall ask their fathers . . .'what do these stones mean to you?'. . . These stones shall be for a memorial . . . that all the peoples of the earth may know the hand of the Lord, that it is mighty, that you may fear the Lord your God forever. Joshua 4

You shall teach them diligently to your children and you shall talk of them when you sit in your house, when you walk by the way, when you lie down and when you rise up. Deuteronomy 6:7

The New Testament gives us memorials as well. In John, Jesus refers to Himself as the bread of life. During the regular observance of the Passover, Jesus instituted the Lord's Supper, which he defines in Luke 22:17-20 and Paul restates its purpose in I Corinthians 11:23-26, "To do this in remembrance of me." Remembrance of His death and resurrection is the centrality for the Christian faith. It signifies a communion with Christ by faith. It has a past, present, and future remembrance for our daily walk.

There are many other passages on remembrances for us and our children. Deuteronomy stresses the covenant responsibility of parents for their children. My favorite summary of it all is Deuteronomy 6:1-7. ". . . you shall love the Lord your God with all your heart, with all your soul, with all your strength, and all your mind. And these words which I command you today shall be in your heart. You shall teach them diligently to your children and you shall talk of them when you sit in your house, when you walk by the way, when you lie down and when you rise up." The character of our children is formed and molded by impressions; unceasing communion with the parent can deeply and permanently impart these impressions. What an awesome responsibility, in that we must hold to obedience ourselves. We should *let* His words live in our hearts. With a heart full of God's love His words will mingle with ours. We can make all the influences and relationships of domestic life the co-support

to the great works of God. I long to make my life an attractive image or example of what God has taught. A spontaneous overflowing of the heart. To take the ordinary and the commonplace, things we often pass by and do not see, and make them extraordinary and significant. To inspire and influence my children's hearts with the flame of my own zeal for life. It will be a sweet and happy work to win the beloved on earth to the Father beloved in heaven.

My original dream for a book was to have each month be a chapter with the interweaving of recipes, tips, thoughts and ideas. The current chapters evolved; I just took what had been growing and developing. This is the image of our life, in a word - our story. Our rhythm. Our voice, as we live our lives in what I refer to as "God consciousness," which to me is "praying without ceasing."

The highest science, the loftiest speculation, the mightiest philosophy, which can ever engage the attention of a child of God, is the name, the nature, the person, the work, the doings, and the existence of the great God whom he (the Christian) calls his Father.
- Charles Spurgeon

Do you feel a lack of glow, therefore a deficiency in inspiring? Is there a void of a spiritual heritage, a generation-to-generation of Christian mentoring? In Joshua 3, the people were faced with crossing a river for the second time. They had to first put their feet in the water. We can't always sit back and wait for God to split the waters. "My home environment can never be like yours." "My children are not my friends. I feel we're in a constant tug-of-war." "My husband and I don't have a deep relationship; we've lost that spark; lost that first love. I don't feel in love anymore." "I've lost that child-like wonder of creation." When God seems silent, when He is nowhere to be found, maybe it's because He is waiting for us to step toward Him. Christians are not hypocrites when they "put on" the image of kindness, when we don't feel kind; patience, when we don't want to be patient; giving, when we haven't much to give. We can put on or build a mold or framework of the act, trusting that God will fill the mold. The deepest form of loving may be play. We must step out and touch the water, step into the stream of God's activity and the Holy Spirit will flow through us. In the first act of empty obedience, God will manifest Himself to us, He will meet us there.

As I typed the book, I had a feeling of harvest. I've been revealing my heart and crafting a message. My goal has been to look at the whole year, either holidays or seasons, and build memories and traditions around them. I am continually reminded of the book *Hinds Feet in High Places*, and think of possible memorials (like the stones in Joshua) that we can keep in a treasure place. Memorials can be of special milestones, victories, learning experiences, and just plain fun, throughout each of our own lives. When in times of doubt or in need of a reminder of God's working in our lives, we can open our "memory bag" and remember. I've decided the most practical format for us is a scrap book-photo album. Currently everything is in file folders, labeled for each person in the family - and not just one. Each person has a number of files to pull and remember. My plan is to have the books done, us working together, prior to each child's leaving the nest. Life then becomes a canvas as we use both God's and our palettes to create a painting as we observe, contemplate, and recognize the hand of God.

A LITTLE HEAVEN ON EARTH

It's a steep narrow road, but it leads to love
That lives in hearts touching heaven above.
With hopes and dreams and family ties,
One word paints the picture in loved ones' eyes.

Home, oh, the vision you bring.
Home, just the thought makes my heart sing.
Home, winsome place of my birth.
Home, a little Heaven on earth,
A little Heaven on earth.

The treasure of children and their laughter.
Their sweet love you never need to ask for.
In the parlor a piano and a wood burning stove,
And memories I'll be holdin' for the day I'm old.

Home, oh, the vision you bring.
Home, just the thought makes my heart sing.
Home, winsome place of my birth.
Home, a little Heaven on earth,
A little Heaven on earth.

A family needs the sonshine and a cool mountain breeze,
To burn the mist, blow the clouds away.
Little prayer at the table said in Jesus' name.
This mystery makes us one and yet not the same.

Home, oh, the vision you bring.
Home, just the thought makes my heart sing.
Home, winsome place of my birth.
Home, a little Heaven on earth,
A little Heaven on earth.

by Monte Swan, 1993

JANUARY

This tradition is for me. People talk of post-partum blues or after holiday lows, and I have not experienced these. After birthing my babies I slept and we got into a routine of feeding, play and sleep. I made it a rule that while they slept, I would take that time for myself. I usually sewed or made crafts. I read while I nursed (45 minutes!!), and did house chores while the baby was awake. After New Year's Day it is so peaceful. I've sat with coffee and last year's and the new year's calendars and transferred birthdays and other details. It's a good time to remember and reflect; a good time to thank the Heavenly Father for the unknown new year and know it will be guided by Him. Sometimes I'll say a prayer for a particular name I've written on the calendar. I don't make new year resolutions. Resolutions, goals, or changes just happen when the moment arises. I have overall visions or directions of what I hope to do, where the kids should be headed, but I don't set an agenda for me or them. That would be asking the impossible of me! It's beyond my comprehension. We don't usually celebrate New Years Day or Eve. As a kid my family stayed up and watched TV. I do remember my mom making big authentic- looking, hot fudge sundaes. The kids and I pick up where we left off before the holidays, with reading aloud together. We do it up to a certain point, while they are working steadily on needlecrafts, carving or whatever for gift giving. (Yes, I let Travis carve in the great room. Just like we've let him shoot a BB gun in his room. Whatever for, you might ask? Why, to shoot a mouse, of course!) Garden catalogs have been sifting in all fall and now's the time to plan next year's plantings and place orders. January holds my birthday.

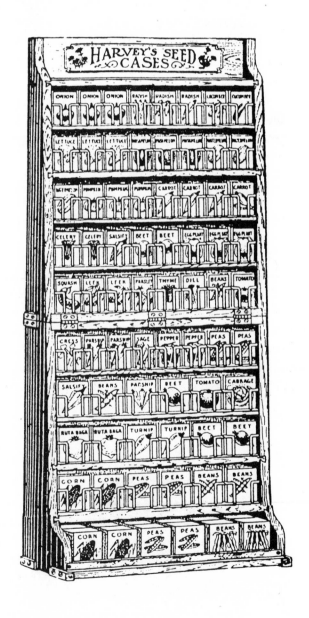

FEBRUARY

Visions of Valentine's Day. Some may remember President's Day, especially those who know the truth of our HIStory and the Godly lives of Washington and Lincoln. I remember my mother's birthday which falls right amongst the presidents. The history of Valentine's Day is fun to read. Some years the kids make valentines to give to friends or relatives with verses on them. I hang a large velvet red heart over the kitchen table. We have vinyl backed decorations that stick on the windows, cloth napkins that have red hearts and red vinyl placemats. I like to decorate the table, not just for company, but "just for the family." By February, I've put away the Christmas decorations, but the last to go after Valentine's Day are the pine cones hanging from red ribbons on all the great room's windows, which includes the kitchen. The ribbons are nailed above the molding and live evergreen boughs are draped over the nails. Of course, the boughs are dry by this time but still pretty. This month's tradition is to clean out the birdhouses. Bugs can be in the old nests and can harm the next babies. If additional birdhouses are wanted, or existing ones need repair, this is the time to do it. Travis and I made a bunch one year and we have looked forward each year to the return of those particular birds. I think Dawson is going to want to do it this year.

MARCH

Spring! Spring doesn't really arrive here yet, but we know it's around the corner. For years I made a "Firsts of Spring" chart. Now the kids automatically tell me when they spot a blue bird, or a crocus, or a robin, or the first aspen catkin. I will make a chart again for Dawson, our youngest, so the memory is etched in his life. The mountain bluebird flitting in the sunlight gives my heart a lilt. Spring is usually our snowiest time with big, wet snows. The phrase "calm before the storm" really applies where we live. We often have the most beautiful days, up in the 70s maybe even 80, and the next day socked in and 30s or 40s. Typical pictures of kite flying don't apply here. We get wind, but it's not steady, and there are lots of trees around. Instead of Easter baskets, we have Spring baskets. Batik Eggs (Ukranian) is the craft of the month. Literally a month! The kids beg to get it out right away. We often invite others to do this with us at various times. We have a pullout table (2-15 feet) in the Keeping Room (off the dining room, a part of the Great Room), that the special dye, candles, beeswax, and tools sit on. Eggs are a part of spring! Our chickens lay in nest boxes, but I've read stories where they often had to hunt for the eggs. An egg hunt is necessary, even for the big kids. When I was growing up, my mom always did it with dozens and dozens of plastic eggs in the yard and house. Then we would do it for weeks with the neighborhood kids! (It's so fun, months or even years later when one was hid so well we never discovered it!)

194

Everybody gets born.
but nobody else
ever came back
from getting killed
Just Him.

From my
college day
sketch book
KS

March is Monte's birthday month. We've made the Passover a tradition. Deuteronomy teaches the importance of Passover as a reminder for the next generation. Passover, the cross, and the empty tomb are reminders of God and His salvation. We never celebrate St. Patrick's Day except by maybe decorating the table in green. I'm usually busy in the greenhouse planting seeds for a head start on the year's gardening. It is cost effective, and getting one's hands in dirt again does wonders for the soul.

APRIL

This is definitely a birthday month; Grandpa, Travis, and Dawson. Many people seem to have been born in the spring. We often go visiting for combined March and April birthday celebrations. "April Showers". . . ours is still snow. I do start seeing some of my bulbs coming up this month. I'm still busy planting and watering in the greenhouse. We find it hard to stay in the house on nice mornings. Mountain mornings are always sunny, still and peaceful. Clouds often move in later, and breezes pick up. It's a time for walks, with little ones (and all); to be still and listen, smell, touch, and see the wonders of God. If we catch the weather just right we can usually have the garden tilled and start planting some of the salad makings, cool weather crops. I take my chances if I put out too much. Most of the spring firsts really occur in this month. I noticed on the calendar two years ago someone wrote - "first stinkbug." We've decided this is not the time of year to plan things. After winter and cabin fever, people may not show up for anything. I anxiously await the sound of the first hummer - hummingbird. They are very noisy here all summer long. We think we've figured out what must be a mating ritual - a very interesting flight dance!

MAY

This is our month for showers and flowers to begin. This is definitely garden-planting month. Our last frost date is the end of the month. So green beans get planted that last week. Most of my greenhouse babies have hardened off and been planted. Dawson is my biggest help around the house and in the garden. I never make the kids do these things with me. I've always waited until they had a desire to help. Sometimes Monte and I will say, "We're going to weed. Why don't you come along." Generally they do. The important thing for them is that we do it together. Weeding or picking alone may be too overwhelming. When the house is out of control and I am overwhelmed not knowing where to begin, all it takes is for one person (usually Monte) to begin, and it's a snap. Or as Dawson just told me the other night, "In every job that must be done, there is an element of fun, you find the fun and snap, the job's a game!" Pretty good memory for a six-year-old who's seen Mary Poppins just once. Better yet is the application he has made to his life. He supposedly thinks this when faced with cleaning. Dawson's always the first to jump in and help. Once he gets on a roll he won't stop . . . (he's like his ol' ma).

I have a friend who leaves flowers in my mail-box for May Day. Each year I say I want to give May baskets, but haven't gotten my act together. I probably need to mark April's calendar as a think-ahead reminder. I almost forgot Mother's Day. It's always a Sunday, so moms are acknowledged at church. Kind of interesting to see what passage they'll use this time, especially when trying to find something obscure. Usually Monte makes me a meal. He doesn't like to go out when the rest of the world is going out, so we go out on another day. Elk have their babies this month and we usually get chicks in the mail. Yes, in the mail, twenty-five of the little day-old peepers sitting in a box at the post office. They call us first thing in the morning, to come pick them up. Last time the kids and I went, they were sitting next to cages of live, buzzing bees! I never got my bees in the mail! Ours always come from a wild swarm. This time of year is spent looking through the hives for bee larvae. Why? Evidence of a queen bee, to see if the old lady survived the winter. If a queen is present, then look for larger-than-normal cells. These could be future queen bee cells. If you prefer the current queen you should kill these cells. If another hive is slow or you don't like their temperament, you may want to kill their queen and put a queen cell frame into that hive for the bees to raise. Two queens? They'll fight and/or maybe fly off taking lots of the workers with them. Interesting huh?

Most of all the other beautiful things in life come by twos and threes, by dozens and hundreds. Plenty of roses, stars, sunsets, rainbows, brothers and sisters, aunts and cousins, but only one mother in the whole world.
- Kate Douglas Wiggin

I never thought that you should be rewarded for the greatest privilege in life.
- May Robert Coker, on being named Mother of the Year, 1958

JUNE

Summer kicks in this month. Some of you probably are saying "Finally!" I used to say that too, having moved to the mountains from the desert. In the mountains it seems we go from winter to summer with spring mixed in here and there. Often times June can be our hottest, driest month. Most of the elk begin to head for the high country about mid-month when the babies are bigger. But some stay year 'round. I think they are waiting to see what delectable new thing I plant. When it rains in the mountains it is instantly cool and usually stays cool the rest of the day. Once the sun sets it cools off drastically. We never put away our winter clothes, sweaters, or coats, and we take clothing with us everywhere in the vehicle and have learned to dress in layers. We built an amphitheater with a fire pit. We had a small one before, but in this new one we can sit comfortably with others. We've had up to sixty people! Sweaters and coats are needed at this time. We sing and the discussions are great. Staring into the fire and coals is therapeutic. A close friend, Gene, spends a lot of time around his campfire. He's picked up all sorts of cast iron paraphernalia (I use this word a lot and Travis always says, "A pair of what?"), and has set up quite a workable cooking area. Gene loves to cook over the fire. He says most of the family's major decisions were made around the fire. Campfires remind people of marshmallows. I try to keep them in stock. Actually, our family's tradition is to have hard marshmallows. What is a hard marshmallow? Don't close the bag! Need I go into more detail? My family thinks they taste better (I'm not a real marshmallow lover). The trick is to heat the poker first, so it slides into the hard marshmallow easier. For roasting, you

can actually eat and roast, layer by layer. We don't *try* for hard marshmallows. It just happens. Father's Day is usually spent working around the yard. That's what Monte likes, simply stay home. Actually, in the past few years, June weekends have been filled with various state homeschool conferences. Monte and I go together, generally flying, so we're not gone long. Some trips, the kids travel with us. It's been fun. We've met so many wonderful people. We often sing and speak as well. June is our last month for conferences. They begin in March. We try to never go anywhere during the summer, since we live where everyone else wants to vacation! We want to enjoy our summer, as well. Since it's dry here, I'm usually watering outside a lot. It's a good time to look my gardens over. I mulch with a cedar shaving and composted horse manure mixture. I guess June is a big wedding month. Not for us. We eloped, and don't attend many weddings, unless they are close friends or we're singing.

The Fourth has always been very special

197

to us since our move to Colorado. Locally an orchestra would perform before the fireworks, which reflected in Evergreen Lake and echoed off the mountains. I loved the orchestra. We'd sit on a blanket on the golf course along with hundreds of others. It was community, a big picnic. The final number was always Tchaikovsky's "1812 Overture" and the fireworks would begin at the sound of the cannon (big kettle drums). Sad to say, the orchestra moved on to bigger and better things (money at a ski resort town) and insurance costs stopped the fireworks. Now we go to the People's Republic of Boulder. I apologize to those of you who may live there, but that is how Boulder is often referred to. We go with friends into Folsom Stadium (Promise Keepers beginnings). It's an evening of sing-along - patriotic, old family fun songs including "Deep and Wide." They play music accompaniment to the fireworks that bring tears to my eyes. The particular coordination of the fireworks to "Glory, Glory, Hallelujah" is quite moving. We love and never miss it. While waiting for the music and darkness, everyone is throwing paper airplanes. Last year, Dawson was making airplanes for two days and filled a backpack and brought a huge ream of paper besides. Travis, though, is the aerodynamic expert! I have a red, white, and blue streamer and a cardboard Statue of Liberty for the table. If the flag is not already out (sometimes I leave it out most of the summer) we put it up. Do kids today still say the Pledge of Allegiance in school? The kids love the Focus on the Family Odyssey tape on the story of "The Star Spangled Banner," our national anthem. We use red, white, and blue watermelon cloth napkins and tablecloth often during the summer. The napkin rings are starched material with stuffed, cloth strawberries glued to the ring. July Fourth usually brings the summer rains called monsoons. I love thunderstorms and the billowing cumulus

thunderhead clouds. We made a labeled poster of the various cloud formations using cotton balls. Heather's birthday falls here. We usually go camping around her birthday to an annual Bow Hunters' Jamboree that we have not missed in thirteen years. Hundreds of people camp in a valley. Lots of target courses are set up. We camp near a stream and hardly see or hear a soul. We do enjoy walking about and seeing all the activities. Some Saturday nights during the jamboree, Monte and I go "out." We leave the kids with hot dogs and marshmallows while we go to a "smokers" booth and have a meal of smoked sausage or ribs, beans and bread. The kids do not let us miss this event either and it goes on the calendar every January. During the summer we often set up a tent in the yard to sleep in. No big change other than walking outside to go to sleep! It's fun reading bedtime stories by flashlight. Canning begins this month, usually with apricots and bing cherries. I often dry a first batch of herbs, too.

AUGUST

Canning, drying and freezing continues. The garden is in full production now. We always take walks throughout the seasons and look for new growth, particularly wildflowers. During two seasons we took pictures and kept track of their "coming out" and found 200 different flowers in our meadow. These were developed into a slide show which the kids presented to many groups. We researched the names and uses and now have a notebook that we can look at to see what flowers grow when, so we can look for them. Most seasons we dry flowers in silica gel or press them. Some years, if the weather is abnormal, like extra late snow or more rain, we see flowers we've not seen before. How long do these seeds remain viable? We hear frogs croak in low area puddles during the two wet months. Where do they go? Do some birds raise two families in a season? I am truly curious. My questioning is usually infectious to the kids. This is part of the process of inspiring them to become thinkers and interested in the Creation which transfers interest in the Creator. I'm glad though, that I don't feel the need to understand all, in order to believe. Would I be fascinated by a Maker who was completely explained and understood?! "It is the glory of God to conceal things, but the glory of kings to search things out." Proverbs 25:2. Our pastor said, "Could creation be like a treasure hunt arranged by a loving Father? Science is worship. Worship is wonder and wonder is the obvious response to glory." Do we adults have this childlike wonder? Are we missing one of the major transcendent Truths? Who steals this gift of wonder from us? Why does the Peter Pan in us die as we "mature"? Have we forgotten how to fly?

We don't start "school," other than me reading aloud. I wouldn't trade reading aloud for anything. I love the family togetherness and the conversation and discussion that thoughts from a great book bring out.

Monte's elk hunting begins later in the month. Archery season lasts a month. As with the spring firsts, I now start looking for fall firsts. This month I write on the calendar the first elk bugle. They start down from the high country with the biggest bulls coming later. The bugles echo, as do the crashing of antlers when they fight. All summer long is a steady progression of wildflowers. This year was exceptional in our meadow mid-August. I also hang bunches of meadow flowers and plants, as well as those I've grown. Some years they adorn one of the beams in the great room until eventually they are bunched in baskets or wreaths. Jean pockets cut off pants make a great gift stuffed with dried grasses and flowers. Glue on jute so it can hang. Mine has a little stuffed animal hanging out of it as well. Sometimes when someone visits for a while, I try to think of an easy craft we can accomplish while yacking. Paper-twist dolls have been one item, as well as the jean-pocket flower holders.

199

SEPTEMBER

Labor Day used to be just another time to spend with family and friends at home. We have now started a camp. Instead of a few friends, we now have close to sixty, for almost a week!! Other homeschool families with similar family goals as ours come from all over the country. The moms represent KONOS, like me, and we get together once a year in Dallas, but we wanted to get the dads and kids together. Our second annual KONOS Kamp was held this past year. It is such a highlight and focal point of the year that kids find ways to scrimp and save all year to help get their families here. It's a way to savor relationship with kindred spirits. Its effect on the kids brings tears of joy to my eyes. Firsts I look for this month are: the first cold day, first frost, first snow, first yellow leaf. This all occurs in September. I note the date the bluebirds and robins leave. They gather in flocks at this time. It is so sad to see the hummers leave, too. It's fun to watch for the ruby throats and the rufus hummingbirds. I always write down when Monte gets his elk and what the weather is like at that time. Canning continues. We don't start school. But what is school?! Heather and I are busy with home-ec. Besides food preservation we start sewing. Heather usually begins baby-sitting for some MOPS group or women's Bible study. Heather and her friend Lura usually begin going to People Comforts a little more regularly. They make quilts with donated fabrics for those in need. This will be her fourth year. The guys are busy gathering the meat. I love this time of year. Indian summer kicks in after the first snow.

Once hunting season ends, the elk come around more. Actually the meadow has browned and the grass and plants close to the house look good. It gets so noisy out there at night that we are constantly awakened. It sometimes sounds like a bunch of kids playing, with the cows "mewing" and calves squealing and an occasional bull grunt or bugle. Our family has become quite knowledgeable in the the birds and bees realm, as we witness elk-mating rituals each year. Oh, the stories I could tell. Late one September, we experienced a magical moment. We were just beginning dinner with some friends and had beautiful classical music in the background, when huge snowflakes started falling outside. As we gazed out the windows next to the dining room table, elk came prancing and dancing past the window in rhythm to the music. Set against the golden aspen trees with a translucent light from a setting sun, it was art.

OCTOBER

The leaves have fallen from the trees by October, but all's not bare. Evergreens abound and are beautiful with white snow, dark branches and trunks with the deep blue sky in the background. Evergreen, Colorado is the blue spruce capital of the world. It's still Indian summer with occasional temporary cold and snow, but it all melts. Sometimes Monte and I go deer hunting, but now Travis goes, so I can stay home and craft. I never cook when Monte's gone because I don't want the interruption. If we're not sewing clothes, we're making a quilted something. We're usually trying to think of Christmas gift-giving ideas. This tends to be the month for cooking, sewing, or crafting classes. I usually do my annual soapmaking. I start reading more and Monte focuses more heavily on work. He's worked at home for ten years now. Some of my friends used to wonder how I could stand it. Now I think they are envious. I love it! We could get snowed in and who cares - plenty of food, good books, a cookstove for taking off the chill, and family coziness, with computer, modem, copy and fax machines for meeting those needs of the outside world. We love it. I like to decorate for the harvest season through Thanksgiving using pumpkins and other squash, Indian corn, straw, fall leaves, cornucopia, and a basket of nuts. In the future I want to make leaf placemats. Each one would be a different tree leaf shape in its fall color. The napkin rings can have an embroidered fruit of the tree - like acorn from oak. Add coordinating plaid or calico napkins. We use cloth napkins often and have many to choose from. Whenever a material catches my attention at the store, I buy a yard or so and rip napkins. Some yardage I put in the center of the table on the diagonal. There's no need to completely cover the table, just a splash of interest. I let them ravel when washed - a natural fringe. Sometimes we use them as placemats. Patterned material looks great under clear dishes. At yard sales and second-hand stores I look for the smaller luncheon plates. We often eat breakfast and lunch on tree plates or apple plates. Memories will include pretty tables for "just family"! Look outside for centerpieces - wildflowers, leaves, etc. I did make fall candle holders from aspen tree twigs bundled together. Monte drilled holes for brown candles. Birch or poplar would do the same - a white and brown. Now we have a true country front porch. It is a very livable

extension of the home's living space. For years, with our mine-area, geology traveling, I've accumulated quite a few rusty items. I collect the smaller ones and Monte, the bigger treasures. These include a welder's forge and two ore buckets - one of which is huge, hundreds of pounds and four feet tall. He tells the story of "rolling it uphill . . ." His latest item is an old rusted, solid iron wheelbarrow found in a canyon with a river. He went back later in the summer to retrieve it with a missionary friend to help him. Monte's story goes something like this: "Jim and I hiked back into a deep canyon near a gold deposit and floated an iron wheel barrow down a river on two inner tubes. Between rattlesnakes, cliffs, rapids, a cave, and a Chinese dinner in wet jeans, Jim said, 'That adventure was more primitive than many of my Africa expeditions'." All these decorate the porch. A rusty barrel ring is my wreath and I add leaves, and other dried items according to the season. A silent man clothed in castaway articles guards the porch throughout the changing seasons. I took old clothes and stuffed them with empty chicken feed bags. Straw protrudes from his pant legs and arms. His head is a stuffed brown paper grocery bag and he's got one of Monte's old battered Stetson hats. During the winter he wears a red plaid neck scarf and a red pointed hat trimmed in white fur. Sometimes I find him in a new pose, usually done by one of the kids.

NOVEMBER

November is the month of Thanksgiving. Usually all the yard work is completed. The plant beds are cut back, cleaned up, and mulched. The kids have to walk around and make sure all the trash in the meadow and play area is cleaned up. They usually find lost balls and all, hidden in the tall summer meadow grass. Travis cleans out his concrete waterfall and pond. He put a sump pump in the lower large pond, then a buried hose extending to the upper, little pond. A buried electrical wire goes to the house. The first summer Travis got goldfish from a local pond. They were doing fine and dandy, until some critter ate them in the middle of the night (probably raccoon). He wants to put in some water plants, but who knows what the elk would do to them. They come and drink and probably walk and wallow in the pond, too! I appreciate the toys up and out of the sandbox safely stored in the playhouse, but there are so many in-between nice days that some end up back out. Plastic filler plants give the porch window boxes some color. Eventually evergreen boughs will fill in more. A lot of the porch pots either go to bed in the cellar with bulbs intact in the dry soil or I've brought them into the house or greenhouse. I do like to have some herbs in pots over winter. Some years we've even had tomatoes in the south window. My kitchen sink is in a corner window and I used to have herbs planted in the bedding area we made, but now with the addition of the porch, it's too shady so I'm trying ferns. Thus herbs are delegated to pots

and to the other windows. I do have a lot of house plants. As you've figured by now, I love plants and needlework/crafts! This truly is a month to be thankful. With the harvest in and a slower pace, we relax and enjoy being a family and reflect on God's goodness. Not that we aren't a family at other times. Until the actual Thanksgiving weekend, we usually have a break with no house guests, the cold weather forces us in, and we start firing up the cookstove regularly. It's a natural gathering spot. We usually read about the pilgrims this month. I have a relative who came over on the Mayflower, William Bradford. It's not the same story each year, though we do have Bradford's own account. God's hand is so evident - location and the lack of enemy Indians; Squanto and his knowing English and able to help them, and so much more. During the holidays we always try and think of those without family and

invite them over. Then, of course, there's got to be kids. What is the holiday season when you're a kid, without kids! That's part of the memories we want for them. We prepare a very traditional stuffed turkey, mashed potatoes, and sage dressing meal. We have one memory that one of us usually brings up now. I got blood

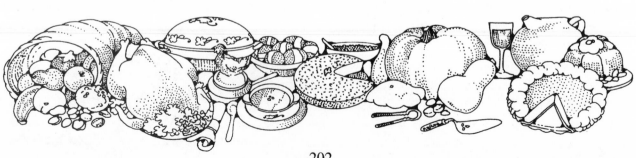

same time, clean up, take care of kids, visit me in the hospital and . . . still fit in his work! I thank the Lord for His plan - the institution of marriage. Each of us with complementary functions - such a beautiful union. The institution of family - oh, how important it is that we as parents are good models, and carry on the responsibility of preparing our kids for their living in the world, walking with the Lord, and developing proper relationships. Thank you, Lord, for your guiding care and who You are!

clots when pregnant with Dawson and one leg was very swollen during preparation for the Thanksgiving meal. Monte made me go to the doctor on Wednesday, so on Thanksgiving I was in the hospital with the whole family eating a hospital Thanksgiving meal in my room. There were little pine cone turkey decorations on the trays. I was in for two weeks and on blood thinner injections, two times a day, for the rest of the pregnancy and beyond. I felt like a guinea pig throughout, having blood tests each week and all sorts of weird variables. (I do not easily give blood. It's not my emotions, but my vein's problem.) It was not the greatest experience, but we are very thankful for Dawson, and Monte is very thankful he still has a seemingly healthy wife. Monte had to come home and put the thirty-pound, home-raised turkey (it didn't fit the oven anyway! We had to quarter it!) in the freezer, and figure out what to do with the bread dough I had stuck in the refrigerator. He gained a real appreciation for moms those two weeks. Sure, he's a great cook, and often cleans the house better than I, but he also has to work. He couldn't see how one can work, plan a meal, cook a meal, and have the right amount of food for the whole family and everything ready at the

203

This is the month we celebrate Jesus' birth. Christmas is good memories, good traditions, good time for relationships and community. Sure it gets busy, but that's part of the good memories and fun. We do decorate, give presents and have a tree. We make cookies. We don't worship these things and we don't forget the Lord. He's the center of the wheel, the hub. Everything else radiates from Him. His creation is extravagant - just look at our meadow of wildflowers; or remember the most breathtaking sunset you've seen; a red cardinal on a barren branch with pure white snow, evergreens and blue sky as the canvas. We are created in His Image and the context of the passage, the image we know, is that of creating. It should be fulfilling then for us to create, and even be extravagant! We feel our home's atmosphere should reflect God, the creator of the universe. Hospitality played a big part in the design and arrangement of our home. It has always been a goal since we were first married and it continues to blossom. Many times rather than just an open door, we have a revolving door (not just at holidays but year 'round). One person out and another in. Because of our home atmosphere, people like to do things here, so will often invite themselves and others. Right after Thanksgiving we go out in the woods and cut down a tree. Monte's dad often shoots the top off a tree. We usually saw off a top.

One year many of my friends were over, everyone making their favorite cookie and we divided them up before everyone left. Monte brought in a big tree and *kind* of put it up. We were all busy yacking and working when there was a crash. The tree had fallen over and little Dawson was standing in the midst. "What did you think you were doing?" "I wanted to climb the Christmas tree!" At least nothing was on it yet. I never thought of, "Don't climb Christmas trees" to a list of "thou shalt nots." There have been a few of these never-thought-ofs that only Dawson thinks of. He has such a zeal for life! He brings a wonderful dimension to our already textured home (he adds his texture). We usually have the decorations up and most presents bought before the first of the month (did you notice I said *usually* and not always!); this way we can focus on relationships. The Advent basket is set out the end of November. I made this years ago and by now the kids have everything memorized. Each day of the month has a little calico bag with a ric-rac tie containing little miniatures and a slip of paper with a verse. The verses are all events in Jesus' life, many of His miracles and teachings. One year I did make my version of a "Jesse Tree" felt wall hanging, with pockets holding felt pictures that go up as ornaments on the tree. Isaiah 11:1 & 10 says, "There shall come forth a shoot from the stem of Jesse...the Gentiles shall seek Him and His resting place shall be glorious." Jesse was the father of King David and out of this root comes the Lord Jesus. This Advent activity focuses more on the Old Testament and who God is. Remember, in John's Gospel, Jesus said, "He who has seen the Father has seen me...I and the Father are one...He who believes in me shall have life." A Jesse Tree instruction booklet may still be sold at Christian bookstores.

Some years we do both these advents. It's such fun to unpack all the decorations. Every year we have made more. We also make new ornaments for us, and to give away. Christmas Eve we have a special Swedish meal and invite guests. Most of the food is prepared that day. We've done it since we were married and Monte's family did it as he grew up. It's been a progression of technology over the years. We didn't originally have a sausage stuffer. We make potato sausage of half meat and half potatoes (10 pounds each) and an onion or two, salt and pepper and a touch of allspice. This is all ground together and stuffed in casings - pig intestines. We used an inverted angel food cake pan to stuff the casings when we were first married! The majority of the sausage is frozen in future meal proportions. This sausage is not fried or baked but boiled in salted water to cover for about an hour. The other main coarse is beef and pork (elk) stew. It's a dipping stew, with lots of bread pieces to dip in (this has a Swedish name). My favorite part is fruit soup. When we were courting, Monte told me about this and I couldn't imagine "fruit" soup. There are a variety of recipes for this. Ours is a grape juice base with tapioca and lots of cherries and dried fruits. In addition we have rice pudding. Some years we make Ostakaka, a cheese-curd pudding made with raw milk, but have decided we prefer the poor mans' version - rice pudding. An almond is hidden in it and the lucky person to get it is said to marry next. Most years it's just been for fun, but last year my brother was here with his girl friend. She got it! - and I didn't even try to have her get it!! Well, she left it sitting on her plate and my brother eventually confiscated it. He kept it and when later asked her to marry him - you know when you open up a little box and there's a ring?! - there was the almond! Christmas morning is present opening time. A tradition is to start the coffee pot first. The kids do this, then papa and mama get up (it has to be dawn, with some light!) and the gifts are distributed. Luke 2 is read (sometimes the

Bible is wrapped in a bright red paper with a label "To the Swans, From God"); we talk about God's gift to us, and the Magi's gifts to Jesus. We give gifts to each other and remember God's gift of His son Jesus. While the kids are playing I make a special holiday breakfast of Aebleskivers. These are spherical pancakes made in a special heavy cast pan with round indentions. Friends used to come for this meal and then we would end up at their house for the night. They always had very special videos for the kids to watch. This was before we had a TV and VCR. Even though their kids were older than ours, we all had a very special time spending the night at their house. Often we cross-country skied and ice skated on their pond. We did this for years until their kids left home. Then my mom moved close by and we spent that day together. Now a new young family is sharing the tradition with us. New memories and traditions are still in process. But . . . the celebrating is not yet done. We believe in spreading it out. We've read of Sweden's darkness at this time and how they celebrate on after Christmas, so we have a Third Day of Christmas Smorgasbord. Again, this is shared with friends, and usually those who get into cooking different food (and unloading holiday leftovers). This spread usually consists of lots of fish dishes with most of the fish from Alaska. Good times. Good friends. Good memories. Another good year.

I love the Paul Harvey Christmas story, *The Man and the Birds*, this time of year: A family attends a Christmas Eve service at church, but the husband stays behind, saying he'd feel like a hypocrite. He didn't believe in this Incarnation stuff, God coming to earth as a baby. A flock of birds hit the front window and he realized they were on their way south and must have got caught in a storm. He tried many things to get them to go into his warm barn. In frustration he said, "If only I could become one of them, speak their language, then they'd listen to me." At that moment, the church bells rang. He then dropped to his knees.

Hope this finds you well and enJOYing life. I'm not referring to happiness and success. Happiness and success are in themselves self-ism. I hope you've seen that HOLY days, and the rhythm of God's creation, can be used to build traditions and memories. Our lives are story. We live in story. Stories give us a sense of value, meaning, and significance. We are not an accident. Poetry and story give us a context in which it is easier to hear the gospel story and let the Holy Spirit work. The Triune God is a relational wholeness and offers us a home ordered by a Father, Son and Holy Spirit. Joy and relationships are based on losing our self and loosing ourselves to the Lord. Mary loosed herself when letting down her hair and anointing Jesus with costly perfume ($24,000 worth!). How extravagant! What about the poor?! What about her dignity? The fragrance was still on Jesus when he was crucified, on his robe when the soldiers gambled for it, and on John when he laid his head on Jesus' breast during the last supper. The fragrance of her worship lingered. She was lost and loose in worship. Whereas the disciples were caught up in image and dignity. The shepherds loosed themselves in leaving their field responsibilities and bowing down to a feed trough. The Magi brought costly gifts and perfume and bowed to a toddler. I'm trying to lose and loose myself in Christ and focus on *being*; focus on my relationship with the Lord, and family and friends. "Now thanks be to God who always leads us in triumph in Christ, and through us diffuses the fragrance of His knowledge in every place. For we are to God the fragrance of Christ among those who are being saved and among those who are perishing." II Corinthians 2: 14, 15 Our purpose is found not in merely doing, but in being. Allowing the Artist of our souls to chisel us until we reflect His brilliant image, rhythm, and voice to the world.

O, little town of Bethlehem, how still we see thee lie!
Above thy deep and dreamless sleep, the silent stars go by.
Yet in thy dark streets shineth, the everlasting Light;
The hopes and fears of all the years, are met in thee tonight.

For Christ is born of Mary, and gathered all above,
While mortals sleep, the angels keep, their watch of wond'ring love,
O, morning stars, together, proclaim the holy birth!
And praises sing to God the King, and peace to men on earth.

How silently, how silently, the wondrous gift is giv'n!
So God imparts to human hearts, the blessings of His heav'n.
Nor ear may hear His coming, but in this world of sin,
Where meek souls will receive Him still, the dear Christ enters in.

O, holy Child of Bethlehem! Descend to us, we pray;
Cast out our sin, and enter in; be born in us today.
We hear the Christmas angels, the great glad tidings tell;
O, come to us, abide with us, Our Lord Emmanuel.

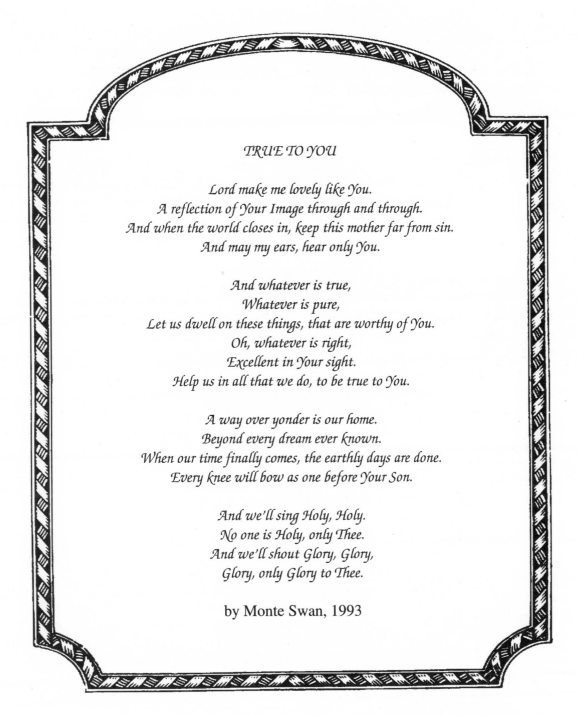

TRUE TO YOU

Lord make me lovely like You.
A reflection of Your Image through and through.
And when the world closes in, keep this mother far from sin.
And may my ears, hear only You.

And whatever is true,
Whatever is pure,
Let us dwell on these things, that are worthy of You.
Oh, whatever is right,
Excellent in Your sight.
Help us in all that we do, to be true to You.

A way over yonder is our home.
Beyond every dream ever known.
When our time finally comes, the earthly days are done.
Every knee will bow as one before Your Son.

And we'll sing Holy, Holy.
No one is Holy, only Thee.
And we'll shout Glory, Glory,
Glory, only Glory to Thee.

by Monte Swan, 1993

Felson's Law: To steal from one person is plagiarism;
to steal from many is research.

Concepts without percepts are empty,
whereas percepts without concepts are blind.
Immanuel Kant

It is the function of creative men to perceive the relations between thoughts,
or things, or forms of expression that may seem utterly different,
and to be able to combine them into some new forms -
the power to connect the seemingly unconnected.
William Plomer

An idea is a feat of association.
Robert Frost

Chapter Fourteen
THOUGHT FOOD
FOR THE FUTURE

What do the super-rich, aristocracy, royalty and homeschoolers have in common? The mentorial style of education. Mentorial means to teach or guide individually in a special way. In the context of this chapter it is examined from the perspective of a Christian worldview and includes speaking and discussing together the great books and the truth they contain. It is the mentor's responsibility to walk alongside and pass on the "tools of learning" to the student - in essence, to inspire and help the student develop a fine mind. The majority of us were public or private schooled with the traditional approach. It is familiar and we tend to bring that system into our home and "school," diluting the most powerful method of education known.

Before I continue discussing educational philosophy and the future, let me give you some background. In human history there have been three major societal eras. The first was the Nomadic age, the second was the Agrarian Age from Abraham to Abe (we're right in the thick of this with our high school KONOS History of the World). People found they could stay in one place - grow their food and store it, build homes, and cluster about walled cities for safety. The third era is the Industrial Age. We've lived close in time to both these last two eras. (Just because we move into another does not mean previous eras entirely disappear.)

Why the history lesson? Because education changes as the society changes. The education focus tends to shift with the eras' focus. The code word for the Industrial Age is "mass." Massified everything. People moved to the cities and living was in mass, concentrated in urban settings. Production and distribution became massified. Media, government, and education followed the same pattern. People became specialized and did one job that fit into the mass - kind of like a worker bee - they became skilled in doing only a portion of the whole. By contrast, in the earlier Agrarian Age, a shoe was fitted and made for you - very individualized. Each person thought more integratively and was more of a Renaissance-style man or a Proverbs 31-style woman. The conveyor belt approach to industry became the symbol of the age and in a sense was adapted by the education system as well. The focus or goal was jobs, and for the industrial era it was an

effective system. Our country is prosperous due to this system. But spiritually we have lost ground because science and technology were touted as our saviors. When alone and autonomous, they destroy civilization and create C.S.Lewis' "Men without Chests." Philosophically, socialism, the natural consequence of runaway naturalism, went out of fashion in the 1980s. The question now is where are we headed and how do we prepare our children for the road ahead?! Let me extrapolate into the future. Keep in mind that these are generalizations and predictions. There are always exceptions when you generalize about people, and there is always error when you try to predict the future.

In the year 2010 most of our children will be in the work force, as will we parents. But will most of the current jobs exist? Many believe we are moving into another era - a transitional Information Period followed by the Knowledge Age. The key word for this time is decentralization. The mode or media is telecommunications, fax, internet, satellite, cable (not big TV networks), talk show radio - information coming from all sorts of different sources. Jobs can be in the home. Distribution is even changing via Internet: grocery shopping and library usage as examples. Even government is trying to decentralize back to the states (will someone tell Washington!). The technology of our day is allowing industry and education to scale down and decentralize institutions. Vertical, cumbersome bureaucracy will become laterally structured. There is a large movement, a human migration, out of the cities. It is the largest in the history of our country and is from the coasts to the Midwest and the Rocky Mountains. Some have compared today with the Klondyke Gold Rush. Many fortunes are being

made overnight for those who see the opportunities - just like the forty-niners who saw and discovered the gold. Monte's brother, Mike, who is very much involved in this movement says that "the dust will not settle for a long time." With the Internet and all, huge capital to advertise or begin a business is no longer needed. In the Agrarian Age land was the key. In the Industrial Age, capital (big factories) was the key and the USA, France, Britain and Japan have been the investors. Knowledge and information, entrepreneurs and little businesses, an increase in efficiency and elimination of middle managers are the keys to the future.

If we are moving into another era, what is the impact on education? How should we educate our children and ourselves for the Information and Knowledge Age? Not that it is the goal of education, but if we continue educating as we were educated, are we preparing our children for the future job market? Here again, would someone please let Washington in on who and where "we the people" really are? I'm thinking about Goals 2000. Do "we the people" know what Washington is doing? When comparing educational systems, public school's purpose has been to educate the masses, but for what? Public schools prepare children to be workers and good employees by teaching them **what** to think - very much a dumbed-down society. The public school method is analogous to industries' conveyor belt approach. Private schools are essentially the same, only more

sophisticated and competitive. They train people **when** to think and to be good managers. Harvard is an example of the highest form of a conveyor belt school. Mentorial methodology, on the other hand, is an individualized method with the goal of helping one learn **how** to think. It prepares leaders - statesmen, analysts and entrepreneurs. In our Founding Fathers' time, sixty percent of the population were tutored and were entrepreneurs. Just ponder upon what they accomplished. They dreamed, designed, and built the foundation for the greatest nation in human history. Currently, only three percent of the population are mentored (Oliver DeMille).

Among the highest paid and most satisfied workers in the country today is the entrepreneur or consultant. The future wave appears to be ideally suited for consultants, researchers, legal consultants, mentors, tutors, analysts, and artists. In other words, public education is training for jobs, private education for careers (career comes from a French word meaning "race track"- running in circles), and mentorial education for entrepreneurship and leadership. Mentorially educated people will make money, live where they choose, and may be more likely to live off one income.

We are homeschooling and hopefully giving our children an individualized, mentorial style of education. With our effort on mentoring all these years, why should we send our kids off to a college that puts them on the traditional conveyor belt?! Will we have wasted our time because that type of college will naturally attempt to fit our children into the old industrial complex with its fragmented, reductionistic, outdated philosophy? What do we do? Monte and I looked into the mentorial style of college.

We discovered there are very few colleges with this philosophy. Michael Farris also discovered this fact and has recently founded Patrck Henry College to help fill this vacuum. How do you work with a traditional college? First of all by developing relationships with the professors and then maybe even requesting reading lists of great books. As these are read, our youth will write papers and have discussions with the professor. Many colleges are trying to shift gears as they discover a high percentage of their top scholars not attending classes but learning via the Internet, discussion groups and by utilizing the library. Colleges are beginning to accept life experience, portfolios and testing out of subjects (usually essay format).

When asked about the most valuable part of their education, the common answer from leaders and great people is their exposure to the classics and the great ideas which come from great books. These thoughts are "great" because they express God's transcendent, absolute truth. A classic is a classic because it survives beyond the culture that birthed it - because it contains truth. In essence, reading the great books is the same as being mentored by the greatest thinkers of all time; for contained in the great books are their thoughts, thoughts that touch God's truth. By inculcating these ideas into our children in the context of a Christian world view we enable our children to stand on the shoulders of these giants and see what no one has ever seen. Additionally, they will be able to act upon what they see and use it through God's power as we aim and launch them like arrows into the future.

With our style of home educating we feel that we have been schooling in the right direction. We have truly learned science in its historical context and the flow of history through all the great biographies and books we have read together. The facts have been presented in the context of meaning and truth. Our children have been given knowledge (Greek style of education) in concrete context with value, meaning and application to life (the Hebrew style of education). We continue on into high school reading aloud the great books because the discussions are so stimulating. Schooling without this sharing of the great literature, Living Books, and the naturally corresponding discussions is too dry for me. When life is hectic and we push aside this aspect of our homeschooling, school becomes a drudgery! With only textbooks and workbooks we miss out on the meaning of learning, there's a lack of both story and content, and we're never introduced to the great ideas that inspire us to learn more, and learn how to think. What is education? Is it only brute fact? With our choice of education, we have opened our children's (and our own!) minds and hearts! The view from here is wonderful!

So many of us are facing the college stage of home education. Monte and I have taken steps in this direction. I've read the *Peterson Guide* to correspondence schools and the *Bear's Guide*. My personal feeling is that when we are working so hard on advanced math, etc, at this high school stage we could be getting college credit for it! We are looking at these mentorial-style colleges (there are some), community colleges and maybe even beginning college at home through correspondence. Whether our children ever go on campus will be dealt with at some future point in time and will depend upon the student. Some of these colleges offering correspondence degrees have great book reading lists and I'm excited about reading these with my kids (I'm still a

homeschooled kid too!). But with this reading together comes the responsibility to mentor. That will be a challenge, because the great books at the college level are not light novels. For example *War and Peace* or Plato's *Republic* will stretch my brain cells to the max - and hopefully grow some new ones. (New research has discovered that we can grow new brain cells.)

Did you catch the educational philosophical message in the motion picture *Shadowlands*? C.S. Lewis discovered through a sleepy student and his perceptive wife, Joy, that the great books are best taught dialectically, not doctrinally. Dialectic mentoring is required to romance a heart with truth.

The traditional mindset is to go to college to get a diploma. The diploma is the goal - the end. Did you know that many businesses are more interested in what is in your brain than in your hand? - they may start giving examinations. If this is a future trend, maybe our goal in education should be education, not graduation.

Another way to look at this is from the liberal arts perspective. Historically, a true liberal arts education has all but disappeared. Prior to the 1900s, liberal arts meant that a four-year college bachelor's degree technically wasn't the end of your education, but the beginning! Liberal meant that a man was free from ignorance, and equipped to grow. He had passed through the Trivium (eg. Grammar stage, the Logic stage and the Rhetoric stage of education) and was now ready to begin to educate himself for the rest of his life. He now possessed the tools of learning - a true liberal arts education.

Today the true liberal arts education, if obtained at all, is acquired in graduate school and/or after ten to fifteen years in the work world. Why not give our children this education from the start. You might ask, as we have, "How will they make a living? And what about a technical education?" First of all, a true liberal arts education, not what liberal arts has become, is precisely what a person needs to make a living. It equips him to identify problems, analyze and solve them. It gives him vision to see opportunities and the courage to pursue them. It importantly gives him an understanding of people and the character to work with them and predict what they will do. A technical education is part of a true liberal arts education and needs to be an integral part, not an isolated specialty. This is what is missing from the Oxford model. Even the great C.S. Lewis failed to hear the sermons preached by science and mathematics during the first half of this century and integrate them into his works. Making science and technology moral can only be done if scientists and engineers comprehend more than brutish fact.

Just as each student is unique, each student's educational track should be unique. This becomes most apparent in the post-high school years. But there are several essential ingredients in common with each track to acquire a true liberal arts education. The first, as I have already discussed, is the great books.

Apprenticeship versus college has been debated quite a bit in homeschool circles. Must we choose one or the other? Education is merely theoretical until it is practically applied in the adult world and workplace. We feel internships, work experience, and, if appropiate, apprenticeship, are an essential part of the rhetoric stage of learning. Until a basketball player actually plays in a game, his dribbling,

shooting, passing and defensive abilities are untested and merely theoretical. Knowledge is not knowledge until it operates.

Monte and I became acquainted with the mentorial style of college through a workshop at a Homeschool Convention in 1995. As our kids have grown closer to college age, we are realizing more and more that this approach to higher education fits right in with our philosophy of education. The workshop helped crystallize our vision. Colleges centered around great books mentioned during the workshop are: Thomas Moore, NH; Thomas Aquinas, CA; Hillsdale, MI; St. John's College, MD & NM; and George Wythe College, UT. Mentorial approach to college should be done through the great books *and* mentoring; we don't know if both occur at these colleges, and there could be other colleges as well. Mentoring inculcates into the heart - Truth.

Dr. Michael Platt recently shared with us that only toward the end of a full year of dialectic mentoring around the great books do students begin to freely discuss the ideas contained in the books. He said at that point, if the teacher does not come to class, the discussion will spontaneously go on without him. Students today are not prepared for this style of college, and take a long time (months) to adjust. In other words, the public/private conveyor belt mode of education does not prepare students to be equipped for a mentorial method of education, i.e. they are not usually readers, writers, self-starters, independent thinkers, and leaders. I'm speaking generally - there are always exceptions. On the other hand, the homeschoolers are typically right at home with the mentorial approach, although homeschoolers are not much better at writing than the traditionally-educated students. The writing deficiency needs to be addressed, especially in regards to thinking and expressing thoughts logically through writing.

We have talked to the vice president of a local Christian university about mentorial-style college for the homeschooled youth and he was open to the concept. One of the professors said they had tried independent study programs but the public/private schooled students were unable to handle that approach. They were intrigued by the idea that homeschoolers may be able to do a mentorial study program, and have recently begun aggressively promoting their school to the homeschool community.

Since we have just started this process and know that many of you may be inspired and moved in this same direction, I think we can get the ball rolling throughout the country. Many of us cannot wait the many years until the country's colleges get the idea, and on top of that, make the changes! We can pursue colleges ourselves and probably will need to contact the visionaries of the colleges before anything happens. We've taken our children's education into our own hands thus far, knowing what's best for our children and our families, and I believe we can change the world in the area of collegiate education, too.

Our current vision is internships and work experience along with limited correspondence college during the high school years seasoned with tutoring in the technical subjects and high-quality mentoring by friends. Advanced Placemant (AP) and CLEP tests will hopefully move our youth quickly through the first two years of college. We feel math, particularly advanced algebra, is essential to the development of critical thinking skills and logic, not to mention its importance for any engineering or science field. Perhaps I should qualify the definition of tutor. As we searched for a math tutor, we discovered a gifted teacher with incredible character. He had lived under communist rule in Poland and you can imagine the

rest of his story. He is philosophically opposed to tutoring. He will only do "consultation" or mentoring because he believes a student must teach himself or will forever be dependent. I must admit that I agree. Another way to look at this is to think dialectically not doctrinally. Jessica Hulcy calls this "discovery learning." But we must be diligent to do this under the over-arching truth of a Christian World view, for to embrace John Dewey's "content neutral" approach to education may produce educated criminals. Some would say to educate under any single worldview is indoctrination or even brain washing. But all education is under some worldview. Even philosophical pluralism (i.e. political correctness or post modernism) is a worldview and, by definition, claims to be inclusive, but in the process excludes Christian theism because Christian theism claims that absolute truth exists.

The correspondence college I envision would ideally have a mentorial slant to it. The value of mentorial college via correspondence is open to question. But, modem, internet, E-mail, conference calls and speaker phones are changing all the rules. We could hustle our children through and put degrees in their hands before eighteen years of age (like some have done) but that would be developmental hurrying in all but a few exceptional cases in our opinion. For college we see the first couple years as correspondence, then possibly moving on campus, to get the full mentorial flavor. Mentorial and traditional college are currently different tracks with little potential for transfer of credits from one to the other except on case-by-case bases. They are preparation for two different goals. How this is handled, we believe, will be different for every student. Although we would like to see some of both, the mentorial track is most important and prerequisite in our opinion, and will probably be the college track we begin with.

Life has become engineered - by autonomously rationalistic arranging, disciplines, and work. With the Reformation through the Enlightenment, came reductionism. Academia brought about fragmentation and specialization. Life has been dichotomized - split into the secular and the spiritual. Life has lost its soul - the integrative, relational wholeness and the large context of God. Life has been packaged into a neat formula. Education has become dichotomized, fragmented, and engineered as well. This reducing has made us feel thin and impoverished. We're nostalgic in paying attention to the older traditions. It's not only transcending into our lifestyle choices, but many are realizing this impoverishment in their spiritual lives as well.

Surveys are showing great increase since the 70s and 80s in religious interest. Much to the secularists' dismay, the polls consistently indicate that 93% believe in a Creator, 84% believe in God, and 40% attend church regularly. Universities seem to be the only major places holding to atheism, naturalism, and skepticism. Our time is called post-modern, which means that philosophically, rationalism has been abandoned in most circles for relativism. If our children are to impact the world as leaders, they must inculcate God's absolute Truth into their very being. Mentorial method in college in the context of a Christian worldview, and a true liberal arts education, hold promise for finishing the work we began when we started down the homeschool road. They will know the truth and have the wisdom to turn the floods of information into knowledge that will nearly drown the masses in confusion! If the Information and Knowledge Age is what the visionaries predict it to be, the "dust will not settle for a long time."

The sources for much of the data, and for further reading:

Fit Bodies, Fat Minds: Why Evangelicals Don't Think & What To Do About It by Os Guinness
Another Sort of Learning by James V. Schall
The Work of Nations by Robert Reich
Futureshock, the Third Wave, Powershift by Alvin Toffler
Preparing for the Twenty-First Century by Paul Kennedy
Megatrends, Megatrends 2000, Megatrends for Women by John Naisbitt & Patricia Aburdene
The Cloning of the American Mind by Oliver & Rachel DeMille.

Readings On Mentorial Education:

Reforming Education by Mortimer Adler
The Closing of the American Mind by Alan Bloom
The Unschooled Mind by Howard Gardner
The Abolition of Man by C.S. Lewis
Some Thoughts Concerning Education by John Locke
Liberal Education by Mark VanDoren
An Aristocracy of Everyone by Benjamin Barber

I know for a few of you this may have seemed rather dogmatic. Especially in thinking we home educators are the thinkers and know the truth. Monte and I are currently working our way through this season of life and have more questions than answers. Not all homeschool environments are going to produce leaders. Not all people can homeschool. Not all children in the established school systems are "going to bunk." This is just food for thought, for the future, from a mom who is trying to prepare her children for their days on earth.

Necessary Skills for Success in the 21st Century Job Market

1. The ability to define problems without a guide.

2. The ability to ask hard questions which challenge prevailing assumptions.

3. The ability to quickly assimilate needed data from masses of irrelevant information.

4. The ability to work in teams without guidance.

5. The ability to work absolutely alone.

6. The ability to persuade others that your course is the right one.

7. The ability to conceptualize and reorganize information into new patterns.

8. The ability to discuss ideas, issues and techniques with an eye toward policy decision.

9. The ability to think inductively and deductively.

10. The ability to think dialectically.

SOURCE: HARVARD SCHOOL OF GOVERNMENT

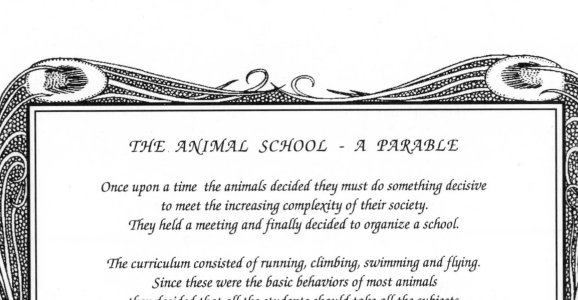

THE ANIMAL SCHOOL - A PARABLE

Once upon a time the animals decided they must do something decisive
to meet the increasing complexity of their society.
They held a meeting and finally decided to organize a school.

The curriculum consisted of running, climbing, swimming and flying.
Since these were the basic behaviors of most animals
they decided that all the students should take all the subjects.

The duck proved to be excellent at swimming, better in fact, than his teacher.
He also did well in flying. But he proved to be very poor in running.
Since he was poor in this subject he was made to stay after school to practice it
and even had to drop swimming in order to get more time in which to practice running.
He was kept at his poorest subject until his webbed feet were so badly damaged
that he became only average at swimming. But average was acceptable in the school
so nobody worried about that - except the duck.

The rabbit started at the top of his class in running, but finally had a nervous breakdown
because of so much make-up time in swimming - a subject he hated.

The squirrel was excellent in climbing until he developed psychological blocking in flying class,
when the teacher insisted he start from the ground instead of from the tops of trees.
He was kept at attempting to fly until he became muscle bound -
and received a C in climbing and a D in running.

The eagle was the school's worst discipline problem; in climbing class he beat
all of the others to the top of the tree used for examination purposes in this subject,
but he insisted on using his own method of getting there.

The gophers, of course, stayed out of school and fought the tax levied for education
because digging was not included in the curriculum.
They apprenticed their children to the badger and later joined the ground hogs
and eventually started a private school offering alternative education . . . .

-alas the author is unknown

To this mother at forty-six, and this father at fifty, each at intellectual top-notch, every faculty having been stirred for years by the dire stress of Civil War, and the period immediately following, Gene Stratton-Porter was born. From childhood she recalls "thinking things which she felt should be saved," and frequently tugging at her mother's skirts and begging her to "set down" what the child considered stories and poems. Most of these were some big fact in nature that thrilled her, usually expressed in Biblical terms; for the Bible was read twice a day before the family and helpers . . . "No other farm was ever quite so lovely as the one on which I was born after this father and mother had spent twenty-five years beautifying it," It was called "Hopewell". . . She had a corner of the garden for her very own, and each spring she began by planting radishes and lettuce, and before these had time to sprout she set the same beds full of spring flowers, and so followed out the season . . "my father would tie a 'kerchief over my mouth when he lifted me for a peep into the nest of a humming-bird, and did he not walk softly and whisper when he approached the spot? So I stepped lightly, made no noise, and watched" . . . In the nature of this child of the out-of-doors there ran a fibre of care for wild things . . . "My regular habit was to lift one plant of each kind, especially if it were a species new to me, and set it in my wild-flower garden." To the birds and flowers the child added moths and butterflies . . .

Her mother and father had strong artistic tendencies, although they would have scoffed at the idea themselves, yet the manner in which they laid off their fields, the home they built, the growing things they preserved, the way they planted, the life they led, all go to prove exactly that thing . . . From the home you could not look in any direction without seeing a picture of beauty . . . Reared by people who constantly pointed out every natural beauty, using it wher-

ever possible to drive home a precept, the child lived out-of-doors with the wild almost entirely . . . To be taken from such freedom, her feet shod, her body restricted by as much clothing as ever had been worn on Sunday, shut up in a schoolroom, and set to droning over books, most

Gene Stratton-Porter

of which she detested, was the worst punishment ever inflicted upon her she declares . . . all her time was spent on natural science, language, and literature.

Through the sickness and death of a sister, Gene missed the last three months of school, but she remarks, "unlike my schoolmates, I studied harder after leaving school than ever before and in a manner that did me real good. The most that can be said of what education I have is that it is the very best kind in the world for me; the only possible kind that would not ruin a person of my inclination. The others of my family have been to college; I always have been too thankful for words that circumstances intervened which saved my brain from being run through a groove in company with dozens of others of widely different tastes and mentality. What small measure of success I have, method of expression . . . whatever I have been able to do, has been done through the line of education my father saw fit to give me, and through his and my mother's methods of rearing me.

"Father knew I was boiling and bubbling like a yeast jar in July over some literary work, and if I timidly slipped to him with a composition, or a faulty poem, he saw good in it, and made suggestions for its betterment. When I wanted to express something in colour, he went to an artist, sketched a design for an easel, personally superintended the carpenter who built it, and provided tuition. On the same easel I painted the water colours for 'Moths of the Limberlost', and one of the most poignant regrets of my life is that he was not there to see them, and to know that the easel which he built through his faith in me was finally used in illustrating my book. If I thought it was music through which I could express myself, he paid for lessons and detected hidden ability that should be developed. Through the days of struggle he stood fast; firm in his belief in me. He was half the battle. It was he who demanded a physical standard that developed strength to endure the rigours of scientific field and darkroom work, and the building of ten books in ten years, five of which were on nature subjects, having my own illustrations, and five novels, literally teeming with natural history, true to nature. It was he who demanded of me from birth the finishing of any task I attempted and who taught me to cultivate patience to watch and wait, even years, if necessary, to find and secure the material I wanted. It was he who daily lived before me the life of exactly such a man as I portrayed in 'The Harvester,' and who

constantly used every atom of brain and body power to help and to encourage all men to do the same."

Gene married, had a home of her own and a daughter, all of which filled her hands, but never her whole heart and brain. The book fever lay dormant a while . . . "I could not afford a maid, but I was very strong, vital to the marrow, and I knew how to manage life to meet my needs, thanks to even the small amount I had seen of my mother. I kept a cabin of fourteen rooms, and kept it immaculate. I made most of my daughter's clothes, I kept a conservatory in which there bloomed from three to six hundred bulbs every winter, tended a house of canaries and linnets, and cooked and washed dishes besides, three times a day. In my spare time (mark the word, there was time to spare else the books never would have been written and the pictures made) I mastered photography . . . using the family bathroom for a darkroom and washing negatives and prints on turkey platters in the kitchen . . . To my way of thinking and working the greatest service a piece of fiction can do any reader is to leave him with a higher ideal of life than he had when he began. If in one small degree it shows him where he can be a gentler, saner, cleaner, kindlier man, it is a wonder-working book. If it opens his eyes to one beauty in nature he never saw for himself, and leads him one step toward the God of the Universe, it is a beneficial book."

I've always liked Gene Stratton-Porter and been inspired by her books. They are true blue story. I thought The Harvester was my favorite, until we read The Girl of the Limberlost and Freckles together. But then too, Laddie is so good. I still kick myself that we passed up her Moths of the Limberlost at a Portland, Oregon bookstore for only $50, but I had my heart set on her Birds of the Bible or The Song of the Cardinal books. (Kind of like Monte passing up a mandolin for only ten dollars at the flea market because his focus was looking for a piece of plumbing!) Any way, I hope these excerpts from "A Little Story of her Life and Work" (1916) inspire you as they've inspired me.

The importance of poetry and novels is that the Christian life involves the use of the imagination - after all, we are dealing with the invisible. And imagination is our training in dealing with the invisible - making connections, looking for plot and character.

Eugene Peterson

. . . there is only one situation I can think of in which they . . . make an effort to read better than they usually do. When they are in love and are reading a love letter, they read for all they are worth. They read every word three ways; they read between the lines and in margins; they read the whole in terms of the parts, and each part in terms of the whole; they grow sensitive to context and ambiguity, to insinuation and implication; they perceive the color of words, the odor of phrases, and the weight of sentences. They may even take the punctuation into account. Then, if never before or after, they read . . . this is what I mean by 'reading.'

Mortimer J. Adler
"How to Read a Book" 1940s edition

The things that traditionally were thought to give adult life meaning - love, courtship, marriage, children - have suffered a tremendous trivialization in recent years, largely as a result of television . . . A young person who reads widely gets more than the pleasure of plot and setting; he or she gets an introductory course in character studies . . . One of the benefits of encouraging a child to read good books is that it saves his parents from doing all the reminding.

William Kilpatrik, Gregory and Suzanne M. Wolfe
"Books that Build Character"

BIBLIOGRAPHY

This listing of books is an unconventional bibliography. A great part of who and what I am today I attribute to books - all the great classics, library books and resource books for all of life 'round and about the home. Our homeschool process has been primarily through real, Living Books. Even today, I am a classic homeschool kid (what does it mean to be an adult?). I develop a curiosity about something and satiate myself with all sorts of books and enjoy a variety of perspectives. This list of books will never be complete when it comes to all the books in our house. It's a compilation of probably the most often utilized books and the ones with the best formatting of information.

Many people make requests for good resource books utilizing whole grains. There are a lot of books on whole grains but not all necessarily palatable! These listed books are ones I trust. All their recipes are good. *Set for Life - Eat More . . .Weigh Less . . . Feel Terrific* by Jane Merrill and Karen Sunderland is an excellent book. The authors were Bosch and Magic Mill dealers and some of their recipes are like mine. They also list the fat, calorie, etc. content per recipe. For finding the contents of our homemade foods when we were calculating fat, I used a book called *Food Value*s, sold at all major bookstores. I added up every ingredient and figured the food portions. This need not be done forever as you see the big picture in a few days. I'm still trying to find out though about the food value of fresh ground grains. If these books base evaluations on foods shelved at the store, then they are not accurate. Has anyone analyzed freshly-ground whole wheat, etc? All the Rodale Press books are good. The ones I use the most are *The Rodale Cookbook* by Nancy Albright and *The New American Vegetarian Menu Cookbook* by Paulette Mitchell. This publishing company utilizes varieties of whole grains, legumes, oils and all, and sweeteners other than sugar, in their recipes. Their books on nutrition, gardening, composting, root cellaring, herbs, quilting, etc, are good too. Be willing to consider vegetarian books because they utilize more varieties of whole foods. *Tofu - Not Just for the Health of It!* by Jana, 2 Crutchfield Park, Charlottesville, VA 22906 (1983) is a great book. All it's recipes taste like regular American, French, Mexican, and Italian favorites. This is an older paperback book and I do not know whether it's still available. Remember, too, I recommended the tofu brand Mori-Nu if you've never used tofu. It is the creamiest I've tried.

In the category of overall cookbooks, the list could be endless. The *Joy of Cooking* has been around for decades and is good for understanding ingredients and techniques, the hows and whys. My favorite resource for the hows and whys and then recipes and equipment analysis is the *Cook's Illustrated* magazine. I've ordered the past years hardbound (I believe to 1993). The magazines are in your bigger bookstores. The *Cook's Illustrated* books are published by Boston Common Press Limited Partnership, 17 Station Street, Brookline Village, MA 02146. I consult my *Harrowsmith Cookbook* a lot. When evaluating why, it's because it uses down- home ingredients. I don't readily have fresh papaya, or salmon and crabs, or endive and caviar. Nor am I going to continually run to the store. So the best cookbooks are the practical ones. Down-home ingredients can be used creatively. You could have some exotics on the shelf and this book can help with the making of them: *Fancy Pantry* by Helen Witty has been a very fun book. For canning, a good basic book that's rather new is *The Busy Person's Guide to Preserving Food - Easy Step-by-Step Instructions for Freezing, Drying, and Canning* by Janet Chadwick. Carla Emery has compiled *The Encyclopedia of Country Living*. It used to be called *An Old Fashioned Recipe Book*, and this is the book I bought before we were married. I loved the format with her ramblings and chattiness all throughout. I believe her personal Christian testimony came out in the egg section. The new book which is the ninth edition is very complete and organized and I've not found the same ramblings. It's still very helpful with details of all the country homestead lifestyle.

Yes this is a bibliography, but I can give you a source for some of the "kitchen servants" I've mentioned throughout this book. Since I have been a Bosch and mill dealer off and on since 1983, you can order the Bosch Universal Kitchen Mixer, Grain Master Whisper Mill, Air Preserve II Dehydrator, and Kuhn Rikon pressure cookers, etc. through me. Monte's songs, which I've quoted throughout this book can be found on our albums "True to You" "What Else Matters at All." They are available through us. We can be reached by mail at: Singing Springs Productions, PO Box 3883, Evergreen, CO 80439, by phone: (303) 670-0673; or fax (303) 674-3431.

Herbs are becoming quite popular. At least there appear to be more and more articles, crafts, books and magazines on the subject every year. Dorling Kindersley books have become popular and their *Complete Medicinal Herbal* book by Penelope Ody is very good for pictures, info and how-tos. I still refer back to my *Rodale's Illustrated Encyclopedia of Herbs* book quite a bit. Good stuff. Another one I like is *The Harrowsmith Illustrated Book of Herbs* by Patrick Lima. My favorite perennial book is a Harrowsmith book by the same author. It lays out the perennials by season. *Rodale's Illustrated Encyclopedia of Perennials* is another. I am striving for color all throughout the growing season with good leaf variations as well. The Harrowsmith books come from Canada where the magazine had its origins. I'm finding everything they suggest for gardening is working for me. Remember, as I said in the gardening section, I've never lived where gardening follows the books. As I write this, my back little salad and herb garden, though surrounded by barbed wire until we build the pergola, and though we've had frost, was looking beautiful, and I was about to put a garden cloth over it for lasting into the winter . . . (sob, sob) it was trod upon and eaten by elk last night!

Along the nutrition line, the most wholesome (not way out) and balanced books are: any Paavo Airola books such as *How to Get Well; Are You Confused*; and *Every Woman's Book* are my favorites. He is noted in the next two books mentioned as *the* top nutritionist (he just recently died). James Balch, MD and Phyllis Balch CNC have written two excellent books - *Prescription for Nutritional Healing* and *Prescription for Cooking and Dietary Wellness*. I've noticed these in many stores and at homeschool curriculum fairs. Another helpful one is *Healthy Habits - 20 Simple Ways to Improve Your Health* by David and Anne Frahm. In writing this book it was stated she had conquered terminal cancer through changes in diet and nutrition. I think she's been on some Christian radio programs.

Victorian anything is resurging as well. Or is it just me and what I'm attracted to? Maybe if I were into Art Deco I'd see it everywhere and think it was popular. 'Tis it in the eyes of the beholder? (When we were first married, Monte never in his life had noticed pregnant ladies. Once I was pregnant, he noticed them everywhere.) Well anyway, Monte bought me this book awhile back for Mother's Day that has been an inspiration, and since, I'm noticing more and more coming out like it: *The Scented House* by Penny Black. I've seen others by her at the library.

If you're interested in making your own soaps, lotions, skin and hair care, take a look at these books: *Soap* by Ann Bramson and *The Complete Soapmaker* by Norma Coney. *The Natural Soap Book* & *Soapmaker Companion* by Susan Miller Cavitch are good too with great info throughout (my likes in info). These two are by Storey Publishing, which puts out lots of how-to homestead info books. Then there's Jeanne Roses' *Herbal Body Book* (this one is a little way out but fun).

As far as homeschooling books, they have become quite numerous as well! Which is exciting, but the danger I've seen as we travel and speak is that the newer homeschoolers have not really re-searched. Many I've talked with don't know the names I mention. Names like Raymond Moore, along with his wife Dorothy, whom I consider to be the grandparents of the movement. Now I know I'll upset someone by not mentioning their favorite homeschool writer, so I'll stick with our early days and the people who got us started. I could fill a book with all the others. Monte's mother sent us an article twenty years ago by Raymond Moore on "Better Late than Early." Then we got to know a family, nineteen years ago, that told us about homeschool. Meeting their girls convinced us to homeschool but, the final turning point for us was Raymond Moore's book *Home Grown Kids* and hearing him on "Focus on the Family." When we moved to Colorado in 1983 we met Ruth Beechick at church. At this time she helped us more than anyone. What a blessing to have her as a mentor and friend. There are two ladies I feel a kindred spirit with and consider grandmothers of the movement, Ruth Beechick and Charlotte Mason. I recommend all of Ruth's books, especially *You Can Teach Successfully* books (Three booklets for K-3 and the big book for 4th-8th grades) and *The Language Wars and Other Writings for Homeschoolers*. With Charlotte Mason's reprinted volumes, I tell people to begin with the last volume because it summarizes her *Philosophy of Education*, volume 6. Then you can go back and wade through the other volumes if you like.

Two young people who give us a hope in ideals and an image of inspiration are Eric and Leslie Ludy. They came to us for inspiration and guidance one evening. I knew nothing of their "story." I don't know who was most inspired as the night progressed - Eric and Leslie, Monte and me, or Heather and Travis. The message of their book *When God Writes Your Love Story - The ultimate approach to guy/girl relationships,* is needed today. They are reaching out in hopes of challenging and encour-aging young people to live at a higher level of purity and commitment to the Lord. They also com-pose songs and minister together through music. Their book includes a CD of "Faithfully," the title track to their next album.

For more information on the "Recipes of Life" chapter subjects, since I threw out bits and pieces, read *Margin* by Richard A Swenson, MD, Thomas Kinkade's *Simpler Times*, and *If Teacups Could Talk,* by Emilie Barnes. My sister-in-law Chris, in Wisconsin, told me about *Margin* a number of years ago since they know Dr. Swenson. I still remember when I went into a bookstore in Arizona asking for it, and did not expect anyone to know of it, the lady said "Yes, and how many copies do you want? Everyone needs to read this!" Among the KONOS sisterhood *If Teacups Could Talk* has been mentioned often because daughters and moms have been using its ideas as a means for hospitality and ministry. Karen Maines wrote a book long ago on hospitality called *Open Heart, Open Home*. Edith Schaeffer's book on the *Hidden Art of Homemaking* is both philosophical and practical for building relationships and traditions. *Simpler Times* by the artist Thomas Kinkade is practical and inspirational with his beautiful testimony and artwork throughout.

A little more specific for the raising of our children (parenting from the heart) is the new book by Steven W. Vannoy, *The 10 Greatest Gifts I Give My Children*. Monte and I intuitively raised our children in this way. I know of no book I could recommend more that focuses on inspiring our children's internal nature, and nurturing their hearts. They in turn make their own choices, right choices, and become self-governed. The closest book, years ago, helping me to focus on their good character was Charles Swindoll's *Knowing Your Child*. Another good book is Tedd Tripp's book *Shepherding or Child's Heart*. Dr James Dobson's book *Hide or Seek* and Dr Ross Campbell's *How to Really Love Your Child* were very instrumental in our training process too. He has also co-authored with Gary Chapman *The Five Love Languages of Children*. All of these help in "knowing" your child and building relationship. John Locke's *Some Thoughts Concerning Education* from 1693 is good. We met Steven Vannoy at a seminar he presented. He is a young, growing Christian and excited about the forward side of life. His mentors and board have advised him to make a wide appeal and target the inner-city and community families not just the Christian community. A publication I have referred to is the PATRIARCH Magazine. We are close friends with the editor Phil Lancastor and his wife Pam. It is a resource for men, aiming to equip them with a fresh vision and practical direction needed to be leaders in their homes. PATRIARCH, PO Box 725, Rolla, MO 65402.

Sometimes I'm asked for literature lists. There are plenty of lists out there. Once you begin to wander down this path you'll notice "lists" in many places. The library is the best and most obvious place to look. A lot of books have been written about books, giving age or subject breakdowns, and summaries of the books. I wouldn't want to write such a book because there is too broad a range of y'all. Some of you may not like something I've suggested and then you'll throw everything I've said out, I'd be labeled. We can't please everyone. Many books I have no problem with, you might. For example, let's say I recommend *Little Britches* by Ralph Moody. The cowboys swear, but, as a boy, how is Ralph going to deal with it? Will he take up swearing too? How he deals with it may give us a weapon. When the problem arises in our own life, we have an image of Ralph, and his response makes our response easier. You may not like fantasy, and I would suggest C.S. Lewis' *Perelandra*, the second book in his *Space Trilogy*. Ah, to imagine the world of Adam and Eve, pre-sin. Eugene Peterson (author of *The Message*) says, "The importance of poetry and novels is that the Christian life involves the use of the imagination - after all, we are dealing with the invisible. And imagination is our training in dealing with the invisible - making connections, looking for plot and character." Do we need faith for the facts and the provable? Isn't faith for the unanswerables and the unseen? *Books Children Love* by Elizabeth Wilson is one resource I've used the most. Its layout is by subjects and is very useful for finding Living Books on most school topics. Gladys Hunt has *Honey for A Child's Heart*, and *Read For Your Life* (for teens). Both are excellent. Don't just read the book lists. The intros are rich! *Books That Build Character* by William Kilpatrick, and Gregory and Suzanne M. Wolfe, is rather new. It's a guide to teaching your child moral values through stories. Another new one is *Great Books of the Christian Tradition* by Terry W Glaspey. I have been plodding my way through many of the suggested books and they're great. I know there are more, but those are what I use. Then of course, all the years of using KONOS Character Unit Study Curriculum, their suggested library book lists for every unit we've studied have been a rich resource.

Book sets are another place to find lists. Since we value the value of story to our lives, we've gone to used book sales and stores for twenty years. Many book sets may be a good starting point. Some we have are "My Book House," "The Junior Classic," "The Children's Hour," "Picturesque Tales of Progress," and "Childhood of Famous American Series." The "Educator Classic Library" has complete and unabridged classics with explanations and definitions in the margin. Another set we are beginning to collect is Compact Classics presents "The Great American Bathroom Book." These compile "Single-Sitting Summaries of All Time Great Books." You might look to see what books are contained in sets like "The Harvard Classics." I like to collect books by some authors as well. Kate Douglas Wiggins or Gene Stratton-Porter are examples. "The Happy Hollisters" series by Jerry West are liked by our kids. Did you know the third book in the Heidi series answers all the questions of Heidi's background? Quite an interweaving plot. Oh, this reminds me, do not let movies substitute for the books. Very few movies stick to the true story and the real message of the book is often lost. For instance, Johanna Spyri's *Heidi* is another version of "The Prodigal Son." Walt Disney made Pinocchio into a rather nice boy, and if they made the "Fox and the Hound" after the book, the title is the only similarity.

Do you enjoy reading? How many books do you read a year? Do you take the time to read? Maybe when it's all said and done, the place for you to begin should be Richard A Swenson's book *Margin*. Then you can try some of the other books I've included in the bibliography.

Well . . . I hope all this has been inspiration rather than intimidation. Remember it has been a process for me, not something I've done all at once. The important thing is to be taking steps forward. Some people take little, some ramble, some skip and hop, others leap, and then there are the great striders. Don't compare yourself.

I love this quote from Mother Teresa,
*"God did not call me to be successful.
God called me to be faithful."*

INDEX

For me, it's the twists and the turns and the curves and surprises that make the journey of life more meaningful and more fun. Some of life's most important lessons, its most resplendent joys, happen when you put yourself in the path of serendipity . . . How can you go exploring when every minute is planned? How can you have surprises when every hour is scheduled? . . . And I guarantee there will be wonderful surprises waiting for you - just around the bend . . . Our best chance of touching, in our own small way, the eternal is to live the life we're given, savoring the now, deciding for the future . . . We can work at establishing a legacy for tomorrow, but we can do this successfully only when we are living fully today . . . a paradox, a mystery of time and eternity. Simply put: We can aim for the eternal, but we can act only in the present moment . . . As a Christian and a man of prayer, it is what enables me to experience the present joyfully and passionately, yet still make plans for the future. . . simpler times are eternal times.

Thomas Kinkade in his Simpler Times

The humans live in time, but our Enemy destines them to eternity. He therefore, I believe, wants them to attend chiefly to two things, to eternity itself and to that point of time which they call the Present. For the Present is the point at which time touches eternity. Of the present moment, and of it only, humans have an experience analogous to the experience which our Enemy has of reality as a whole; in it alone freedom and actuality are offered them. He would therefore have them continually concerned either with eternity (which means being concerned with Him) or with the Present - either meditating on their eternal union with, or separation from Himself, or else obeying the present voice of conscience, bearing the present cross, receiving the present grace, giving thanks for the present pleasure. . . Our business is to get them away from the eternal and from the Present . . . We want a whole race perpetually in pursuit of the rainbow's end, never honest, nor kind, nor happy now, but always using as mere fuel wherewith to heap the altar of the Future every real gift which is offered them in the Present.

A senior devil giving advice to a junior devil in "The Screwtape Letters"
C.S. Lewis

The past is history; the future a mystery;
But the present is a gift.
And that's why we call it the present.
Author unknown

Memoranda for the Cook

Memoranda for the Cook

Memoranda for the Cook

Memoranda for the Cook

Memoranda for the Cook

Memoranda for the Cook

Memoranda for the Cook